50 Cents for a Life

A True Story of

Surviving by Synchronicity

Bernard Rosenfeld, with daughter Nancy Rosenfeld

Copyright ©2024 by Nancy Rosenfeld

Print ISBN: 978-1-958892-05-3
Epub ISBN: 979-8-88531-678-1

All rights reserved. No part of this publication may be reproduced, restored in a retrieval system, or transmitted in any form or by any means, electronic, mechanical, recording or otherwise, without the prior written permission of the author.

Disclaimer. The author, publisher, nor any other representatives, will be liable for damages arising in connection with the use of this book. This is a comprehensive limitation of liability that applies to all damages of any kind, including compensatory; direct, indirect, or consequential damages; loss of data, income or profit; loss of or damage to property and claims of third parties.

Published and Distributed by Booklocker.com, Inc., St. Petersburg, Florida, USA. Please contact Booklocker.com for individual and quantity sales.

Library of Congress Cataloging in Publication Data
Rosenfeld, Nancy
50 Cents for a Life: A True Story of Surviving by Synchronicity, by Bernard Rosenfeld, with daughter Nancy Rosenfeld
Library of Congress Control Number: 2024902036

Booklocker.com, Inc.

Author contact: www.50centsforalife.weebly.com

NancyRAloha@gmail.com

Dedication

To Bernard Rosenfeld, his siblings and mother, and millions of others who came here with a challenging destiny. May their lives be remembered and honored. May humanity evolve with compassion and respect. May belief in synchronicity inspire holding on to embrace divine openings of possibility.

Acknowledgements

This book would not exist, with its rich details and vivid images, without the emotionally raw manuscript written by my father, Bernard Rosenfeld. A role model in perseverance and determination, his story is shared at his request, to give hope for what can be created in life and to remember that we are here to help each other, to not abandon during difficult times.

Thank you to Shelley, my sister, for her inspiration, awareness, and always being there to talk stories and memories. Thank you to my sister, Tina, for her support and continuous involvement with our parents' care, and to Diane for her early years of big sister helpfulness. To Ryan, my son, heaps of gratitude for his patience, understanding, humor, and kindness – I am so blessed.

Vast appreciation extends to the U.S. Holocaust Museum for incredibly detailed timelines, archives, and registry matches. Thank you to hundreds of researchers, writers, film producers, and documentaries that educate, inform, and help create awareness to be a better society.

Thank you to my friends, from childhood to current island home, for listening, encouraging, cheering, and supporting this timeless endeavor.

To my publishing team at Booklocker – Angela, Ali, Todd for cover design – and more, thank you for your patience, upbeat attitude, and continuous helpfulness.

A huge cast of characters exist within this life story who contributed through their mighty and intricate actions. I am forever grateful to be able to share this story, of one more unique soul who endured greatly, who survived at times with pain impossible to smolder, and other times, with joy that decorated his spirit.

I am grateful to you for reading this book, to complete my father's last wish, that his story be received, known, and the lives of those who could not speak, be honored.

The legacy of this book seeks to inspire belief in unexpected, outrageously positive, possibilities!

Nancy Rosenfeld, Co-Author

50 Cents for a Life

Table of Contents

Prologue ix

Introduction xiii

Chapter 1: Like Leaves on a Tree, Family Destiny Disperses 1

Chapter 2: Playful Innocence in Lithuania 13

Chapter 3: Inviting Fate 23

Chapter 4: Destiny Strikes 33

Chapter 5: The Journey Out 49

Chapter 6: Secrets of the Forest 63

Chapter 7: You're in the Army Now 73

Chapter 8: Escalation Peaks in Europe 83

Chapter 9: Surprise Meetings 91

Chapter 10: Homeward Bound 105

Chapter 11: From the Depths of Love 113

Chapter 12: The American Dream 119

Chapter 13: Search and Release 127

Chapter 14: A New Voice 133

Chapter 15: Hello, Are You There Lithuania? 139

Chapter 16: Momentous Milestones 147

Chapter 17: Passions of the Soul 163

Chapter 18: Life Moves 179

Chapter 19: Visions of Transition 191

Chapter 20: The Final Chapter 199

Chapter 21: Unveiling 217
Chapter 22: Favorite Mystical Connections 225
Appendix I: Map of Europe During WW2 235
Appendix II: Bernard's Family List 237
Appendix III: What Does it Mean to be a Survivor? 239
Appendix IV: Validating Data 243
About Co-Author Nancy Rosenfeld 253

Prologue

Dangerous Nazi Germany was already terrorizing during the early moments of World War II. Anyone planning to depart Lithuania must get out now, within the next 72 hours to be exact. After that, transport routes and borders would be heavily guarded without mercy for a young Jewish man's desire for survival.

At only 17 years old, Bernard, the youngest of six siblings, would be leaving everything he ever knew - his rural village, his large family, close lifelong friends. Options were perilous, risky no matter what action he chose.

With the clock ticking, panic spread rampantly throughout his village. He held no money and no papers. It was a treacherous fate. The chances of escaping from eastern Europe were nil. The thought of crossing fierce military borders was enough to not even try.

Young friends teased Bernard: *"You won't go to America. You'll stay here and die with us!"* Bernard responded with certainty: *"No, I will go to America! And I will return to visit your graves."*

But there would be no graves. Cruel Nazis viciously forced Lithuanian Jews to dig deep pits in the forest earth, exhausted until they could barely stand. Then shots were mercilessly fired, all of them collapsing dead upon one another. Massive body counts were piled skin-to-skin in each killing pit, including Bernard's family and friends.

"How can I get out in three days?! It is impossible!"

"I feel numb, floating, hearing sounds but no words," echoed in Bernard's mind two days after receiving the urgent state of affairs from

the consulate. Only 24 hours remained to flee. He pleaded for a miracle as news worsened, leaving many hopeless with fear.

And then, out of nowhere, the opportunity to escape descended upon Bernard like a mysterious spell. He had a way out. Whether or not he would be protected, destiny would reveal at each dangerous border.

Raw emotions were buried in disbelief at the surreal scene before him on this final day to leave. The only sound was the crunch of pebbles beneath his feet as he walked upon his village road in the chill of the dark morning.

He paused to turn around slowly, solemnly waving goodbye to family and friends who gathered to witness the moment with envy, fear, or wonder. His eyes saw familiar faces with smiles and tears, but their words were mouthed without sound. His ears did not want to hear their voices speak about his sudden dangerous exodus into the unknown.

In the wake of the ominous alert signaling imminent border closures, the events of the previous day held an air of mystery, revealing a story that could only be described as a divine twist of fate.

He was oblivious that his life ahead would be steered by angel-like synchronicities, painful empty paths, and miraculous safety.

This is the brave true story of Bernard Rosenfeld, a strong stoic man from a poor Jewish family in a village of Lithuania. He narrowly escaped the worst atrocities of humanity, while his family and over 90% of his town did not survive. This is the story of magical synchronicity, inspiring hope and belief in oneself to continue on when the path appears impossible. This is an example of unstoppable determination and the ultimate acceptance of letting go to find peace.

Bernard silenced the painful memories of his story by refusing to read details about the horrendous killing pits of his town until decades afterwards. He refused to share his emotional journey of immigration with his daughters until almost fifty years after his escape. He stubbornly tried to bury the pain in his heart, afraid of what might occur if he allowed himself to feel, afraid he would lose control as a strong husband, father, and businessman.

The threatening eruption of fierce grief and sorrow had to be buried. It was safer that way. Life was in the deep South of the United States, isolated from a larger supportive Jewish community. Diverse immigrant cities, like New York and Chicago, were abundant with knowledgeable and experienced resources to help deal with this severe emotional trauma. Not so in Shreveport, Louisiana.

Finally, a critical life-changing and gut-wrenching decision flared; it was time to talk by releasing in writing the desperate fate of family. He never read his own manuscript after it was completed. It was enough to shed the throbbing story to honor his family.

Bernard Rosenfeld is my father and this book is a collaboration beginning with his original manuscript and expanded by research and current life events. My additions to his original manuscript are in italics, explaining his local references, as well as the unbelievably complex World War II theater surrounding his journey out of Europe.

I believe this act of collaboration was a soul promise between daughter and father. It was the topic during our final in-person conversation, looking each other directly in the eyes, and the subject of our last telephone call softly whispered from his dying bed. I promised him that I would do something with his manuscript, because he wanted the story to be shared. He wanted others to know what can happen if we don't help each other. He wanted to honor his family, friends, and millions of others who were insensibly murdered in the Holocaust.

My wish is that in sharing my father's life story, others will be knowledgably informed from an eyewitness account of the Holocaust and WWII years, to expand compassion and respect for the effects of diverse life stories. May this inspire each of us to live life with utmost goodness, love and harmony, and appreciate the many blessings from angel-like synchronicity.

Thank you for reading and entering this story.

Nancy Rosenfeld

Introduction

Much of this candid memoir is written by Bernard Rosenfeld, born in 1922 in the small rural village of Raseiniai in central Lithuania. His home country shares borders with Poland in the south, Latvia in the north, and the Baltic Sea on its west coast. To the east of Lithuania was Russia, part of the Soviet Union from 1922 to 1991, also known as the USSR.

Nearby, Germany bordered Poland to the west, making the countries of Poland and Lithuania an unfortunate intersection of the most violent mass murders during the 1940s, known as the Holocaust. Six million Jews were tortured to their deaths, two-thirds of all Jews in Europe. Millions of non-Jews died during this war also. While this is devastating human behavior, its description is not the motivation for sharing this story.

Bernard's life was, most importantly, a demonstration of mystical-like protections through unexpected synchronicities. Moreover, his tough determination and perseverance to live to the fullest is a message of hope to anyone painfully grieving or feeling the emptiness of loss, which can be a joy-devouring force.

Our focus is on survival, both physical and emotional. Survival takes many forms, including how we choose to cope, how or if we heal, and the many pathways to a life rich in balance and fulfillment even with painful memories of the past.

It is helpful to understand several words, events, and conditions as you enter the landscape of Lithuania.

First, what was the Holocaust? This darkest period for humanity occurred throughout Europe between 1933 and 1945, with highest counts of radically cruel massacres during the latter years. The Nazi regime of Germany and its allies, conducted a systematic, state-sponsored persecution of six million European Jews. Many non-Jewish Europeans were also mercilessly murdered by Nazi's.

A basic tenet and philosophy for Nazism under its delusional and power-obsessed leader, Adolf Hitler, was antisemitism, enacting discriminatory laws and organized violence starting with Germany's Jews. Hitler promoted a plan referred to as the "Final Solution to the Jewish Question," a genocide implemented between 1941 and 1945.

The Nazi's began blaming Jews for Germany's defeat in World War I, which ended in 1918. Nazi hatred and paranoia of Jews escalated to horrific status when Germany panicked in the 1930s due to political crises, fear of Russia's communism, and economic shocks of the Great Depression. All of this contributed to many Germans being open to Nazi ideas, needing to blame dire conditions on someone, namely the Jews, who were defined by Hitler as a separate, inferior, and most dangerous race.

Jews were denounced as a threat that could corrupt and destroy Germany, and they needed to be removed from all of society. And Hitler, ultimately, wanted to be the leader dictator of all of Europe. It was the Jews who were his obstacle, with their skills, intellect, and influence in politics, banking, industry, science and general society.

How "The Final Solution" occurred around Bernard's miraculous journey unfolds in chapters ahead. For further information about details of the Holocaust, there are many books, museums, and online resources that share data and eyewitness stories by country. The Appendix at the end of this book includes a few of these references.

Lithuania, where Bernard was born, in northern Eastern Europe, is similar in land size to West Virginia in the U.S. The country was ruled

A True Story of Surviving by Synchronicity

by Russia for over one hundred years until WWI, when Germany briefly occupied it from 1915 to 1918. After World War I, Lithuania was independent until 1940, when Russia, part of the Soviet Union, regained control.

Lithuania had a total pre-WW2 population of close to 2,000,000, with 155,000 Jewish citizens in 1938. By 1945, over 90% of the country's Jews had been killed. For comparison, in the 1970s, still under Russian rule, the total population had grown to almost 3,000,000, but with only 24,000 Jews, less than one percent. Closer to current time, in 2023, the total population is 2,700,000 and Jewish citizenship has declined to around 2,500 to 4,000, with the majority religion being Catholic.

The village where Bernard was born and lived until teenage years, Raseiniai, was in inner Lithuania. Prior to the year 1900, the population was around 10,000 with 80% to 90% Jewish. From 1926 to 1939, Bernard's growing-up years, the total population in the village dwindled to less than 10,000, with 40% Jewish.

It is also relevant to understand while reading this memoir that there is a form of PTSD, post-traumatic stress disorder, associated with surviving a trauma when others do not survive. It is known as Survivor's Guilt and is considered a serious emotional trauma symptom of PTSD. Individuals grappling with this anxiety find it challenging to shift their thoughts, enduring anguish and at times displaying irrational behavior. This heightened anxiety, in turn, contributes to both physical ailments and emotional distress, creating a tormented experience.

For Bernard, his heart suffered physically due to the emotional anxiety ignited from survivor's guilt.

Survivors often question why they escaped death while others lost their lives. They may also wonder whether there was something that they could have done to prevent the deaths of others. More thorough information about this type of emotional trauma and helpful modalities to begin to heal can be found in the Appendix.

In addition to his original manuscript written in 1987 shared for the first time with his daughters, this book relies heavily on historical records from the U.S. Holocaust Museum in Washington, DC. Their timeline of data integrates complex world war events surrounding Bernard during his divinely-protected journey out of Lithuania. Additional research and articles enhanced details of what occurred in forests, concentration camps, and liberation discoveries.

Bernard's life treasures included hundreds of photographs that tell a visual story of beloved family, friends, army adventures, paintings, and an expansive life well-lived in America, which aided in the piecing together of this memoir. A photo gallery illuminates his story and can be found at www.50centsforalife.weebly.com.

To embark on this journey, we unveil the cover letter to his clandestine manuscript, which Bernard surprised his four daughters with in 1987. This glimpse opens a portal into the depths of Bernard's emotions. You immediately recognize his deeply entrenched symptoms of trauma. There is no hiding it. However, magical synchronicity and an unyielding will to live balance and captivate. A kaleidoscope of colorful blessings is sprinkled with moments of lightheartedness, with the ultimate gift being 50 cents that saved his life.

April 1987

Dear Diane, Tina, Nancy and Shelley,

I'm writing about my family and myself so that you may know not only about your father but also who you are, that you come from a large family, and had they lived, you would have been loved by many.

I want desperately for you to know where I came from, how I grew up and about your grandparents, aunts and uncle and cousins, even though they are dead. They died a horrible death. I will never forgive or forget those who did the killing and the world who didn't do anything to stop it.

I could never before write about myself or my family. You were too young and I was worried that you may not understand what I have written. I am sorry for waiting so many years to tell you about myself and the family I left behind. The time has come for me to tell you.

To live with a guilt that no one could understand or give comforting words, to feel guilt for being alive is at times almost impossible to endure. I am sorry that your mother had to be, and still is, a witness to my personal tragedy. I am grateful for her patient silence, for no comforting words will help.

I hope that someday you will tell your children. Remember!

Love you, Daddy

Chapter 1:
Like Leaves on a Tree, Family Destiny Disperses

Dear daughters, I'll start by telling you about my mother's family, to introduce you to people who were part of my everyday life growing up in Raseiniai in the 1920s and 1930s. My grandfather's name was Benche Marcus. He was a strong, big man who liked his tea boiling hot directly from the ornate metal Samovar, which he kept on the table next to him.

Grandmother's name was Rive Roche. She was a small woman, sickly with Rheumatism. She didn't get around much. My older sister, Hedva, lived with them and took care of their day-to-day needs.

My mother was one of Benche and Rive's six children. These are aunts and uncles who you will hear much more about later as part of my journey. First, the boys. Uncle Morris, went to Leeds, England and had six children. Uncle Meyer went to America in 1905 and also had six children, settling in Baldwin, Missouri. He was soon followed by Uncle Isadore who settled in McGehee, Arkansas, and had two children.

The oldest daughter of Benche and Rive was Leah, who first went to Leeds, England, had four children, and ultimately settled in St. Louis, Missouri. Aunt Leah will become important to my story. Aunt Elke and my mother, Feige, remained in Raseiniai, Lithuania. Aunt Elke had no children. My mother, Feige, had six children. I am the youngest of the six, born August 4, 1922.

When I was about one year old, my Uncle Morris from England came for a visit to Lithuania in the early 1920s to visit his parents and family. Uncle Morris was a fine fisherman and quite well known for his fishing skills. I have a photo of Uncle Morris, my grandparents and me during that visit. The horse and wagon belonged to Grandfather. The river in the picture is called Dubishe in Yiddish. It was a shallow river and in warm weather, we would play in the water.

Grandfather Benche Marcus made a living from leasing orchards about five miles from town. Jews were not allowed to own land. I spent a lot of time with him in the orchards. When the cherries began blooming in early spring, we would go to the cherry orchard, build a roof out of long sticks over a small sitting area and keep the birds away from the trees by making loud noise. Every day, we rode back and forth in the horse-pulled wagon until the cherries were all picked and sold.

During summer, I spent all my time in the orchards with Grandfather. We built a hut from sticks, covered with straw to keep the rain and wind out. There was enough space to sleep in our little hut and store apples and pears until we went to market on Mondays and Thursdays. For cooking, we built a fireplace from rocks and placed three poles over the fire to hang a pot for cooking. We dug a hole in the ground to store milk and cheese. It was always chilly at night, even in summer.

It was so beautiful early in the morning when dew covered the entire orchard. I would walk out in search of a fresh apple that fell during the night. The apple was always ice cold, crisp, and so juicy sweet. I can taste that memory. When the sun rose, we would pick the ripe fruit and let it dry in the sun, then store the delicious crop until market days.

When I was older and out from school for summer in the 1930s, I could hardly wait to go to the orchards. During harvest, I would help a landowner by riding in wagons loaded with hay or wheat, take it to the barns, unload, and go back for more. My payment was fresh honey, eggs and bread. I loved that time of year. Everything was beautiful and peaceful.

During early fall, usually end of September, right before the Jewish Holy Days of Rosh Hashanah and Yom Kippur, we would pick the remaining apples and take them to town where they were stored to be sold. Apples that were kept for winter markets were covered with straw so that they wouldn't freeze, and the others were sold. To this day, I love all kinds of apples and eat them fresh and cooked, with happy memories of the orchards and time spent with Grandfather Marcus.

Rozenfeldas, Raseiniai, Lithuania

Father's name was "Nothel Easher," translated to Nathan Irving. I do not remember his parents, my grandparents on his side, other than my grandmother being on her death bed.

My father, Nathan, had two brothers and three sisters, for a total of six children in his family. One brother and sister went to South Africa. Another brother, David, and sister went to Brooklyn, New York, in America. My father Nathan and Aunt Seine remained in Raseiniai.

Nathan married Feige Marcus, my mother, and they also had six children, as mentioned earlier, four girls and two boys. My name alternated among: Berale (Yiddish), Dov (Hebrew), and Berelis Joselis (Lithuanian). Little did I know what fate awaited me, a boy from a small village with a large family in Lithuania.

My father engaged in commerce. We had two horses and a large wagon that were used to bring goods from the capital (Kaunas) to local merchants. That is how he earned money. My mother had a store where she sold everything from herring to a needle. Everything was fine in my early years, 1922 to 1927.

During the festive holiday of Hanukah in December 1927, the sixth night of lighting candles, my father died from a heart attack. I was five years old and alone with him, finding him dead. *(Hanukah is the* celebration of light, for the miracle of one vial of oil used for light lasted, not one day, but eight days. This miracle of illumination from the oil allowed light in order to clean inside the holy Temple, which was desecrated during a violent battle of war over two thousand years ago.)*

The last day of my father's life is forever etched in my memory. All day, Mother and others were running around bringing hot water to Father, yet it was also very quiet. I was completely ignored, only five years old. I never felt sure if I remembered details correctly until my sister, Hedva, told me sixty years later.

On that Friday of Hanukah in 1927, I was playing in my sister's room. I covered an entire wall with newspaper and set it on fire! That's what can happen when a five-year-old boy is ignored. Well, the fire was put out and I must have been punished. After dinner, I had to stay in my parents' bedroom. My father was lying in his bed and I was sitting on Mother's bed. It must have been around eight o'clock at night. Father looked at me and said: *"Why don't you lay down, Berale?"* I listened to him and did what he suggested. Soon after that, my beloved father made three sounds and then he was dead. I was alone with his body in the bedroom. I'll never forget his sounds followed by silence, the image of his lifeless pale face, and my fear and confusion at age five.

Since Father died on a Friday night during the Sabbath, the funeral was delayed until Sunday. *(Jewish custom is for no embalming, preservation or cremation of the body. Burial occurs in a simple pine casket with no nails, as soon as possible, "ashes to ashes, dust to dust." Sabbath is from sundown Friday to sundown Saturday, during which no work, parties, or funerals occur.)*

My father was lying on the floor in the bedroom covered with a white sheet from Friday evening to Sunday. Being young and curious, I picked up the sheet cover for a peek and observed him lying there appearing so very sound asleep. I still can see that image of death. He had some sort of band that covered his forehead. On Sunday, a horse and wagon covered in black cloth carried my father to the cemetery. He was only 49 years old. Everyone was walking behind the wagon and crying. That was quite an experience for a five-year-old.

Afterwards, every morning at five o'clock, my older brother, Motl, and I walked to the synagogue to say Kaddish prayers for our father. I think we had to walk to synagogue three times a day, maybe even for a whole year, which was the religious orthodox custom in our Jewish community. Being so young, I was scared to death to go through the long alley by our house in the dark of the morning. It was below freezing and windy and my hair stood up from the weather and being frightened because there were ghosts in the warehouse along our walk! I could almost see the ghosts in the warehouse windows. Since that time, I was always frightened to walk through that long alley.

As we travel along my past, I will come back and continue my story, years will have passed from these memories of 1927.

Life after Father Passed

After my father died, things started to get tougher for my family. I began to study Hebrew and the bible. The Rebbe *(Yiddish for Rabbi and teacher)* was very old and could not hear or see very well. He kept the book about two inches from his eyes. We would play all kinds of tricks on the poor man and he would beat the daylight out of us if we were caught.

When I started to attend regular school, which was a Jewish school, I wasn't the best student. It was very difficult to grow up without a father when all the other students had both parents. I remember one year the school put on a play. I wanted to be in that play in the worst way, especially the part of an old man. Naturally, the boys whose fathers were wealthy got the parts. But I kept on learning the old man part anyway. I was perfect for that role! God must have wanted me to have the part because why would the boy who played the old man character get sick a few days before the performances began? I was the only one who knew the part. *(Synchronicity and perseverance are important frequent themes in Bernard's life as you will see unfold. Opportunities seem to magically appear to help him, and his determination denies obstacles in his way.)*

In our town, Raseiniai, the Jewish community was considered quite large, about 3,500 people. We had a Jewish grammar and high school. We were like a country within a country. Our schools marched in parades proudly carrying both the Jewish and Lithuanian flags.

In the meantime, life went on. Mother's store wasn't doing well at all so she started to come along to the orchards to help Grandfather. Since we leased two orchards about a half-mile apart, it was a big help having her there. However, Mother would still work in her store several days a week, as well.

Grandfather swore that one evening as he drove the wagon by a cemetery, a ghost came out, grabbed his horse and wouldn't let go no matter how hard Grandfather tried to beat the ghost away. Another time, ghosts were dancing as the sun was going down. Our orchard overlooked the cemetery and this is the truth about the ghosts, no question about it.

One day everyone was running and hollering: *"Close the windows! Lock the doors! A fish is in the sky larger than a house!"* Finally, when night came, we saw lights inside the fish and heard music coming from that fish in the sky. It turned out that was the Graff Zeppelin. Oh well, someone made a mistake.

Grandfather Marcus, my mother's father, the strong man with a long beard, died leaving Grandmother alone. My sister Hedva had previously departed to learn how to become a farmer and how to prepare herself to go to Palestine in 1935. Grandmother moved in with us, taking over Mother's room since it had doors and she could rest comfortably. So now my sister Beilke took care of Grandmother in our home. Mother's store finally closed since it wasn't doing well and our only earnings came from the orchards. Mother rented a basement where the apples were stored in the winter and sold from there. The cellar was open twelve hours, six days a week. Most of the time, Mother didn't sell enough to buy a meal. I still went to the orchards with her and helped as much as I could.

My Siblings

My oldest sister, Taube, was a beauty and worked in a fabric shop. She married Eudke Greenblath from our town and they moved to Memel, on the west coast border of Lithuania. In spring 1939, after Passover holiday, Adolph Hitler invaded and claimed Memel as belonging to Germany. Memel has a port and had belonged to Lithuania since 1923, located across the Nieman river from Prussia. Taube and her husband hurriedly moved back to our town prior to Hitler's takeover. They had a son, Yaakov. Taube's husband was a fine tailor for men's clothing and made a good living, coming from a nice and large family. I do not remember Taube much. She was ten years older than me.

ALL ARE DEAD.

Sister number two was Dveirke. She was a brilliant student, especially with math. Since we had to pay to attend high school, we just didn't have the money for her to continue school so she had to drop out. Later, the people who ran the school came and asked her to come back at no cost. My Aunt Elke, Mother's sister, said, in no way would she let Dveirke return to that school, I guess out of pride.

Dveirke began working in a fine shop that sold a variety of notions and electronics. Her boss was a fanatic when it came to keeping records so Dveirke was a natural at helping. Dveirke and Orke Ludgin were very much in love but his family was against marriage because they felt she wasn't good enough for him. But they married anyway and moved to nearby Telsiai (*Telz in Yiddish*.) Her husband opened a small factory and manufactured leather uppers for shoes. They had a son named after our father, Nothale (*Nathan*).

I remember when Taube and Dveirke lived at our home. They were already fine young girls and dressed and acted accordingly. They would hide their soap and toothpaste from the rest of us, but we would find it and use it anyway.

One holiday we were all sitting at the table. I must have been punished for something or became angry. I threw my fork on the plate as I was ready to leave the table but the fork bounced off and became stuck in Dveirke's wrist. I was so scared and started crying. Thank God, the fork was pulled out and she was alright.

Telz, where Dveirke and her husband lived, was a beautiful town. It had many hills and was famous for the fine Telzer Yeshiva for advanced Jewish studies. I visited Dveirke during the festive Jewish holiday of Simchat Torah. It was something to see! The students from the Yeshivah were singing, dancing and carrying the Rabbi on their shoulders while he held onto the Torah.

Dveirke will later go mad when the Germans grab her child, Nathan, away from her arms. She never recovered from that vicious tragedy and died in the Shavier Ghetto, so I was told.

ALL ARE DEAD.

Sister number three is Freidke, Hedva in Hebrew. A few years before Grandfather died, Hedva decided she wanted to go to British Palestine *(current day Israel.)* However, in order to go to Palestine, one had to go through a two-year training program sponsored by a Zionist organization. Not everyone would qualify. You had to be strong, willing to endure hardship, learn to work on the land and also learn how to use a gun. The other requirement was that you had to get married and be willing to live on a Kibbutz *(community housing, a co-op lifestyle, with shared costs, food, education, housing, childcare and more.)*

Hedva, with her new husband and her best girlfriend, and others, left for Palestine in 1935. The next time I will see her will be 35 years later, in March 1970. We wrote to each other at least once per month for decades, but I felt I was writing more to a good friend since I was only 13 years old when she left home, plus most of my life she lived with our grandparents.

When she moved to be a pioneer settling in Rehovot, they were having a rough time. There was little comfort in Palestine for anyone. A few more years will pass until our uncles, my mother's three brothers, will help Hedva and her husband buy a lot to build a house of their own. About 10 years later, I received a letter from Hedva that she could no longer live with her husband and she wanted a divorce. By that time, they had three sons.

I don't recall what transpired for the next 10 years or how she was able to support her family since she was sick most of the time. One day, I received a letter from Hedva that she met a man who had grown children, a widower who wanted to marry her and she wanted my opinion. They married and lived a happy life for many years. He loved her boys, Natan, Rani, and Yossi, and took good care of her. His name was Zvi.

(Hedva escaped death during the Holocaust and stayed in Israel where her grown sons have fought protecting Israel in many wars and tensions, as Israel is surrounded by hostile countries. Her three sons and their families continue to live in Israel.)

My brother Motl was next, the fourth child in our family, and a handsome man. He had blondish hair and blue eyes. He was six years older than I.

When Motl was very young, he was walking by the stove in the kitchen. Someone was taking boiling water off the stove, and not seeing him, they ran into him and spilled the boiling water, burning him. Since it was winter, he wore a wool sweater and when they tried to pull off the sweater, skin pulled off from his chest. The skin on his chest looked horrible for the rest of his life.

Motl stuttered badly, especially when he was excited. There were people who worked with him to teach him how to speak slowly. That would eventually help him to speak without stuttering.

I was told that he did not stutter when he was a young boy. The reason given was that one Purim holiday while the traditional text was being read and the children were playing with noise makers and cap guns, one of the boys shot the cap gun right into Motl's ear and, since then, he stuttered.

I don't remember much about my brother. I don't recall growing up with him but I'm sure we shared experiences. He was an excellent ice skater. When he moved to a nearby town, his barbershop clients included many Army officers and he would teach them how to skate.

I visited my brother before October 1939. He was very proud to have his own barbershop. I believe that his wife came from the town where they lived. I don't recall the visit other than from photos. We loved to take photos and I am sure glad we did. I have many.

On November 10, 1940, I received a letter and a picture of Motl with his wife and our mother, Feige. That was the last time I ever heard from Motl.

ALL ARE DEAD.

The next sibling was Beilke and she was two years older than I. When Hedva went to Palestine in 1935, Beilke took care of Grandma in our house and also did the cleaning and cooking.

Everyone is gone by now. My four older siblings are all married and it is 1938. Beilke, Grandma, Mama and I are the only ones left at the house. Aunt Seine, Papa's sister, and her husband and two children live next door. We share one roof in a duplex-style house. She would tell us all kinds of stories and sang love songs to us. Aunt Seine was a very good cook and she always brought us something to eat.

By now, our situation has become acute. Mama didn't sell hardly any apples. The only money we had was from our uncles in other countries sending us money to take care of Grandmother. Once in a while, we received a check from our aunt in Africa. Beilke is unhappy but doesn't complain. All our friends are in the same boat with nothing to look forward to and without any hope. Poor Beilke. I wish life was different for her. Grandmother never came out from her room in our house. I slept in there and was age 16 in 1938.

(Bernard drew a layout of the area where his family lived. Outside of the duplex house, there was a large garden to grow a variety of vegetables and potatoes. There was an outhouse also. Imagine how cold it was walking there in the winter! Bernard maintained a personal garden for flowers and trees, and loved gardening his whole life. They had a stable for the horse and wagon. Inside the house, the stove was used to bake and keep warm. He spoke of a "shared wall" with the stove that helped warm the adjoining room. The very long alley, with ghosts in the warehouse, led from his family's property to the main street.)

In later years, a professional photograph of my parents, Nathan and Feige, was given to me. The photo was taken when my parents were young, possibly after their wedding, which I assume was around the turn of the century, 1900. The photo was found by my father's nephew, my cousin who lived in New York. My cousin's name is Seth Gaffin and he originally gave the photo to Uncle Isadore Marcus, my mother's brother living in Arkansas. When Uncle Isadore gave the photo to me, it was the first time I had ever seen the beautiful photograph of my parents.

Bernard's parents in early 1900s

Chapter 2:
Playful Innocence in Lithuania

We have now reached a point in my life when I have to tell you about myself. Earlier, you met your great-grandparents, grandparents, aunts, uncle, and also some of your second cousins. ALL ARE DEAD EXCEPT FOR HEDVA AND MYSELF.

How can I begin to tell you the rest of the story? It is very painful, yet, a warm feeling and closeness that I haven't felt in many years envelops me as I write. I don't exactly know why I have chosen now to tell you about myself.

As I was getting older and Mother still had the store, I would help her sometimes. She made the best ice cream and all the kids loved coming to her store for an ice cream treat.

I was fortunate to have many friends and we were always getting into a lot of fun trouble. One day, a friend and I took all the Russian cigarettes that were left over in his father's store and smoked most of them. Boy, did we get sick! Once during harvest time, a few of us were helping some non-Jewish friends unload hay in their barn. There was a little girl who was playing with us probably around nine years old. The boys asked her who she wanted to play with and she picked me. I was 11 and took off running away from her because I was scared. Boy, did my friends laugh and make fun of me. Around that age, I used to get on our roof whenever a plane flew by. I would sit looking up there until the plane flew completely out of sight. When I was 13, in 1935, it was time for my Bar Mitzvah ceremony. I only recited the Sabbath prayers and did not read from the sacred Torah. There was no party. What can you expect from a boy without a father, so it was said.

I used to hang out a lot with my cousin. His father was related to relatives in Africa so that made us some relation. One day, his family was missing some jewelry. They searched all over the house but couldn't find it. Since I visited often, their three-year-old daughter pointed to me and said that I took the jewelry. You can imagine the shock! The news spread all over our village and feeling shamed was unbearable. They made me go to the Rabbi to swear I didn't take it. Several months later, as they were cleaning the house for Passover, they found the jewelry. The father came to my house to ask for forgiveness, but my family didn't want to hear him, for the shame had cut deep for all of us when he publicly claimed I was a thief. He even went to the synagogue to ask for forgiveness before the congregation. I have never forgotten this incident. It taught me a lesson I will always remember.

One day during our freezing winter, a small plane was forced to land on the solid ice behind our house. The pilot ran out of fuel. Well, that was the most exciting thing that happened in our town in a long time. People came running to the field where the plane landed and I want you to know, that wasn't all. After about three hours, another plane came and landed on the ice next to the first one! The second plane brought fuel and then they both took off and that was that.

Around early September, the weather began to change. It became cool with lots of rain. Winter was coming and soon it would get very cold. This was the season that we picked the winter apples and stored some in the attic and some in the cellar, covered with straw so they wouldn't freeze. Some apples we would eat after they froze and thawed and froze and thawed again. Oh boy, that was delicious, tasting like wine!

Raseiniai was a very nice town of about 10,000 people, and records show that 47% were Jewish. Most of the Jews engaged in commerce. We had our Jewish doctors, dentists, butchers, tailors, barbers and more. If one had a trade, he could make a living. The houses were pretty nice and Jews lived all over the town. We got along with the non-Jews fairly well. The Rabbi would take care of most of the problems except when it came to criminal or political cases. We had several synagogues and many religious Jews went three times a day to pray.

I can see it clearly in my mind to this day. Before the Jewish holy days, or even for weekly Sabbath, the streets and sidewalks would be cleaned and men with long beards and prayer books in their hands, walked down the street to the synagogue. All was quiet and fresh sand was sprinkled on sidewalks to make the place look pretty. Delicious smells from freshly baked and cooked Sabbath meals danced in the air. It was such a beautiful and peaceful time. Visible from house windows, two Sabbath candles burned a warm glow, respecting and honoring tradition.

On Friday before sunset, we would run to the baker to place our cholent in the baker's oven so that we didn't have to cook on the Sabbath, which was a religious custom. *(Cholent is a type of stew that usually simmers overnight and then is eaten during Sabbath day.)* After services on Sabbath morning (*Saturday*), we would pick up the meal from the baker for Sabbath dinner. The only time we would eat meat was for Sabbath. Usually, we ate fish soup or chicken.

Winter came and snow covered the entire world around us. Before the snow, it rained a lot. The rain flooded the fields and then they would freeze. We ice skated on those frozen fields. The wind was so strong, all we had to do was just let the wind push us, but there was no way to skate back. Many times, we would just hold onto a sleigh and get pulled back to town, otherwise it was a long cold walk back.

One night during a winter storm, it was so cold and drafty in the house. Beilke, our cousins from next door, and I all sat in my sister's room next to the oven for warmth. We heard this dreadful howling sound from outside and were terribly scared, even crying with fear. All of a sudden, we were shaken by a knock on the door. We screamed and all ran to the door together. It was only our friend. She was deaf and dumb, but we were able to speak to her in sign language. We told her that a wolf was outside making a frightening loud howling noise. Well, she walked right to the oven, closed the chimney draft, and there was no more wolf.

Winter was now in full force and we were running out of wood. The house was extremely cold and everything was frozen inside and out. We couldn't even go out to the outhouse. Mama was seldom home. It was just Beilke, Grandma and I. You could get frostbite if not dressed properly to just walk across the yard to our stable. That's how freezing it was. There were only a few logs remaining. I began to tear down some of the boards from the stable, fence, anything I could find. The snow was so thick that houses in low areas had to dig a tunnel in order to get out through the door. Even birds would freeze. I tried whatever I could to keep warm, even wrapping newspaper around my legs to protect from strong winds.

When sunshine appeared, I loved to go outside of the town and walk slowly through snow up to my knees, appreciating the brilliant white snow not yet disturbed by animal or human. I didn't feel the cold when the sun was out.

***

To help create more understanding of Bernard's world and writing during his early years, some historical references are important. Before World War I, Lithuania was under Russian rule for over one hundred years until 1915, when Germany took control of Lithuania. After WWI ended, in 1918, Germany was defeated and Lithuania gained independence, yet there was instability with conflicts against southern neighbor Poland and Russia. In 1920, Poland took over Lithuania's capital, Vilnius. The new Lithuanian capital became Kaunas, also known as Kovna.

Bernard was born in 1922 during what was considered a brief "Golden Age" for Lithuanian Jews, with more equal rights and the ability to create a thriving community. In 1926, a right-wing coup installed an authoritarian leader and Jewish rights were weakened and anti-Semitism increased.

Meanwhile, in the United States, there was a concern that too many immigrants were arriving taking jobs. There was also a hysteria created in 1917 over perceived threats from Communist Russia, known as the Red Scare. Anti-Semitism existed in America and Adolph Hitler studied this, such as the KKK, eugenics laws that forced sterilization and discouraged births of "undesirables," and misinformation that led to prejudice. In the early 1920's, the U.S. restricted immigration from Asia and set a quota country-by-country, especially restricting immigration from southern and eastern Europe. Lithuania was located in northeastern Europe.

Hitler was aggressively rising to power in Germany. Hitler believed that Nordic and Germanic races were superior. All other races were inferior and ripe for expulsion, forced sterilization, and capturing of property. Jews were hated most by Hitler and he labeled the "Jewish race" as most inferior and dangerous of all, threatening German society, He believed Jews were the reason for Germany's defeat in World War I, that they had links to feared Communism, and that they dominated professions and skills that led to too powerful of opportunities economically and intellectually. Jews were an obstacle to his desired plan for Germany's takeover of Europe and creating a white supremist race.

The 1929 Great Depression struck, creating fear and panic globally. By 1932, more people left the U.S. than arrived. One third of all Germans were without work and Hitler wanted a scapegoat. He found his chance to blame the Jews for dominating banks and commerce, destroying the German economy and denying jobs to others. He rallied German young men as superior and promoted the hatred of Jews to a growing Nazi culture.

In 1933, Hitler was appointed Chancellor of Germany, ultimately an absolute dictator, with horrid abusive practices by his forces. History considers this the beginning of the Holocaust era in January 1933 when Hitler and the Nazi Party came to power. They enacted discriminatory laws and organized violence against Jews and had a plan known as the "Final Solution" for systematic mass murder of European Jews.

The U.S. government and American public learned about the Nazi persecution of German Jews from American diplomats abroad and from the media. The U.S. response was limited in 1933 because of suffering from the Great Depression. Unemployment was 25% and the new president was Franklin D. Roosevelt. Only 8,200 immigrants arrived in the U.S. in 1933 with quota laws, a 95% decrease from previous years.

In New York City in 1933, a gathering of tens of thousands of Americans denounced Hitler and Nazi's, with additional rallies in many cities. However, the Depression limited traction of support. In 1936, after much controversy over the Olympics in Hitler's Germany, a prominent Nazi publisher pronounced that to secure the safety of the whole world, Jews must be exterminated. American media reported on this, but with still high unemployment in the U.S., rallies did not build.

In 1936, Hitler sent troops into the Rhineland, a demilitarized zone along the Rhine River in western Germany, after France signed a treaty of friendship and mutual support with the Soviet Union. By 1937, European wars were spreading and Hitler was eager for power gains. Lithuania, located northeast of Germany and all the conflicts, was not directly involved, but was learning about Hitler's dangerous threats through newspaper and radio, for the few who could afford that media.

***

It was Spring 1937 and I was 14 years old. Food was a problem. Aunt Seine, father's sister living next door, would bring food to us occasionally, which we appreciated. As far as Mama earning a living to feed us, well, that was almost impossible. Mama had to borrow in order to keep us fed. Things started to change. Many of our friends were leaving. The high school was about to close and the rooms were empty and quiet. Zionist organizations were being organized. We belonged to the Haluzim. News from other countries in Europe was bad. Hitler was gaining strength from Germany.

Since the high school was no longer active, the Haluzim organization used some of the rooms for meetings to learn about Palestine and speak only in Hebrew. It was loads of fun. Boys and girls would hang out in the large empty building. I'll be honest, it was scary in there. I had a couple of girlfriends and the whole gang would just sit around and talk about current events in Europe and in Palestine. My sister, Hedva, is now in Palestine and the letters we receive from her are not always good.

It is August 1937 and I have just turned 15 years old. With my school education ended, I started to work as a painter and can remember my first job. The government was building new barracks with a wooden fence all the way around the property. The painting was to be completed by a contractor I was working for. To my surprise, I was assigned to paint the fence of at least several miles! I earned fifty cents the first week and I felt proud and good to earn money.

As I continued to work as a painter, my sisters thought I should at least have a uniform so they sewed me a new uniform. That was the first time in fifteen years that I ever put on a new garment. My clothes were mostly second-hand sent from American relatives. When I put on this new outfit, all brand new, not a spot on it, I asked, *"How could I be a painter without a spot on my clothes?"* Well, I took the brush and painted all over my new uniform. Now I felt and looked like a professional painter! A lot of the friends who hung out at our house worked for the same contractor also.

The year of 1937 was coming to a disturbing end. There was much talk in town about socialism and communism and about Germany and Russia. It was getting very bad for the Jews in Germany, due to Hitler. Some of the people I knew were arrested for handing out leaflets about Communism. My friends and I started to meet secretly with some men at the cemetery. We couldn't see their faces and we never knew their names. They would give us literature to read and set dates for other meetings. Anything was better than the monster Hitler.

With all this uncertainty and fear being talked about, I started to blame God for taking my father away. Getting involved in organizations, and with Socialism being the thing of the future, I started to think very seriously and question whether there was a God at all?

Deep in my heart I was scared of God. For the first time in my life, I started to rebel against God and his laws. How could I get even? First, I smoked on the Sabbath, but I didn't want God to see me so I smoked in the outhouse of the synagogue. I knew He couldn't see me there. Next, on Yom Kippur, the holiest day of the year, when religious Jews do not eat anything for 25 hours, I bought some ham! *(Pork is forbidden, unkosher, and never eaten by religious Jews.)* I ran to the stable and ate the horribly sinful food. I was sure He couldn't see me because there was a roof over the stable and who can see through a roof? I did feel very guilty and scared. I never told anyone about that.

I still remembered when my father died 10 years previously, the bitter cold and early mornings when we walked to synagogue to say Kaddish prayers. Part of the prayer was, *"My father, my teacher, my guide."* My father was not there to teach or guide. People talked down to me. Why did Father have to leave us?

This experience would stay with me for the rest of my life. When I did go to synagogue as a teenager, I wouldn't listen anymore. We still had our permanent seat, but I would just make it look as if I was praying. I spent more time looking up where the women sat upstairs, watching the girls wave. It was another distraction from the life we were living, waiting, hoping and uncertain.

Would things take a turn for the worse or the better? We were hundreds of miles away from the chaos and threats of Hitler and wars. It was hard to imagine anything beyond the tranquil simplicity of Raseiniai, distant from intricate complexities and dangers of the outside world.

Bernard, standing in center on ladder, in his painter's clothes.

Chapter 3:
Inviting Fate

It was a somber beginning to 1938 - nothing to do, no place to go, feeling useless. To break the monotony, some older boys who were friends of mine and my sister, would come to our house and we would sing, play cards called keno, and joke about our nothingness. These friends were not accepted into college since they were Jewish, so even the smart ones were faced with a limited future.

The big excitement once a year was around New Years. An international car race event brought cars racing through our town. We stayed awake almost all night to cheer the cars noisily passing through and could see their lights from far away. Cars would skid on icy roads and the street level could sometimes be higher than houses from snow moved off of sidewalks. Snow was piled high on the dirt street and, with a little rain and freezing temperatures, you had solid ice.

I almost forgot to tell you about our beautiful ice-skating lake. During winter, when the lake froze with ice at least two feet thick, the fire department would clear snow every day from the area until they made like a snow fence border around the lake. Christmas trees were placed all around the frozen lake with lights and music played. It was a magnificent sight! We skated at night with the moon shining down on us while the wind slept. You didn't feel the cold then. When buckets of new snow fell from the sky, the white blanket was thick and all was hushed quiet. I can still feel the fresh, cold air on my face along with the calm quiet peacefulness. Life was beautiful at moments like that.

My brother-in-law, Orke, you remember Dveirke's husband, made me a pair of new hi-top shoes. They felt so good and were shiny. I was sure proud of those new shoes. I would attach my ice skates to the new hi-top shoes in the house, go out in the street, hang on to a passing sleigh pulled by a horse, and skate to the lake. The shoes got wet every time I skated and soon my feet were getting bigger or the shoes were shrinking. My feet hurt but I was scared to complain, afraid my shoes would be taken away. My two little toes will bother me every time I buy new shoes for all my life.

When the ice started to melt, spring was surely in the air. It was almost impossible for a horse and wagon to ride through the alley because mud was knee deep. As the weather became warmer and the Passover holiday was near, it was time to prepare with Jewish customs for the holiday of freedom. Dishes were changed and glassware was boiled clean to be kosher for Passover. Wine, matzoh, and an alcoholic drink made from hops and honey, mead, were ordered. I had fun watching the baker make round matzos, the flat cracker made of only flour and water.

Passover was lonely at our house with only Mama, Grandmother, my sister Beilke, and I. Aunt Seine, my father's sister, was busy next-door cooking creating delicious smells. Her Matzah balls in chicken broth took your breath away! They were big, round and golden, filled with schmaltz and gribenes *(chicken fat and skin cracklings with fried onions and salt.)* She brought us almost a whole meal that was very special for us.

When the weather became even warmer, it was time again to prepare the garden for planting. It was also time to clean inside and outside. Beilke spent days scrubbing the wooden floors until they were white again. It was also time for the police to come around to inspect the grounds to make sure everything was painted and clean.

After Passover in 1938, a very significant event occurred. We never could have imagined the importance of a letter received from Mother's family in America.

The letter was from Mother's sister, Leah, asking if Mother wanted to send one child to America. My mother and grandmother decided I was the one and I should feel lucky that my family wanted me to come to America.

Well, to tell you the truth, I was 15 and not too excited about America. In our small town in Lithuania, who knew anything about America? We surely didn't. Now, if it was Russia or France, that would have been something to be excited about! We knew and were told how good it was for the Jews in Russia, after all, weren't many of the leaders Jewish? Okay, I will go to America. When or how I would actually go, no one knew.

***

It was no small task for Bernard's family in America to sponsor him given the rigid U.S. quota system and required documents and money to enter America. The U.S. had severely restricted immigration quotas since 1924, supported by public opinion favoring economic and national security priorities. There was also no special refugee quota policy during the Nazi persecution crisis period.

The U.S. process involved registering with the American consulate for Bernard to be placed on a waiting list for entry into America. Documents required to obtain a visa included identity paperwork, police certificates, exit and transit permissions, and a financial affidavit showing you had money and would not be destitute upon arrival. In most cases, a $5,000 deposit was required by the sponsoring family who received the funds back after a period of time. This deposit represented more than a year's income for most families. Many of the documents had expiration dates and you had to start over if one expired.

Application for immigration also required a valid ship ticket before receiving a visa. As Germany became more aggressive, fear of their submarines targeting passenger vessels further concerned Atlantic crossings. Many vessels stopped entirely or reduced the number of crossings, increasing the cost and demand for berths on a ship.

In America, "Hebrew" was a racial category for immigration at this time. There was a significant presence of antisemitism in American politics and industry. During the period of 1939 to 1940, over half of all immigrants to America identified themselves as Hebrew/ Jewish. The actual percentage is believed to be higher with some refugees selecting a different category to hide their identity.

The timing of Bernard's family inquiry to sponsor him, in spring 1938, coincided with Nazi Germany invading and annexing Austria in March 1938. This launched a refugee crisis, as hundreds of thousands of Jews joined the waiting lists for U.S. immigration visas hoping to escape a worsening situation in Europe.

In July 1938, a meeting of 32 countries convened to address the Jewish refugee crisis caused by Hitler's cruel march. The countries said they had no space. Two-thirds of Americans agreed. President Roosevelt tried to ease the quota system but it did not pass. There were many antisemitic members in U.S. Congress and among influential corporate leaders. It is likely that Bernard did not know the details of the difficult demand and process for acquiring a visa.

At this point, Germany was already the most powerful nation in Europe. Hitler declared that Jews must be removed and Germany needed more space and resources. His eyes were on invading Poland, Ukraine and Lithuania, all with high proportionate Jewish populations.

***

Summer of 1938 came and went. There wasn't much to do. We met regularly with the Zionist Haluzim organization at our empty school and were told that the future for Jewish people was in Palestine. I was still involved with the socialist group and we held our secret meetings. More of my friends were arrested for Communist activities.

I was still working as a painter when work was available. A new modern jail was being built across from the old cemetery. I started to work painting at the jail. One day, I was looking across to the cemetery and was reminded of Grandfather's funeral. That gave me a funny feeling inside. I could see the image of Grandfather's body at his death, dressed in traditional white burial garments, being placed in the freshly dug grave. As they lowered him in the ground, I looked down and saw him, his eyes closed as if asleep. Soon they placed a few boards to cover him and piled dirt on top of my grandfather, never to come back again. These old memories and images stay with me clearly.

One day, as I was painting window frames that overlooked the jail yard where they kept political prisoners, I saw a guy down there, one of the prisoners, who I knew. He waved at me. I waved back. Then he pointed for me to come down by the wooden fence. There, he spoke quickly to me through the fence and gave me a piece of paper. He told me to deliver it to a known Communist. I was surprised and before I could back away and refuse, two secret policemen roughly grabbed me. I was jerked away and whisked hurriedly to headquarters.

Boy, this was it. I was incredibly frightened! Soon, the police began questioning me. It seemed that there was no end to their unrelenting questions. I was crying by now, only a 16-year-old teen terrified. I kept repeating that I knew nothing about Communism and I thought he just wanted to say hello. The chief of the secret police came in and, after getting a report from the guards, he asked me a few more questions. He told me to follow him. We walked outside and he got on a motorcycle, instructing me to get on behind him. I was so fearful that I vigorously shook my head no, refusing to get on, and instead, I ran after the motorcycle next to him all the way into town, several miles!

Well, the news spread quickly and it took my town by storm. Many people started to gather in front of the police station. Soon my mother and Aunt Elke arrived. Aunt Elke operated a small hotel with meals. Many people would just eat there and others also lived at the hotel. The Chief of the secret service was well known by Aunt Elke. She kept assuring him and pleading with him that I had nothing to do with politics. After the badgering questions continued for what seemed like an eternity, I was finally released to Aunt Elke. Thank heavens she personally knew the police chief! I don't want to think about what could have happened if she didn't. But that wasn't the end of the ordeal.

I could sense the changing attitude of the people in town towards me. Some parents wouldn't let their children associate with me. That felt sad and unfair. Later that summer, I had to go to the capitol where the trial was being held. I was to be a witness for the prosecution. Mama came with me. After waiting nervously near the court room almost an entire day, they never even called me, so we went back to Raseiniai. Staske, the man who gave me the note was sent for a prison term. He was a nice guy even if he wasn't Jewish, but he spoke Yiddish like a Jew.

My life wasn't exactly dull all the time. However, more and more people were leaving. Some were getting married and moving to another place, while others left the country. Life went on. Once in a while, some of us would walk to the synagogue just to listen to the old men study the sacred Talmud text. They would debate and argue for hours about the meaning of one word or sentence. It seemed confusing, but could be entertaining. More importantly, it was one way to pass time when we had nowhere else to go and not much to do in our village, shrinking of people, commerce, and activity.

***

On November 9 – 10, 1938, Nazi forces coordinated violent antisemitic attacks against Jewish communities in Germany. Houses were invaded, hundreds of synagogues burned, thousands of businesses destroyed. Jews were beaten and killed. This horror is known as Kristallnacht, or Night of Broken Glass, for so much shattering of glass windows as a result of the brutality. Radios and cars were confiscated and Jews were banned from being in public or conducting commerce. Some German Jews were able to escape to Amsterdam and reported the horrors. This appeared on the front page of U.S. newspapers. President Roosevelt was in shock of such cruel violence and recalled the U.S. ambassador of Germany. Nazi threats were rampant throughout Europe now. Bernard's village often received delayed, incomplete news. Many were in disbelief that it could get any worse or closer to home.

***

Winter 1938 arrived early with heavy snow and winds, not letting up for the rest of the year. Beilke's friends and my friends came to our house some evenings since there wasn't anything else to do. We discussed the situation in Europe, told funny stories, sang, and even got drunk when we were able to scrape up enough money together to buy a bottle of schnaps. As bad as times were for us, there was always someone who had it worse. Germany seemed far away from us. Even though schools had been closed for a while, Raseiniai appeared safe.

One cloudy, cold evening in November, snowfall entertained the night. It must have been around eight o'clock and I decided to go for a walk in the darkness, bundling up in my usual winter layers of hand-me-down clothing. Streets were completely empty and it was so very quiet you could hear snowflakes land softly on the pillow of a blanketed ground. I walked all the way around the village square, past the big synagogue, which faced the market. By the time I returned home, I was walking in over a foot of soft new snow, alone, in a painting of a wonderland. I loved beautiful peaceful moments like that.

The hygiene situation presented a problem, but not knowing any better, we didn't really consider it a problem. There was no such thing as a bathroom. At its best, if you had a portable tub such as you might have seen in western movies, you had it made. You could take a bath once in a while, like several times a year. However, one could always go to the public baths. Also, lice and bedbugs were no strangers either, especially in the winter time.

I wish I could describe winters in Raseiniai in such a way that you can actually feel the brutal coldness in your bones, slapping your face, and chilling your lungs. The winter of 1938 was bitterly severe and caused hardship on many people in the town. There were some who didn't even have enough clothes to keep warm. At least we had clothes that came from America. They were used garments but so what? We had clothes.

One of our friends, in particular, will stay in my mind always. His name was Faifke and he was a nice man in his early 20s. He came to our house often. I can't remember whether his father died or went to America. Anyway, one day when Faifke came to our house, his face was chilled blue from the brutal winter storm. He kept jumping around rubbing his ears, trying to warm up a little. He had no overcoat. Instead, he wore a worn-out sport jacket that showed a simple white shirt with white cuffs under it. Why was I thinking about him? He was very smart and talented, but so poor. When he came into our house, seeing him without an overcoat almost frozen and blue, I realized somberly that there were others worse off. I became more thankful for what I did have. But when I got near him, I saw that there was no full shirt under the sport jacket! He had sewed a white collar, front bib, and wrist cuffs to the jacket, appearing as if there was a shirt. I'll never forget what I saw, a worn-out sport jacket over bare skin in minus freezing temperatures.

You may be wondering why I write so much about the winters. It is the winters that made us feel hopelessness in our hearts. Look at my photos to see summers. Life was different in the summer. Study the pictures. They tell so much - more than a thousand words.

***

Bernard kept many original photos from the 1920s and 1930s from Lithuania. It is unclear how he preserved them so securely without damage from weather, transport, and time. His deepest emotions and memories during his whole life were connected to these photos of family, friends, himself, and his village.

Many more photos from early years to final years can be found at www.50centsforalife.weebly.com.

Bernard at bottom, with friends

Chapter 4:
Destiny Strikes

As the bitterly cold winter of 1938 tightened its grip on our village, world news of Europe's worsening situation surpassed our ability to envision what lay ahead. Each piece of information left us more on edge, weaving a pattern of tense uncertainty into the frigid air.

Germany was on a terror march to gain power. Newspapers filled columns with stories about what happened when the German army took over a country, creating heightened worry and fear. Antisemitism was on an ugly rise. So far, we had no problem in our town. Raseiniai was located in central Lithuania and that interior protection made a big difference. We had one or two German families living in our town and all the Jews did business with them.

In December 1938, I was 16 years old and became very sick with a dangerously high fever. My chilled body shook uncontrollably. The bed that I didn't move from was dragged into the living room next to the warm wall with the kitchen oven heating on the other side. I felt awful and weak from likely a bad case of double pneumonia. Nothing mattered.

We had received letters from my uncles in America telling Mama that they were still working on my immigration papers for many months. These papers would enable me to leave Lithuania as soon as possible. I didn't care at all. I wasn't thinking about America. I felt too sick to think or care about anything.

One evening, my group of friends came to the house and played cards, keno, as usual. I guess they were trying to cheer me up by being nearby. As I lay in bed with my eyes closed, weak and chilled, on yet another cold winter night, I could hear soft voices in the background. Muffled talking continued, saying something about the Jewish newspaper in our capital of Kaunas trying to raise money for the Zionist movement. The newspaper was selling raffle tickets at 50 cents each. I didn't have 50 cents and besides, couldn't they grasp how utterly lousy I felt? Why bother about this? Who cares about a raffle ticket fundraiser?

Little did I know, they were quietly pulling nickels from their pockets until 50 cents was collected among them. Around that table, my friends pooled their coins and bought me a raffle ticket as a surprise gift.

In that powerful moment, a life-altering destiny unfolded with their kind gesture. Unbeknownst to me at the time, they were giving me the gift of life, a secret that would remain hidden for months.

Winter faded and spring of 1939 arrived. It was the same routine starting all over again. Nothing but scary news about Germany's aggressive march for power.

One day that spring, I received an official-looking letter from the Jewish newspaper informing me that I had won the raffle grand prize with the 50-cent ticket purchased by my friends! The thrilling news spread through our village like wildfire. But what was the grand prize?

We anxiously awaited the arrival of the prize. A few long days later, we had our answer when a big box was delivered to the house. My friends gathered around excitedly as I tore it open, laughing and joking about outrageous possibilities.

And then we saw it. Inside the huge box was the most beautiful, large short-wave radio in a genuine mahogany case. No one had ever seen anything so big, majestic, and importantly valuable. We were mesmerized by it! Very few people even owned a radio at all, we surely didn't. Cheering and celebration swept through the house, and my good fortune was beyond comprehension in that moment.

Well, there was one important detail for the grand prize radio. We didn't have electricity in our house. Yet. That changed quickly when Mama, Grandma, Aunt Seine next door, and my oldest sister Taube, all pitched in and, somehow, we were able to get electricity installed. We were limited to a ten-watt bulb.

People began to come to our house often to sit in front of the beautiful large radio, smiling as they listened to music, and disturbed to witness Hitler's deranged speeches.

The news was very bad as Hitler's vicious troops were invading more and more countries. Somehow, we felt shielded being far away in Raseiniai where it was quiet with no sign of trouble. The war atrocities were still distant, although some people began talking about leaving.

Life continued that spring of 1939 and we sensed an uneasiness growing in town. The younger Lithuanian goyem *(non-Jews)* were getting braver and meaner as they became influenced by Germany's aggressive supremist rise. They mocked and disrespected elderly Jewish men with long beards and scoffed at any gathering of Jewish people.

Our newspaper began to quote other papers in other countries. Germany continued its ugly power march. Harsh ultimatums were given by Germany to Poland, who we shared a border with in the south. We were uncertain what this might mean for Lithuania.

***

In March 1939, Germany also gave an ultimatum to Lithuania, demanding that Germany gain the vital port city of Memel territory on the Baltic Sea. If this demand was not met, the current Lithuanian capital of Kaunas would be immediately bombed. Kaunas was only 50 miles south of Bernard's town of Raseiniai. On March 23, 1939, Lithuania ceded the Memel territory to Germany. This resulted in a major further downturn in Lithuania's economy and escalated tensions for all of Europe as Hitler advanced his power east. Most of the Lithuanian and Jewish population fled Memel prior to Hitler's arrival, including Bernard's sister, Taube, who returned to Raseiniai with her husband.

In New York City, in March 1939, a huge parade of 20,000 marchers and half-million viewers shouted "Stop Hitler!" Congress refused to listen and Jewish children and adult refugees faced impending death at home as severely limited immigration into America worsened. Much smaller countries were accepting more immigrants than the U.S. Bernard's place on the waiting list for a visa was unknown.

***

Summer of 1939, I turned 17 years old and the outlook was grim for all of us. My friends who bought the winning raffle ticket joked with me. They sneered, *"You won't go to America. You'll stay here and die with us."* I countered with, *"No! I will go to America. And I will return to visit your graves."*

That was a pitiful way to joke and it still hurts me to this day, but making light of hopelessness was what we teens did. It eased the true fear and distress.

Finally! In August 1939, my official documents and vessel tickets arrived from America. We were stunned that our relatives managed to arrange this, considering the extremely low count of visa's issued due to restrictive U.S. immigration laws. I was to leave in one month, September 1939. Mama cried. My friends were overjoyed for me. Yohevet, my girlfriend, cried. Everyone was happy and excited for me.

And how did I feel about going to America? Well, to tell you the truth, I felt numb. I guess that was easier than to feel anything else, such as fear of bidding farewell to everything I knew. And, fear of traveling alone for weeks across oceans to an unfamiliar country and culture. This fear grew with uncertainty about crossing borders amid dangerous threats from Hitler's regime that terrorized Europe, adding a profound concern to my journey. Yes, numb was safer.

With the tickets to America came a ten-dollar bill. This was proof that I had money upon arrival. You had to have some money on you, that was the law to be allowed in and stay. My papers and tickets were all made out for a departure sail in September from Bremen, Germany. Hitler's Germany.

September arrived quickly, bringing with it a brutal war between Germany and Poland. Our hearts sank as news of these attacks reached us, marking the onset of a full-fledged World War, engulfed in horror and destruction. The illusion of immunity vanished as the Lithuanian Army mobilized since Poland touched us to the south.

As country borders were about to shut tight, this terrifying situation changed everything for me. Trapped inside Lithuania, it seemed my friends' warnings were true. Was I destined to share their fate? Fear and despair gripped our village, with panic and hopelessness racing through our thoughts. The looming question hung heavy: What would become of me and my family?

***

On September 1, 1939, Germany invaded Poland initiating the official start to World War II with 1.5 million Nazi troops. France and Great Britain had previously signed a pact to protect Poland triggering their declaration of war on Germany.

A couple weeks earlier, in August 1939, Germany and Russia had signed a 10-year non-aggression pact with a secret plan to destroy

Poland and divide it. Lithuania was added to this deal in September. Three million Jews lived in Poland and 160,000 in much smaller Lithuania.

During those early weeks in September, Polish synagogues were burned by Germans, 50,000 Jews were murdered, and 400,000 Jews were pushed into a Warsaw ghetto within an area of two square miles. They were used as slave labor or just holding pens for later determination. Meanwhile in Germany, Hitler issued ration cards to Jews limiting them to a starvation diet of 200 to 300 calories per day. Bernard's family did not know these details as he waited to depart.

Between September 17 to October 6, 1939, Russia invaded Poland from the opposite side, the east, as part of the deal with Germany. Russia took back the city of Vilnius from Poland and returned it to Lithuanian control. In return for that deal, a treaty was signed on October 10, 1939 where Russia demanded the right to install 20,000 Russian troops in five military bases in Lithuania.

It is relevant to Bernard's story that Russia blocked the harbor of Tallinn, Estonia at this time in September 1939, north of Latvia and Lithuania. Tallinn is the exit to the sea, located across from Finland. There was Russian air activity and troops along this Estonian northern border including 600 tanks, 600 aircraft and 160,000 Russian troops. By September's end, a pact was signed with Russia promising peace to Estonia in exchange for 30,000 Russian troops to be based there. Russia then invaded the last of the three Baltic states, Latvia, just north of Lithuania. All of this activity is pertinent to what happens next for Bernard.

On October 12, 1939, Russia demanded that Finland relinquish a military base to them near Helsinki. By late October 1939, the British government released a report identifying that concentration camps had been verified as being built in Europe for Jews. None of this information was known by Bernard.

***

FATE

(Bernard often said it was his destiny to leave Lithuania. He believed in fate, all the actions leading up to the present moment were fate, which helped his destiny come true.)

After Germany invaded Poland by bombing on land and air in September 1939, Nazi Germany stood worryingly on Lithuania's southern border. We were told the fighting had stopped. There was an eerie fear of doubt hanging in the air because Russia was approaching Lithuania from the east. Hope was fading fast. I was 17 years old and at 18, I would have to join the Lithuanian Army.

Feeling disoriented by the chaos, and fearing being surrounded by hostile Germans and Russians, the most jolting news of all arrived at our door in early October.

I opened the official letter from the American consul in Kaunas, confused as it declared that I had only three days to get out of Lithuania and depart for America.

Three days?! If I was told to walk to the moon, it would have made more sense. None of my passage tickets and visas were good anymore. I couldn't proceed through Bremen, Germany. There was no way to get in touch with my uncles in America for new tickets and no time to start the rigid visa process over. Money didn't exist for us here anyway. It was an impossible situation!

Reading that letter again to make sure my eyes weren't deceiving me, tears blurred the print, as all hope crumbled. I felt utterly defeated, weighed down by a heaviness of sadness as if shackled to the ground, imprisoned by despair.

Confronting the frenzy of obstacles in leaving Lithuania, with no papers and borders closing amid terrorizing from Germany and Russia, demanded nothing less than a miracle. I was short on time as the clock sped forward.

I had no money, all I had was three days. Fear for our lives and impending dangers, along with desperate pleas for hope, collided together as news of my letter spread through our community, broadcasting the shocking reality of our situation.

(The three days would have been October 6, 7, 8, 1939. This was the same time as Russia's deal-making with Lithuania to install 20,000 troops in the country, which was officially signed on October 10th. The consulate likely was aware of this negotiation, telling Bernard to exit now, before troops arrived. Russia was also invading Estonia and Latvia to the north, Bernard's new exit route out, since traveling west through Germany was out of the question. The three Baltic States' freedom and independence were facing an imminent end.)

All of a sudden, as if a bolt of lightning struck the town, fate intervened miraculously - a wealthy man emerged out of nowhere, eager to buy my grand prize radio!

The identity of this unknown savior remained a mystery. I'll never know who saved my life. The man handed Mama enough money to buy documents and a new vessel ticket for passage to America from a different port on a new date. Was he an angel? In a state of disbelief, I lifted the large, beautiful radio in its mahogany case, offering it to the generous man, with my heart pounding in bewilderment and gratitude.

All of these incredible events of fate were interwoven for my destiny - my friends purchasing the raffle ticket, winning the grand prize radio, family in America able to sponsor me, this wealthy mysterious man appearing, the consulate notifying me just in time and willing to issue new documents despite quotas, space for me on last-minute transport, all working to save my life and pave the way for an immediate escape from Lithuania.

God must have wanted me to live. I don't know why I was protected, especially after turning against God when my father died. I believe it was my destiny to live.

Fifty cents for Berle's life.

Remaining hours were a blur of preparation. My oldest sister brought me a coat and cap. I had an old suit sent previously from a cousin in America. Someone packed a small weathered suitcase, which included a beloved box of photos. I was ready. The clock was ticking.

In the dark, chilly morning of October 8, 1939, I went in to say goodbye to Grandmother. With tears in her eyes, she softly whispered in my ear, *"I only want to live long enough to know that you arrive safely in America."*

I lightly kissed her aged cheek and silently left the room. I was 17. I didn't know what to say. I didn't know how to feel. It was safer to remain silent. Don't speak, just move through this confusion as told. For the last time, I walked out of our simple small duplex house, closing the door on all I had ever known. I was leaving my town of Raseiniai, Lithuania, never to return again.

I am trying to find the right words to describe how I felt on that unforgettable morning. Numb. Disoriented. I felt as if I was floating. I couldn't quite understand what was going on around me. Everything sounded far away, distant. I only heard muffled sounds but no words. This was not real. It was confusing. Was this really me? Was I dreaming? I lived my whole life in this village, with family, orchards, friends coming over to joke, play cards, and ice skate on frozen lakes.

At seven in the morning, it was dark and drizzling, adding to a sense of blurred illusion. Mama, sisters, cousins, and aunts were all walking me to the bus station. We walked down the narrow alley from our small house and stables and onto the main street. It was a long walk to the station and people came out as we walked to wave goodbye. No one said a word. It was so quiet. Was it really me that they were escorting on this journey? It was impossible to consider that was the truth. Mama was coming with me to Kaunas, our capital, then I would be traveling on my own. That was something I could not even imagine.

My older sisters, Beilke and Taube, Aunt Seine, the whole family I had in Raseiniai, plus friends, all were there at the bus station, waving a quiet goodbye. Some had moist eyes, staring at me through tears, wondering if this would be a last glimpse of each other. We hugged and kissed. I remained in almost denial that this was happening, observing as if a stranger from afar.

Finally, it was time to board the bus. As the bus slowly moved, passing one familiar street after another, I saw my girlfriend, Yohevet, standing near the road, watching the bus pass by. My hand instinctively lifted for a small wave to her. I doubt she saw it. As the bus approached the outskirts of town, I turned around and took one long last look at the village where I grew up.

When we arrived in Kaunas, Mama and I went directly to a cousin's house and then on to get my passport, followed by reporting to the American consul. We accomplished all the required preparations within the three-day period, thanks mostly to Mama, especially the miraculous selling of my prized radio. Every action seemed both rushed, since time was quickly ticking away, and also distorted in slow motion, surreal. I still felt numb and emotionless, floating along as if my feet met no ground.

At the American consul, my exit route was explained, although I didn't fully understand what was said. A lot of countries and a lot of officials to approve crossing borders. Mama and I were informed that I had to obtain visas as I traveled north through the Baltic States of Latvia and Estonia, and some Scandinavian countries, until I reached Gothenburg, Sweden. I'll never forget the stern Lithuanian official's remark as he handed me my passport. *"Be sure to come back when you reach your 18th birthday to serve in the Lithuanian army."*

***

Bernard makes no mention of the precarious and risky surroundings of his exit route out of Lithuania. It is assumed that he, his family, and most in Lithuania are unaware of specific details and locations of war tensions and invasions.

To put this in perspective of place and time, Germany is brutally killing to the south of Lithuania, in occupied Poland. Russia has also invaded Poland to divide that country with Germany. Lithuania's original capital city of Vilnius was in the process of being returned. Two days after Bernard departed, Russia was bringing 20,000 troops into Lithuania, with menacing border control. This aligns with the American consul informing Bernard that he must depart by October 8, for after that, borders would close.

The harbor in Tallinn, Estonia, where Bernard would sail across the Gulf to Finland in early October, had only been allowed to re-open less than two weeks previously, after Russian blockades brought 160,000 troops, 600 tanks, and 600 bombing aircraft to this harbor area. There were still 30,000 Russian troops remaining in Estonia where he would sail from. But first, he had to pass through Latvia, where Russia had invaded and occupied.

Finally, two days after he passes through Helsinki, Finland, Russia invades to take over the military base there. Any delay in arriving or departing from Helsinki could have resulted in detainment and possibly the end of his journey west to safety. Border gates opened one after another, just in time for his safe passage, without his full awareness of war events before, during, or after his immediate departure. As he said, he was "floating" through time, surreal, moving along as he was told, guided and protected.

***

On October 8, 1939, I murmured goodbye to Mama at the Kaunas railway station, embracing in a gentle hug, not grasping the magnitude of feeling her comfort and warm breath next to me in that moment. I would never see her again. There was a group of people waiting near the train with their meager belongings. I saw a man from my town that I recognized. He had returned to Raseiniai from America many years ago. My friends and I used to call him the Americaner Goy (*non-Jew*). I said hello to him, then silently joined the line, commencing my long solitary journey to a foreign land.

We boarded the train and I found a seat in one of the cramped cabins. Silence enveloped us as the train rolled away from the station, leaving behind my home country and all that I knew and loved. I had no idea where we were going and joined others peering out of windows, occasionally waving as the train passed through towns and villages.

Our first stop hours later was at the train station in Riga, Latvia. Riga was a large capital city on the Baltic Sea. We made a brief halt there, long enough for Latvian officials to walk through cabins checking our papers. No problems, just felt a bit anxious. The train continued north for a long overnight journey. We arrived in Tallin, Estonia on October 9th.

That first night away from my family was painfully long, filled with loneliness and physical discomfort. With no space to lie down, some people talked throughout the hours of darkness. At the border station between Latvia and Estonia, we repeated the same routine again of preparing our papers for inspection when the train stopped. Late in the afternoon of October 9th, my second day of travel, we transferred from the train in Tallin, Estonia, to a ferry boat, crossing north over the Gulf of Finland to Helsinki. I can't recall if we disembarked in Helsinki, but I do remember the sight of hundreds of bicycles.

A True Story of Surviving by Synchronicity

On the afternoon of October 10, 1939, we sailed west from Helsinki, Finland and the whole time we were firmly instructed to be very quiet. The reason remained curiously unknown. *(They might have been told to remain quiet to avoid attracting attention from potential nearby Russians. Just two days later, the area in Helsinki was invaded and occupied.)*

After an overnight sail, we reached Stockholm, Sweden on the morning of October 11. In Stockholm, we had the freedom to explore on our own, as long as we returned to the railway station by four o'clock sharp. We were being transported by train to a ship's location that would take us to America. I tried hard to understand all of these instructions correctly and, feeling adventurous and excited, I disembarked from the ferry.

Here was my first chance to explore a new country! As a teenage boy with no worldly experience or means for communication, I left the safety of what I had known and set out alone to explore this unfamiliar land.

As I walked around the bustling city of Stockholm by myself, every direction I turned was filled with wonder. It was a maze of new experiences - wide, long streets stretching as far as my eyes could see, towering buildings making me tilt my head back to view their height, and a variety of unfamiliar trees and plants, all so beautiful and pristine.

I stopped in front of a modern building with a peculiar door, feeling puzzled. How do you open and pass through a door that moves in a circle? Pulled by curiosity, I walked closer, and as I approached the circular door, it began to rotate forward into the building! I reached out, grabbed its outer edge, but my fingers got wedged in as it moved forward. Now my fingers and hands were stuck along the edges of the door!

Before I knew what was happening, people came running towards me, talking fast in a language I didn't understand. Finally, my hand and fingers released from the door and someone spoke to me in German, asking if I wanted to see a doctor. Shaking my head, no, I said I was alright and hurriedly left that scene. That was my first experience in the modern world. If you want to go through a revolving door, be sure to keep your hands inside the door and push!

I didn't want to get in trouble or miss the transport, so I returned to the railway station and boarded the train early. We were soon traveling west to our final destination of Gothenburg, Sweden, where a big ship awaited to sail us to America. Another new experience not knowing what to expect. I just moved along as instructed at each place, hoping that I was understanding directions. Every single encounter was new and many were bewildering to me.

***

Bernard's Destiny Route Out of Lithuania

Bernard and his mother traveled by bus from Raseiniai south to the capital city of Kaunas (aka Kovna), Lithuania, which was approximately 50 miles away. In 1939, Kaunas was also the largest city in Lithuania and 25% of the population was Jewish, about 32,000 people. They were primarily merchants, artists, and professionals. There were about 40 synagogues and Kaunas was an important center for the Zionist movement.

Bernard then boarded a train alone in Kaunas, Lithuania, traveling north to Riga, Latvia, 160 miles. Riga is on the Baltic Sea. Russia had signed a treaty with Latvia three days earlier, preparing to bring in 25,000 troops, which likely could have endangered border crossings.

Next, was an overnight train ride north from Latvia to the capital city of Tallin, Estonia, a distance of 190 miles, with a valuable port outlet.

Tallinn, Estonia is across a body of water, known as the Gulf of Finland, and closest to Helsinki, Finland. Today, the ferry ride takes a little over three hours to cross the Gulf between the two cities. Less than two weeks before Bernard's crossing, the exit port was closed with 160,000 Russian troops disturbing the area.

Bernard sailed west from Helsinki, Finland to Stockholm, Sweden, and then onward by train to the west coast port city of Gothenburg, Sweden, the largest seaport in Scandinavia, which feeds into the North Sea. Gothenburg, Sweden is known as the gateway to the world beyond, and lies across the North Sea at a latitude similar to northern Scotland to its west.

It's a mystery how Bernard swiftly obtained revised documents and visas in Kaunas, just a day or two after the American consul's alarming notice. Immigration to America was extremely restricted with country-specific quotas and waiting times that could stretch for years. From 1938 to 1941, only 123,000 Jewish refugees managed to immigrate to America, with hundreds of thousands more trapped in countries massacred by Hitler.

Bernard's family in America was not wealthy or influential. They likely pooled resources and worked together to navigate the laborious document process. When his documents and ship tickets became invalid due to the onset of war, there was not sufficient time to contact family in the U.S. for assistance.

The process to expedite his new documents, secure approval for a new arrival date in the U.S., and find available and immediate transportation, with extremely limited space on full trains and ships, remains unknown. Bernard was unaware of these complex and seemingly impossible obstacles. Once his prized radio was sold generating money, all he believed was that his destiny was to arrive in America safely. The remarkable openings of fate that allowed him to escape harm, thus far, are truly mystical and incredible.

Yohevet and I, summer 1939 outside town, a place we use to hang out The Sand Pit

Chapter 5:
The Journey Out

On the evening of October 12, 1939, we sailed away from the busy port of Gothenburg, Sweden. I was on a ship headed west to America! Imagine, less than a week ago, I was a penniless 17-year-old in a country threatened by German and Russian invasions. Whoever made this happen, however it came about, my astonishment knew no bounds. At the time, I didn't know that the hands and synchronicity that made it possible had just saved my life.

The next morning, October 13, while sailing along the Norwegian coast, I was captivated by the breathtaking scenery. The view of surrounding majestic mountains was truly a magnificent sight, forever etched in my memory.

The ship, The Drottningholm was huge, the most colossal ship I had ever seen. It was beautiful! Everything was white and spotless. Passengers were dressed in fine clothing and lively, moving around, laughing, and having a wonderful time.

(The ship was owned by the Swedish American Line, at 538 feet long, with steam turbines, and held 1,300 passengers, travelling at a speed of 17 knots. It is highly possible that this was the last passenger voyage out of Sweden to America. The ship was officially taken out of service in November 1939. It became a "mercy ship" by 1942, chartered to the U.S. for the exchange of diplomats and prisoners of war. The Drottningholm made 14 mercy voyages carrying over 18,000 total passengers.)

We were scheduled to arrive in America on October 24. Twelve days at sea - unbelievable. Everything on the ship, the people, the fancy dining room, the vast ocean, was so new. I was floating through this surreal situation like an observer with wondrous eyes.

My small cabin squeezed four people onto two double bunks. Sea sickness hit hard on day two, and I battled it for a grueling seven days. Couldn't eat, couldn't leave the bunk bed. On the eighth day, I finally mustered the strength to step out of my cabin, even thinner than when I began this journey.

The first thing I saw when I opened the door, way down the long empty hall, sitting in an open cabin door, was the Americaner Goy from my town! He motioned for me to come and join a small group sitting together. They gave me a large piece of black bread, hard salami, and a glass of very strong schnaps. Well, since I hadn't eaten in seven days, this surely would kill me or cure me, so I drank and ate the delicious familiar food. I felt very grateful to that man and happy that the food stayed down.

The unfamiliar food on the ship made for difficult eating. It looked good but it wasn't to my stomach, so I ate plenty of bread and other food that appeared more familiar. To communicate with other passengers, I used my hands to point or gesture. Most all others spoke English and I primarily spoke Yiddish. Ocean waves were so rough at times that holding onto the rail while walking on deck was a necessity.

I remember an older couple who befriended me. They asked me if I would keep a cigarette case for them until we arrived in New York. They were so nice to me. Wherever I went, they just came along following me. Little did I know, they just wanted the cigarette case taken through customs for them. I never knew why. At some point, this cigarette case was taken away from me and that was that.

Eleven days at sea were over! As we approached our final destination scheduled for the following day, we had many forms to complete. I was worried because no one knew that I was even on the way, let alone when. I was assured that Jewish organizations would take care of getting me into America safely.

Some of the passengers were talking about the war and escaping to America, saying that this was the last ship out of Europe. They were distressed that so many wanted to leave but quota policies, money, or waiting lists blocked immigration. I didn't understand the magnitude of their words. Europe and Lithuania seemed so far away now. I last walked the streets of Raseiniai to the bus station on October 8, weeks ago. It was uncomfortable to think about my family and friends, so I pushed thoughts away to avoid the discomfort.

Finally, the day arrived! The ship docked in New York City on Monday, October 24, 1939 at six in the morning. The engines quieted. Cheers erupted, goodbyes were shouted between new and old friends. I was in America! Excitement was in the air, combined with confusion due to my lack of understanding the English language.

We were ready with our belongings to disembark and wait in long lines for paperwork to be reviewed and processed. I felt a mix of relief to finally be off the ship in America and tense uneasiness, unsure of what awaited me when it was my turn. In a new land with unknown rules, arriving unannounced, would they let me stay? Holding tightly to my ten-dollar bill, I hoped it wasn't required for payment upon arrival. Relinquishing it would leave me with no money at all.

After a long anxious wait, it was my turn. Stepping forward to the busy, no-nonsense official, I handed him my immigration identification documents, in the name of Berilis Joselis Rozenfeldas. He looked at the documents, then looked at me, a thin, dark-haired, wide-eyed teen standing alone.

"What is your new name now that you are in America? Is it Joseph?"

"No! Not Joseph. Joe. Bernard Joe." Okay, he said. And then, without saying a word, he changed my last name. My official new name in America was Bernard Joe Rosenfeld.

Now what? I couldn't speak much English, so I waited a long time for someone to come claim me. At one in the afternoon, a Yiddish-speaking couple approached where I sat. I told them my story and gave them the name, Wasser, a distant cousin in New York City whom I knew from Raseiniai. I also told them that I had an uncle, my father's brother, in Brooklyn. They told me not to worry - they would handle everything.

I waited for hours, just sitting there and watching people greeting their relatives and friends, laughing and leaving together. I felt very lonely and uncertain about my next steps. Would the couple who spoke Yiddish return? When? I didn't know what to think.

Around four o'clock, I finally saw a familiar face! It was Schmulke (Sam) Wasser from my town. Happy handshakes and greetings exchanged, he wanted to know everything about Raseiniai and how I managed to get out of Lithuania. On the way to his parents' apartment, I described the unbelievable and eventful journey. He was overjoyed and stunned by my story that I was able to escape, since he knew more details about the frightening invasions of war. He mentioned the difficult and limited quotas for immigration to America that I had heard ship passengers speak about. When we arrived at the apartment, I met the entire family. Excitement buzzed throughout the room, we had so much to talk about. Their questions were unending and they were astonished to see me in America. Meanwhile, my cousin worked on finding my Uncle Dave, Papa's brother.

The details of my first meeting with Uncle Dave are a bit hazy now. The whole family gathered to meet me. Uncle Dave had two daughters, and Ruth was one of them. I can't recall the other's name; she died much later. Over the years, I lost touch with my cousins. Later that evening, I met Papa's sister's children - so many cousins!

Everyone was just fascinated with me and intrigued by how I got out amidst war dangers, quota restrictions, transport limitations, and border closings. They all wanted to know about the situation in Lithuania, eager to confirm if what they read in the papers was true. Questions flew at me from all directions, and some questions they also answered for me, since they were more informed. Conversations flowed in a mix of Yiddish and English. It felt comforting to be with them, a sense of relief being with family from a familiar place.

The next day Uncle Dave and his daughter Ruth took me shopping. They bought me a suit, hat, shoes, and underwear. I was now an Americaner. Uncle Dave called my mother's sister, Aunt Leah, in St. Louis. She couldn't believe that I was in America! Uncle Dave wanted me to stay a while in New York, but Aunt Leah wouldn't hear of it. She insisted on getting me to the train as soon as possible to see her nephew for herself.

Before traveling to St. Louis, Sam Wasser from Raseiniai, had a surprise for me - visiting the 1939 New York World's Fair! My eyes could barely take it all in. The strange futuristic displays left me amazed and sometimes perplexed. We had loads of fun, leaving me feeling that America was an incredible place to be!

More cousins, including Seth and Ruth Gaffin, came to greet me and bid farewell. On Thursday, October 27, only three days since landing in America, I said goodbye to Uncle Dave and family in New York. I told him how happy I was to meet everyone, and thanked him for all the clothes he generously bought me.

Once again, I was on a train. But this time, I wore the finest clothes I had ever worn and had a new American name and family expecting my arrival. I looked out the window at farms, towns, and people. The train went fast, with stops every few hours. People tried to talk to me, but I didn't understand the language. I wanted to tell them that I was from Lithuania and traveling to St. Louis. I believe that some of the passengers did understand what I was saying when I handed them my ticket and pointed to my destination.

The train ride felt endless. America was a vast country. Food details escape me, but I think it was sandwiches provided from family in New York, because I still had the ten dollars in American money and ten cents in Lithuanian money. (Later, I would drill a hole in the coin, keeping the ten cents on a chain or key ring for many years, a reminder of how little I had when landing in America. Unfortunately, I lost the coin years later.)

Finally, on October 28, 1939, the train reached St. Louis, Missouri and there was an eager Aunt Leah and her quiet husband Uncle Itzig.

Upon arriving at their apartment in University City on Eastgate, cousins and Uncle Meyer, Mama's brother, were there. Uncle Meyer looked like his father, Grandpa Marcus. After warm greetings, we sat down to eat and the conversation flowed in Yiddish and English. Some cousins spoke only a few words of Yiddish, but we managed to communicate. The room buzzed with chatter, everyone talking at the same time, especially eager to learn about the family I left behind, particularly Grandma.

Aunt Leah surprised me with an unexpected question, *"Do you still have the ten dollars we sent?"* I handed it over, and she replied, *"I'll send it to your mother."* And just like that, I was back to having no money.

Aunt Leah had three sons—Jack, Abe, and Morris Simberg, and a daughter, Ethel. The first night I slept in the bed with Jack. I was so exhausted I didn't even hear him come to bed or get up. The next day was quiet when Ethel and Morris went to school. Uncle Itzig and the other two sons went to work at their poultry store. They sold live chickens, slaughtering and cleaning them while customers waited. I stayed in the apartment where Aunt Leah was most of the time. Everyone spoke to me in English, and I answered in Yiddish. I was glad when Ethel returned home from school. She was nice. Morris was in love with a girl named Sylvia, and they would hug and kiss in front of everyone.

One day, while I was alone, the delivery boy from the Jewish grocery store brought some groceries. I couldn't understand what he was saying. He was a black boy in his twenties. So help me, you could have knocked me over when he started to speak to me in Yiddish. I will always remember that. This reminds me of the first time I saw a black man. It was at the New York railway station. He was at the train engine, and his face was very black and round with bright white in his large eyes. I can still see his face. It was black and shiny unlike anyone I had seen before.

I enrolled in night school to learn English. There were quite a few people from a variety of countries. For a while, I also attended a day school for language. I wanted to learn to speak English as quickly as possible. I went to the movies, and that too helped me to understand English.

Aunt Leah kept talking about how hard her three boys worked. Even son Morris had to work after school. She often said to me how wonderful it must be not to work. She tended to pick on her husband too, although he was such a nice man.

I distinctly recall my first Christmas and New Year's in America. It was New Year's Eve 1939, soon rolling into 1940. Jack, Abe, Morris, and Ethel were getting ready to go out. They sure looked sharp in their white shirts and dark suits. I left the festive mood for a walk and it began to snow. Music played and Christmas lights twinkled from the houses. People sang and laughed as they passed by in cars. I felt incredibly alone and homesick. The scene reminded me of a winter night in 1938 in Raseiniai when I walked alone in a snowstorm.

Remembering that felt heavy and sad, making me wish I was back home with my family and friends.

On Sundays, we piled into the car and drove less than an hour to Baldwin, Missouri where Uncle Meyer lived, Mama's brother. He named his property Marcus Farm, and rented out a large room for weddings. It was beautiful out there, everything being green and fresh. One Sunday, Uncle and I took a walk around the place. We came to a little pond and stopped to watch small cows drink from it. As I was viewing, I said, *"When they grow up you will have plenty of milk."* He laughed and replied, *"They are not milk cows. They are young steers."* Oh well, that goes to show you that I wouldn't make a good farmer.

The whole family visited Marcus Farms on Sundays: uncles, daughters, Fanny with her large family, Dorothy, Babe, and sometimes his sons Hy and Iz. Poor Aunt Chipe Lae, she cooked for an army, surrounded by little children running around. But Uncle Meyer loved having the family over. On the drive back to St. Louis, Aunt Leah talked about everyone. I looked out the open window of the car and read all the signs out loud, even if I didn't know their meaning, just to show off my progress in learning the English language.

I had a toothache, and another one. Always on Saturdays, it seemed. Some teeth had to be pulled and Aunt Leah was not pleased by the expense of it at all. Well, it was time for Bernard to go to work in the chicken store. It was summer 1940, and the smell of the chickens made me swear never to eat chicken again. But they tasted so good when Aunt Leah's maid fixed them.

I quickly learned that the work was really tough. The chicken cases were very heavy, and being thin, I was not all that strong. Abe and Jack knew how to carry the weight. Jack was smart and invented a machine that removed feathers from the chickens in a snap. He could build a radio from scratch. Abe was really nice to me. Morris always walked around with a silly smile on his face.

One day, Abe took me to lunch at a small diner. He proudly announced to his friends that I had just come over from the old country, and they were so impressed. I just smiled. I waited for Abe to order, since this was my first time ordering food while dining out. I told him I would have the same. Oh boy, the cream of corn was not for me. I couldn't stomach this kasha (*buckwheat porridge*) or whatever it was.

In the summer of 1940, Jack, Aunt Leah, Uncle Itzig and I went to visit Uncle Isadore, another of Mama's brothers, and his wife. They lived in McGehee, Arkansas. The drive seemed to last forever, almost seven hours, and inside the car was hot. Jack had to stop several times because I got carsick, which didn't make them too happy. Aunt Leah made several remarks, Jack was impatient, while Uncle Itzig didn't say a word.

Uncle Isadore lived in a town of 3,000 people and owned a dry goods store. There were about thirteen Jewish families in McGehee and most had stores, but some were farmers. Many of those Jewish families were somehow related to us. Uncle Isadore's daughters, Fay and May, were in school, so I didn't get to meet them. Uncle Isadore was a wonderful and good-hearted man.

Uncle Meyer's daughter, Freida, worked for Uncle Isadore in Arkansas. I was told that when she was a young girl she had a bad accident. She went to the bathroom one night, using a candle for light. That was before they had electricity. She dropped the candle and set herself on fire. That is why she had horrible scars on her face. It looked just like my brother's chest. She had many operations, and they told me I should have seen her before.

Aunt Leah continued to make her little remarks, telling me how hard her three boys worked and how I was afraid of hard work. One day, she told me that I should go work at a feed store where her friend would give me a job. I loaded trucks with heavy sacks of feed and bales of hay. I think the hay weighed more than I did. My back and arms ached with throbbing pain.

Seth, my cousin from Brooklyn, came to St. Louis on business. I shared with him how challenging it was to get along with Aunt Leah and that the work was too strenuous for me. He promised to talk to Aunt Leah and, in the meantime, introduced me to a friend who owned a shoe store. Seth asked him to help me find a job.

Uncle Meyer spoke to Aunt Leah one day, telling her that I was going to live with a distant cousin of ours. Their names were Bessie and Ben Figus and they didn't have any children. Bessie was born in Raseiniai. Although my room there was small and hot in the summer, it was like heaven to me. Things were looking up as I started a new job sorting eggs according to size, color, and quality. After a few weeks, some workers went to the office asking for a raise, and not knowing any better, I joined them. We all got fired.

Letters were welcomed from my mother and sisters in Lithuania in 1940. Beilke wrote that the Russians treated the Jews well and many of my friends got important jobs in the city. They were all learning to speak Russian. It sounded good and I was happy for them. Mama wrote that Grandma was very sick, but she wanted to live long enough to know that I had arrived safely in America. She died soon after that.

Seth's friend called, telling me to go to B&R Dry Goods at 1401 Washington Avenue to talk to them about a job. I started working there the following Monday at $14 a week. My bosses were Maushe Rabinowitch and Sam Beilenson. I reported for work promptly at eight in the morning. Soon, a major project was assigned to me. With broom in hand, I was told to sweep the entire basement. And a large one it was, but I did my job happily.

The next day, my boss said to expect a large shipment of facings. What were facings? It wasn't long before we received a large wooden crate, about three feet by four feet, containing hundreds of rolls of ribbons and facings, in a variety of widths and colors. After my boss explained what the facings were used for, I sorted the rolls by width and color. It didn't take long to catch on. I soon learned about style numbers, fabric, and everything else we carried as jobbers to be sold to the small merchants. I liked this job, and my bosses were pleased with my work.

Now that I had a steady job and even received my first raise, I began to relax. I spent much of my free time at the museum or strolling in the park. Paintings captivated me and I started experimenting on my own. Bess and Ben were kind and supportive, urging me to keep painting. I observed some art classes at the YMHA, the Young Men's Hebrew Association, and met young people my age there. My English was improving rapidly. A friend named Sam, would take me home and even came up to see my paintings.

Visiting Aunt Leah several times a week and always on Sundays was still part of my routine. We also continued driving to Uncle Meyer's property to meet with the whole family. They were always eager to hear about letters that I received from home. A lot of time on those Sundays was spent listening to radio talk shows. Aunt Leah loved the Jack Benny show.

News from Europe was disturbing, filled with stories of violent invasions. England was already at war with Germany, and Hitler's armies were destructively taking over most of Europe. Talk was circulating about America getting into the war, making the near future look grim.

In late 1940, the United States initiated the first peacetime draft in its history, drafting young men into the armed services. Everyone had to register and wait for the call to duty, unless there was an exemption, such as for medical reasons. I was 18 years old and stepped up to enlist in the Marines, thinking that was the right thing to do. But I was told that I couldn't enlist because I wasn't a U.S. citizen.

Germany and Russia signed a non-aggression pact, opening the gates for Germany to occupy the rest of Europe. Mail was slow in coming from home and that was worrisome. What was happening in Lithuania and to my family? All I could do was hope for responses to my letters, feeling helpless and concerned.

***

In November 1940, Bernard unknowingly received his last letter from home, unaware of the cruelty taking place and the inhumane treatment of his family and friends.

Aggressive war activity had been initiated earlier in the year. In May 1940, Russia was organizing a total takeover of the three Baltic States. Russia staged conflicts and accused Lithuanians of kidnapping Russian soldiers. By mid-June, there was a total military blockade with Russian troops ready to enter. On June 15, 1940, an ultimatum to surrender was given to Lithuania by Russia. The president escaped the country and Red Army troops entered, attacking border guards as they trampled forward. Lithuania, Latvia and Estonia were all soon occupied by Russia.

In mid-July, rigged elections were organized by Russia for control. The next month, Lithuania was formally annexed into Russia. Many were killed under their ruthless occupation.

Jewish national activity was prohibited and cultural and religious institutions were banned. Nationalization of private property and mass arrests occurred, with thousands disappearing to Siberia. Concurrently with Russian hostilities, pro-German Lithuanian nationalists secretly distributed antisemitic literature falsely blaming Jews for the Russian occupation. Lithuanian Jews were facing aggression from Russia, Germany, and within from their own countrymen.

Meanwhile, Hitler began planning Operation Barbarossa, the German invasion of the Soviet Union, completely disregarding their non-aggression pact. This placed Lithuania in a vitally important and vulnerable location for Germany's march East to attack Russia. When Hitler initiates Barbarossa, it will become over its duration, the largest military ground invasion in history, with 3.8 million troops, thousands of tanks and aircraft, and more than half a million horses advancing East.

Chapter 6:
Secrets of the Forest

Time was moving quickly. It was already 1941, over a year in America! Lithuania seemed far away, yet I still felt an emptiness in my heart, greatly missing my family and friends. I tried not to think about them all the time.

Days went by with my English language and job improving. I went to the YMHA and even met a few girls who I liked. We went to the movies or spent an evening at the Y. My favorite eating place after a show was a little diner on Delmar, right across from the movie theater. They made the best hamburgers for a nickel and the biggest piece of pie for only ten cents. Boy, was that good!

Then really disastrous news struck. But I didn't fully understand the horrific implications at the time.

On June 22, 1941 Germany invaded Russia. I couldn't quite understand what that meant to everyone at home in Raseiniai. I kept wondering, why haven't I heard from family in such a long time, over six months? I couldn't comprehend the atrocities of war and what might happen to my town and its people.

I wished I knew more, yet at the same time, was afraid to know more. How could I go on living a happy life when my friends may surely die? Why didn't I go to pieces when I didn't hear from home? Because it was easier to not know?

Questions, nothing but questions, and no understanding or response. Not one sensible thought went through my mind. Did I forget the time when my friends were kidding me, saying that I would stay in

Raseiniai and die with them? Is my reply coming true? Did I know or even dream that when I replied to them, *"I will go to America and come back to visit your graves,"* that there would be no graves?

I knew no details of the tragic events that were occurring for a very long time. Maybe this was another angel protecting me from being consumed by a horror that I could not change?

The last letter and pictures I received from my mother was dated November 1940. I didn't think in my wildest imagination that I would never hear from my mother or anyone else from home ever again. It was and is still impossible to grasp that they had all been brutally murdered.

***

World War II was in full blaze. London had been bombed again by Germany and Buckingham Palace was hit.

In May and June 1941, Russia deported over 17,000 Lithuanians to Siberia, where many died due to inhumane conditions. This was the major event that incited popular local support for an uprising against the Russians by Lithuanian nationalists and initiated a positive bias toward a German invasion, which occurred in June. Lithuanians who escaped the deportations or arrests organized themselves into armed groups, hid in the forests, and waited for a wider uprising against Russia.

Nazi Germany was ready to betray their nonaggression pact with Russia by invading their territory and occupying Lithuania. Initially, Germans were welcomed as liberators by many pro-German Lithuanian nationalists. The Nazi goal of removal of Jews remained and was assisted now by Lithuanians, carrying out brutal mass shootings of Jews.

Known as the June Uprising, Germans amassed 700,000 troops, 1,500 tanks, and 1,200 airplanes for the attack beginning on

Lithuanian land. The Soviets had about 400,000 troops, 1,500 tanks, and 1,300 airplanes. Within a week in June, the German army took control of the whole of Lithuania, defeating Russia. Lithuanian nationalists greeted the Germans as liberators from repressive Soviet rule and hoped that the Germans would re-establish Lithuanian independence or at least allow some degree of autonomy. That support never came from the Nazis, who steadily replaced Lithuanian institutions with their own administration.

The Battle of Raseiniai, Bernard's home town, occurred June 23 – 27, 1941 and involved a large tank battle that took place in the early stages of Germany's invasion of Russian-occupied land. The Red Army tried to destroy the advancing German troops that had crossed the Neman River but failed quickly as Russian forces were overtaken.

Despite a generally friendly Lithuanian reception, Germans selected Lithuanian and Jewish men, age 15–50, and executed them in groups of 20–25 at a time. Additionally, more atrocities in Raseiniai and beyond were carried out by the retreating Russian army.

On July 2, 1941, the Ponary massacre killings began by the Nazi's and their Lithuanian helpers, with the shooting of Soviet POWs captured the previous month. Jews from Vilnius were marched to large open pits in this forested area, where they were horrifically shot in mass or buried alive. Later reports by survivors were said to be hallucinations, denying that these killing pits existed.

August 31, 1941, in Vilnius, Lithuania, Nazi forces staged an attack on their own German soldiers by Jews, leading to a 'retaliation' mass arrest of residents of the old Jewish quarter, to be murdered at Ponary forest, three days later. Most of the Jewish population in rural Lithuania had been shot by this time, including from Raseiniai.

German officials established a ghetto in Kovna, also known as Kaunas, Lithuania to provide forced labor for the German military, such as construction of a military airbase. Work inside the Kovna *ghetto for women, children, and elderly who could not participate in the labor brigades, employed about 6,500 people. The hope was that the Germans would not kill Jews who were producing for the German war effort. Each section of the ghetto was enclosed by barbed wire and closely guarded. They were overcrowded, with each person allocated less than ten square feet of living space.*

In September 1941, all Jews under German rule must wear the yellow star of David badge with "Jew" clearly written on it. They were forbidden to leave their towns or conduct any commerce. Meager food rations led to weakness and illness.

In early October, 1941, the Germans liquidated part of the Kovna ghetto and killed almost all of its inhabitants. Later that same month, German officials selected close to 10,000 ghetto inhabitants they deemed "unfit" for forced labor. Half of these were children. On October 29, 1941, the death toll on that one day was 9,200 Jews shot and killed.

By November 1941, most of the Jews who had been forced into ghettos in larger cities had been massacred. Those who remained lived in primitive housing with no clean running water.

Most of Lithuania's Jews, ultimately over 90%, were killed by the end of 1941. The remaining suffered from lack of food and disease. A total of 40 locations of mass killings will later be identified in Lithuania. Killing pits, death camps, and destroyed ghettos will be found. Bernard, and most people in Allied countries, did not know any of this, yet.

***

In 1941, my work progressed and raises rewarded my efforts. I paid Bessie $10 a week, and once in a while I gave her more. We were busy at work with a lot of merchandise arriving. My boss, Maushe, a smart man, said that we need to be prepared. If there was a war for America, we wouldn't be able to buy much - inventory and sales could disappear.

On November 19, 1941, at work, a heavy trapdoor fell on my head as I was walking down to the basement. Rushed to the hospital, x-rays were taken, revealing a fractured skull that required a six-week hospital stay. My bosses were visibly concerned and visited me often. As the weeks passed, many friends and get-well cards arrived. My roommate, a Jewish guy, had also been in an accident. Both of us started to feel better, except that I had to remain in bed most of the time.

The nurses were afraid to come into our room because we liked to have some fun with them. After a while, they teamed up in pairs to enter. Nighttime turned into a party, sending out for barbeque ribs and other crazy things. Our reputation spread throughout the hospital, and the nurses, determined to retaliate, boycotted our room until we promised to tone down the mischief.

On December 7, 1941, we heard a lot of excitement from loud voices outside of our hospital room. We didn't understand what was going on. Someone came bursting in, frantically shouting about Pearl Harbor, which bewildered us. I turned on the radio hearing panicky news announcing that Japan had bombed Pearl Harbor, with heavy casualties. I didn't know where Pearl Harbor was and couldn't quite make out what it was all about. Soon I understood, the President declared that the United States was officially at war.

After Pearl Harbor was attacked in the U.S. territory of Hawaii, young men lined up eager to enlist. War bonds were sold and soldiers seemed to be everywhere. The news from Europe and the Pacific grew increasingly alarming. People stayed glued to radios, and the papers overflowed with troubling updates. It was a tough time, anxious and concerned.

During the first week of January 1942, I returned to work. The doctor said to take it easy and come see him in three weeks. He also said that I couldn't be drafted into the military due to my accident. Throughout most of January, my boss was away buying as much merchandise as he could find. Soon there would be a shortage, since everything had to be directed to the war machine.

The year 1942 started out with a cold wave and lots of snow in St. Louis. Work was as usual. Merchandise began to arrive for spring. My boss traveled to Chicago where he visited large department stores to buy all the leftover goods. We sorted items and sold to other stores. Another employee, a black girl, and I became experts in changing the sizes and making the clothing look great.

One day, we received about a hundred dozen long housecoats with small dots and zippers, all one size, mostly navy and white with a few red ones. When we were finished packaging them, we had small, medium and large, in lots of assorted navy and red. They sold like hotcakes.

Aunt Leah's sons, Jack and Abe Simberg, were already in the Army. Morris went into the Navy. Rail and bus stations were full of uniformed young men traveling to their units or reporting to duty for the first time. It was not pleasant wearing civilian clothes within an atmosphere of war duty.

I felt I needed to try again and registered for the draft, still not a U.S. citizen. To my great surprise, I was accepted! I was placed in Class A and just had to wait to be called.

In the meantime, life continued on. The YMHA was filled with soldiers and the girls were having a ball in the company of men in uniform. Elsa Hoenisberg and her older sister were regulars at the YMHA gatherings. Elsa liked me a lot, often lingering nearby, hoping that I would walk her home. She was a pretty little girl, but I thought she was too young for me, as I was almost 20 years old. I also met Francis, who lived in University City. Her father owned a factory and they lived in an affluent neighborhood with a fine house featuring a cellar complete with a bar and fireplace. We spent many evenings there, listening to the radio, talking, dancing, and having a lot of fun. We talked about the war, but it seemed distant and disconnected from our lives in America.

I was concerned about my family, but didn't go to pieces. Mail had stopped coming and going to my family over a year ago. No news is good news, they said. I had no idea that wasn't true.

I did receive letters from my sister, Hedva, in Palestine, and they were just as bad as the ones I wrote to her. We were terribly worried about home. There was no news at all about Lithuania, as if the country didn't even exist!

On August 6, 1942, I wrote a letter to the American Association of Lithuanian Jews, asking them if they had any news from Lithuania. On August 13, I received a reply:

Dear Mr. Rosenfeld,

In reply to your letter, we wish to inform you that none of the names you have inquired about are listed amongst the ones who have survived from Lithuania. However, we do not have a list from the ones who have escaped to Russia. If any of your family are in Russia, you will hopefully hear from them, if they have your address. Many relatives in the United States are sending their inquiries to the Red Cross. We would like to suggest that you go to your local Red Cross and give them the information regarding your family in Raseiniai. We are sorry that at the present time the Red Cross is the only hope there is. Kindly let us know should you hear anything at all from your family in Lithuania.

Sincerely yours,

Roz Avusk, Executive Director

P.S. Regarding the Marcus Family, we are keeping in touch with your Uncle Meyer Marcus in Baldwin, Missouri.

This letter hit me hard. Its profound impact and true significance will unfold years later. My family wasn't on a list of survivors in Lithuania? They might have escaped to Russia? My mind was both alarmingly confused and in disbelief. This sounded impossible, leaving me unable to comprehend where they might be or the potential horrors they might have faced.

The truth of what really happened to my family I may never know or accept. The pain I carry is a mystery to others, hard to put into words. It's a burden of heaviness, yet I strive to appreciate this life granted to me in America. It was a confusing jumble with no one to confide in, other than Hedva in Palestine, though her own daily worries and health struggles kept her preoccupied.

Every Sunday was spent at Aunt Leah's. Sometimes Bessie and Ben joined me there. It was a repeat loop: eat dinner, listen to the radio, and talk about everyone else. Bessie loved baseball, entertaining us with her excitement, shouting at the radio if the game didn't go her way.

Painting had become my true passion, a place where time would slip away unnoticed. I rose early on Sundays, painting before and after our visits to Aunt Leah's. One day, a small picture in the newspaper captured my attention: Moses, with raised arms, supported by his brother Aaron and nephew Ur, stirred memories of a Biblical tale. The news article shared the story of the English artist and how the painting was destroyed over a century ago. Sparked by curiosity, I went to the library and searched through a book about the Bible and art, and there, in vibrant colors, I found the masterpiece that had fascinated me. I was awestruck by its beauty and could not get the painting out of my mind.

Inspired, I started sketching the picture and returned to the library again, inspecting hundreds of painting images. I even cut out pictures of biblical paintings from Life magazine. Soon, my paintbrush strokes attempted to recreate the first picture I had seen of Moses, which I titled "Forsake Me Not My God." I guess there was meaning in that title that I would not recognize until decades later.

(The painting of Moses was Bernard's second painting. With money earned from early jobs, he purchased art supplies and collected magazines with captivating images. A photo in Life magazine of a bald statesman with vibrant, cheerful eyes ignited his desire to experiment at creating. He later declared that this first painting in 1941 of "The Senator" stood as his finest work. The extraordinary detail was remarkable for any artist, and even more so as a first portrait painting.)

Every few weeks, I visited the doctor as instructed to check on the fractured skull I got from the trapdoor falling on me. My doctor, who happened to also volunteer as the medical doctor for the Army draft three afternoons a week, emphasized that my injury meant no military service for me. Boy, was he surprised when I replied that I was already in the service, just waiting to be called. I had gone to the draft office when I knew my doctor wasn't there, keeping my accident hush-hush from everyone.

***

In early 1942, the United States was firmly establishing bases in England and organizing into major command units. A U.S. tanker was torpedoed off of America's east coast in Cape Hatteras in March causing great concern with the war so close to home.

Jews in occupied Belgium and France were now ordered to wear the yellow badge star of David identifying themselves as Jewish. In

June 1942, the first reports that gas was being used to kill Jews was met with horror and disbelief. General Eisenhower arrived in London ready to assume the post of Commander of American forces in Europe.

In July 1942, over 250,000 Jews from Warsaw, Poland were deported to an extermination camp, Treblinka, and murdered. This became a model for other Nazi camps. Remaining Jews in Warsaw began to build bunkers and smuggle weapons and explosives into their ghetto. Jewish underground military groups formed and began to train. This would surface the following spring.

In August 1942, Germany focused on invading Russia, taking oilfields, and continuing their advance toward Stalingrad. Meanwhile, the U.S. planning team included George Patton who joined a combined allied planning team from London, England.

Massacres of Jews in Poland continued, including women and girls who were raped beforehand at Gestapo headquarters. There were public hangings of Jewish leaders and Jewish police.

In November 1942, Winston Churchill stated: "This is not the end. It is not even the beginning of the end. But it is, perhaps, the end of the beginning." Hitler's troops surrounded the Russian city of Stalingrad. In response, Russian forces encircled the Germans in the city, turning the tide of battle in Russia's favor.

In December 1942, gasoline rationing began in the United States. The United Nations issued its first declaration to condemn the Holocaust.

Chapter 7:
You're in the Army Now

It was official! The U.S. Army called me into war duty. Still not a U.S. citizen, I followed orders and departed St. Louis, Missouri, at age 20 years old, arriving near Abilene, Texas on the early morning of January 28, 1943.

Camp Barkeley was a stern, cold sight. There were many small temporary barracks lined in straight rows waiting for us. Twelve men were assigned to each barrack. No sooner did we unload our stuff than a whistle blew, followed by a loud voice shouting: *"Fall out! Everyone fall out and line up!"*

The lieutenant came forward, followed by the master sergeant and another sergeant. They quickly introduced themselves and the sergeant called off our names. His voice blared out: *"Now you guys listen to me! When the whistle blows, I want your asses to get moving. For the next six weeks, you are mine. And I am going to work your asses off!"*

It didn't take long to learn what he wanted, first how to clean the barrack and how to make our bunks. Roll call was at 4:30 every morning. It was incredibly cold, even colder than I remembered in Lithuania. Most of us wore long underwear, fatigues, ODs *(olive drab green-color garment,)* plus an overcoat. We obediently lined up with our mess kits in hand. After roll call, we ran to the mess hall to wait in a long line. The men often complained about everything.

Our unit was assigned to the 130th Station Hospital. After basic training, we would then train in first aid and how to treat casualties.

Other units would join us. When we were at full strength in numbers, we would move to a port of embarkation and await further orders.

Days were ticking by fast, getting to know the guys, training, and wondering what our fate would be in this war. When I was inducted into the Army, I was told that after 90 days, I would become a citizen of the United States. I assumed that would happen as told.

***

Camp Barkeley was built during World War II and became one of the nation's largest military training centers. At its peak, it housed more than 60,000 men on over 70,000 acres of land. Soldiers who trained there served in many critical roles. A special distinctive role was training how to liberate Nazi concentration camps.

The 130th Station Hospital was officially activated at Camp Barkeley in Texas. The hospital's mission was to prepare for overseas duty as a 750-bed station hospital in Europe. The early months of 1943 were spent assembling the unit's personnel and equipment and in accomplishing their training.

On July 25, 1943, the hospital unit moved to the New York Port of Embarkation and at full strength, sailed for England. The station hospital established itself at Camp Chiselden, Wiltshire, located about 70 miles west of London. Its mission there was to provide station medical service to nearby troop units.

Station hospitals provided general medical and surgical treatment for military areas in need and were smaller than General hospitals, which contained over 1,000 beds. They were set up far from the war front to keep patients safe from danger, but also to keep them in the war theater, which made it easier to return the soldiers to duty.

Of historical note, General George Patton died at the 130th Station Hospital as a result of injuries sustained in an automobile accident.

***

A True Story of Surviving by Synchronicity

After ten cold weeks in Texas at Camp Barkeley, training was completed and New York was our next destination. In New York, we boarded a huge ship - ironic that I was now sailing back to Europe across the Atlantic, from whence I came. We were sailing to England as a complete Station hospital, with 450 soldiers, nurses, and doctors. Our vessel was the Queen Elizabeth, the largest ship to sail the oceans at that time. She was known for moving at relatively high speeds, outrunning hazards, specifically German U-boats. On August 25, 1943, we reached England's port.

Becoming a citizen while in the Army was a lot more complicated than just waiting 90 days. Before we left for New York, I received orders to report to Austin, Texas to be sworn in as an American citizen. Too late, there wasn't enough time. When we eventually arrived by train at our new camp in Swinden, England, the first mail call arrived and there in my mail were new orders to report to the port of embarkation in New York to be sworn in as an American citizen. Too late again. The back-and-forth paperwork effort was lengthy and slow. Documents continued to be delayed, lost, or incorrect. In the meantime, I was in the service of a country of which I was not a citizen, on foreign land, and unbeknownst to me, closer to where Jews had been massacred.

***

Earlier in 1943, while Bernard was in training, Russia defeated Germany in the Battle of Stalingrad. The German public was informed of this disaster, marking the first time the Nazi government had acknowledged a failure in the war.

In the United States, it was announced that shoe rationing would go into effect in February 1943. In April, U.K. and U.S. leaders met in Bermuda to discuss the plight of the European Jews.

In April 1943, the Jewish underground resistance movement in Warsaw, Poland stood up to Nazi Germany's final effort to transport the remaining Warsaw ghetto population to death camps. The ghetto refused to surrender to the Nazi police commander, who ordered the burning of the ghetto. A total of 13,000 Jews were killed, about half of them burned alive or suffocated.

This uprising was the largest single revolt by Jews during World War II. The Jews knew they couldn't win and that their survival was unlikely. Their inspiration to fight was to "not allow the Germans alone to pick the time and place of our deaths." After years of degradation, they rose up against their destroyers, to determine what death they would choose.

Simultaneously, in occupied Belgium, a German railway convoy transporting 1,600 Belgian Jews to Auschwitz stops. The driver engineer halted the train after seeing an emergency red light in the near distance, set by Belgians. After a brief fire fight between Nazi train guards and only three resistance members – equipped only with one pistol between them – the train started again. Of the 233 people who attempted to escape from the train, 118 got away, and others were shot or recaptured.

In September 1943, with the Gestapo starting to round up Danish Jews, certain Danes were secretly sending their Jewish countrymen to Sweden by means of dangerous boat crossings.

In Lithuania, the Germans destroyed some ghettos and converted others to death camps. Some 15,000 Lithuanian Jews were deported to labor camps in Latvia and Estonia. Another 5,000 Jews were deported to German-occupied Poland, where they were murdered. Children and the elderly were sent to Auschwitz concentration camp in Poland. Few survived.

The Kovno ghetto in Lithuania had several Jewish resistance groups. They secretly acquired arms, developed hidden training areas in the ghetto, and established contact with Soviet partisans in the forests around Kovno. During 1943, the General Jewish Fighting

Organization was established, uniting major resistance groups in the ghetto.

In early November, 43,000 Jews were shot at three camps in Poland in a two-day Nazi "Harvest Festival."

On November 28, 1943, U.S. President Roosevelt, British Prime Minister Churchill, and Soviet Leader Joseph Stalin met in Tehran to establish an agreement concerning a planned June 1944 allied invasion of Europe against Germany, codenamed Operation Overlord, and later known as D-Day.

In late December, U.S. General Eisenhower became the Supreme Allied Commander in Europe.

***

We arrived at our new camp in England and the living quarters were made up of individual wards in Quonset huts (*prefabricated lightweight steel structures with a curved roof, half-cylinder shape*.) Showers and bathrooms were in the middle of the camp. Our hospital was separated from the living quarters. There was no time to get settled in; the immediate priority was setting up the hospital and the landscape area, resulting in long and challenging days of physical work.

Well, that kind Angel was looking out for me again. A captain from the dental clinic soon learned that I was an artist. He asked that I paint a portrait of his wife from a photo for their anniversary, and I gladly took on the task. Oh boy, good-bye cleaning detail and even exercise hikes, I was too busy painting!

Once I finished the portrait, word spread throughout the camp about my artistic skills. Soon after, I was asked by the executive officer to paint murals on the walls of the officers' mess hall. The officer I collaborated with was Jewish, and together we selected subjects, mostly landscapes. I painted them just the way I saw it.

Picture my astonishment when a jeep rolled up with a private driver, exclusively for me - a foreigner with no rank or credentials! He drove me to town whenever I needed paint or other supplies to create the murals. It was an incredible blessing, shielding me from physical risks and distracting me from worries about family far away.

The guys in the camp came to admire my paintings, and so did the officers. While the work was going on to prepare the hospital for action, I just kept on painting. I felt grateful that no one had hard feelings due to my being excused from tough physical work details. The only problem I had was that I was consumed with painting. Once I started, I could not stop. I still have one painting of a soldier giving first aid to another soldier. This was hung in display in the Army recreation room.

One day, Major Wallen tasked me with painting the Allied flags over a doorway. The Commander of the camp wanted this painted before a party he was giving for Allied officers. Not knowing when the party was to be held, I decided I needed a break and stopped painting for the weekend, with encouragement from the guys to join them in London. Boy oh boy, when I returned everyone knew I was in serious trouble!

I met with the Major who explained why the flags had been whitewashed over. The Commander had seen my work and went into a rage. I had stopped painting before outlining all the flags so it appeared that the American flag was in the wrong place. The American flag would be in the center once all flags were included. The Major instructed me to start over. Of course, I worked extra quickly, completing the flags as originally planned, well aware that critical eyes were on me.

My painting days soon came to an end. One morning, the same Commanding officer came into the Officer's Club. I was at a table, waiting to meet with Major Wallen, and picked up a nearby newspaper to read. After a while, I put my feet up, and continued reading. I guess the Commanding officer saw me. Major Wallen rushed in all excited telling me: *"That's it! It's over, no more painting. That's an order from the top!"* My buddies thought I got a raw deal due to early bias from the Commanding officer about the flag paintings and felt bad for me.

Since I had been painting from when we first arrived, everyone else had been assigned to duties. So initially I was placed in the casualty receiving office and later in another detail. Major Wallen tried to get me assigned to a good worthwhile job with a higher rating, but it was a no-go. Finally, I was promoted to PFC *(private first class)* and that was as high as I could be promoted without the Commanding officer's approval.

One day, I was surprised by a request to meet with the executive officer. He wanted me to paint again! This made no sense. I didn't understand what was going on with opposing orders, and responded respectfully that I preferred not to paint since no rating or opportunity for promotion would be possible. His reply was straightforward and clear: *"If I were you Rosey, I would paint."*

So, there I was, painting again. My reward was not far behind - a position as an assistant in the dental clinic. No further promotions were ever received again no matter how many times I was recommended or how well I performed. The Commanding officer would never approve any advancement for me.

Once again, I felt protected from danger upon learning that by serving in the dental corps, I could not be called into combat. Sadly, a lot of my Army friends were not as fortunate. Many were returning from battles to our hospital by air, coming back as casualties or mental cases. Those were rough moments to see them.

I liked working at the dental clinic. Everyone was very nice and I was taught how to clean teeth and develop x-trays, plus how to assist doctors. At one point, this assignment was interrupted for temporary duty at a Military Police training camp. I learned how to guard Prisoners of War.

I knew that my uncle lived in England but I hadn't heard from him and didn't know exactly where he lived. When I was in London one day on leave, I tried to locate him. No luck. That same day, dressed in my U.S. Army uniform, I walked right into the Russian Embassy in London asking if there was any news from Lithuania? A man came out to talk to me and said that all is well in Lithuania. Of course, that was absolutely false, especially after receiving the letter in 1942 from the Lithuanian organization. The Russian embassy was censoring news profoundly since (I now know) over 90% of Jews in my home country had been killed by then. It must have appeared somewhat strange for an American soldier in 1943 to walk into the Russian Embassy on his own and alone.

When I returned to camp, a stack of mail and two packages awaited me! In my sister's letter, she shared her terrible worry about our family. Stories of Raseiniai were brought from new arrivals in Palestine and were beyond horrible. My mind did not grasp the extent of tragedy from her vague words.

Surprise, a letter from my previous girlfriend, Elsa! She was sorry to tell me but she was getting married. I wasn't so surprised, since it had been a long time since I last said goodbye. One of the packages was from my boss in St. Louis sending a large salami – boy was that welcomed. Finally, the second package, from Bess and Ben, was just what my stomach and tastebuds were waiting for – six cans of sardines and hard cheese, delicious!

While stationed in England, I traveled to several cities, including Bristol, Salisbury, Oxford, and Bath. Sometimes these were solo trips, and sometimes with my Army buddies. For the Jewish holidays on October 1, 1943, I visited Bournemouth. The city and gardens overflowed with beauty, with vibrant colors that reminded me of my painting days. Those moments were a refreshing contrast to the constant stream of incoming casualties and the olive drab green Army barracks.

England was getting bombed almost daily. More and more troops arrived from the States and our camp bustled with activity. Working long hours helped to distract and push through somber times. American planes bombed Germany and many troops didn't return. It often felt surreal. Even being there, still not a U.S. citizen, seemed as if I was living a life inside someone else. But at least I was alive, and protected from dangerous combat by being assigned to the dental clinic.

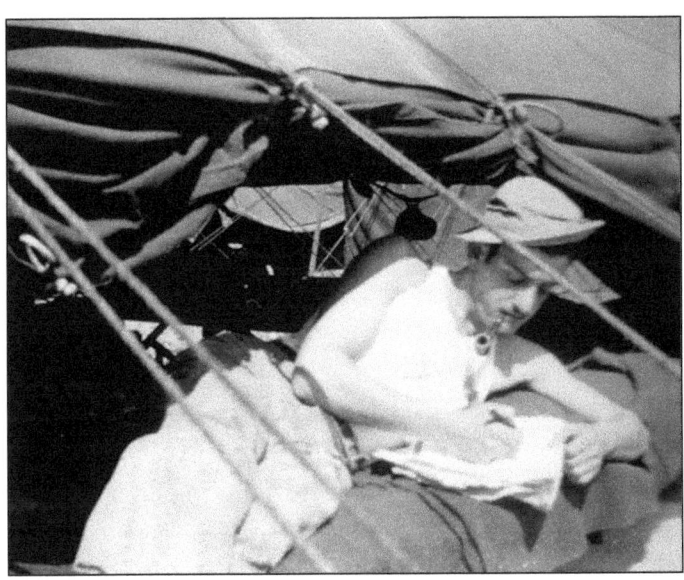

My Hut, Swinden

Chapter 8:
Escalation Peaks in Europe

Something significant was unfolding, and I had no idea what it was. In April 1944, I was directed to join a group of men and two doctors to leave our camp and help set-up a sick call station to serve thousands of troops gathering from all over England and the States. This was a temporary assignment near Plymouth, England. Military Police were everywhere and the camp was off-limits to all civilians. The air buzzed with a sense of urgency, certain that a crucial mission was underway.

German air bombers attacked the city of Plymouth soon after our arrival. The next day, I went into town with another Army guy. We were astonished to view the destruction everywhere - buildings flattened, timber and debris scattered as far as you could see. The Germans missed their target, which was a bridge, but the devastation demonstrated the ugly power of war machines. Despite the chaos, we surprisingly found a little restaurant open and stopped for lunch. I ate rabbit for the first time and it wasn't bad at all.

We returned to our temporary camp near Plymouth and later that night, a German bomber plane flew over us. Sirens blared in shrill alert and we all tore out from barracks, running for the trenches, which had been dug earlier. I buried myself low but turned my head to steal a look up from the trench. It was an amazing sight. Powerful search-light beams brightly lit the sky following the German plane. Anti-aircraft fired from all sides working to chase the bomber away from our camp over to the Channel where the Air Force was ready to shoot it down. The noise of men breathing hard running and diving into trenches, screaming sirens, thundering aircraft engines, and intense bright search lights, appeared like a heart-racing action scene from a movie! The harsh reality of being in that frightening scene at that moment increased my pulse and all my senses to high alert.

The next morning, I walked back to where I had been lying in the trench. I found a bullet shell piece right there. Protected again.

***

Bernard's temporary duty in Plymouth aligns with the timing of a secretive mission, known as Exercise Tiger, to train Allied forces for the upcoming massive invasion in Normandy, France scheduled for early June. Plymouth had been severely bombed by German forces since 1940 and through May 1944.

Exercise Tiger was a full-scale rehearsal for D-Day in France, taking place at Slapton Sands beach in England, about an hour's drive from Plymouth, and one of the most ambitious simulations ever conducted. The Commander in Chief in Plymouth was in charge of the safety of the rehearsal. It was highly secretive and an appalling disaster as German boats intercepted the Allied training ships at sea. The casualty list shockingly reached almost 900 Allied troops.

Exercise Tiger's failure was kept strictly under wraps and remains one of the most underreported stories of World War II. One reason for the mass rehearsal was that General Eisenhower was concerned by the youthful inexperience and relative naivete of the flood of new U.S. troops arriving into England. He believed they were not ready for real combat and this unfortunate rehearsal proved him right.

The actual D-Day, known as Operation Overlord, was scheduled on the coast of France for June 5, 1944. Due to high seas and poor weather, it was delayed until the next day, June 6. It is estimated that 36,000 troops departed Plymouth early that morning for the beaches of Normandy. Among the first to depart from Plymouth and arrive in France across the channel, were 110 ships carrying U.S. troops. In total, 155,000 Allied troops landed on the beaches of Normandy, France and quickly pushed inland for the largest amphibious military operation in history. It took until the end of August 1944 before Germany finally surrendered France.

***

It's June 6, 1944, D-Day. All morning and throughout the day, thousands of troops, planes and ships were on the move, truly a theater of complex and purposeful action. The town was off limits. We waited anxiously at camp. At around ten in the morning, the first casualty arrived back at our station in Plymouth. All I remember was a blur of activity for the loss was great, yet the mission enabled Allied troops to advance into the European continent to fight the Nazi's.

I still wasn't a U.S. citizen, after 18 months of Army service. My citizenship seemed to slip through the cracks during this demanding, busy time. I was on war duty for a country I was still not a citizen. Word circulated around the camp in England that our unit would soon move to France. That news brought anxious concern for if I fell into German hands, who do I belong to legally and who would protect me? I requested a moment with the company commander, explaining my status and the late, lost, and incorrect papers. Fortunately, he agreed with the concern and took action.

On July 11, 1944, I quickly became a naturalized American citizen at the headquarters in Plymouth, England. Now officially an American, I was proud to serve my new country. (*At this time, Bernard is a few weeks shy of his 22nd birthday. The document states that his complexion is "dark", eyes brown, hair black, height 5 feet 11 inches, weight 155 pounds.*)

On July 20, 1944, our group departed Plymouth to return to the Station hospital in Swinden, England, except for me and one other. We were sent for guard duty at a POW camp where we stayed until the end of the month.

When I returned to our Station hospital camp, the atmosphere and energy had dramatically changed. Our troops had entered war from England and the tension, alertness, and casualties were now undeniably real. No more practice or rehearsals, no more joking or laughter.

Evidence of active war surrounded us, and a rushed busy weariness gripped the personnel. Our hospital overflowed with casualties, each bearing their own story and struggle for life. It was the first time we witnessed what war could do to a person. Surgery was conducted all day and night, with bright lights and adrenaline rushes betraying midnight hours. We looked away to avoid seeing arms and legs separated from bodies. The smell coming from surgery made you want to run far away into fresh air. Some soldiers recounted when they fell, with slow, pained words and dazed expressions, still in shock.

As soon as casualties were operated on or treated for gunshot wounds, they were transferred to a larger General hospital. One day the head doctor at the dental clinic instructed me to assist a dental case soldier who was about to be taken to the General hospital. I soon found out why I was going along for the ride. The soldier's entire lower jaw had been shot off, and his tongue was pinned to his upper lip with a type of safety pin. It was awful to see that, but the doctor assured both the patient and me that he would be all right and that his jaw could be restored.

My work at the dental clinic at our Station hospital continued, taking care of personnel plus soldiers in dire need. When the whistle blew, we knew (or it was announced in advance) to be ready for casualties. The roar of planes was heard as they landed not far away, and ambulance sirens blared with speed and urgency. Whoever was near or available unloaded soldiers and took them swiftly to the proper wards.

At one point, replacements for all these casualties slowed to a concerning pace. Where were the new U.S. soldiers? The war effort was in full force in France and casualties were high. Some men based in non-combat duty at the camp began to receive orders for nonessential personnel to report for combat training. First, the guys not currently assigned, mostly kitchen patrol and troublemakers, were sent. Next, guys from the offices. While most of us were watching with concern, we believed that no one from the clinics would be sent for combat. Our questions were answered with more questions and no one knew what was going on. It was unsettling, nerves were on edge. We knew the next step was most likely France, but when, and in what form of duty? I had so many questions now as the calendar approached the last months of 1944. Both for myself and my family.

***

The Allies would eventually commit a million troops to the Normandy invasion in France that summer of 1944, forcing Germany to surrender southern France by late August.

Meanwhile, in July 1944, the Germans were forced out of Vilnius, Lithuania by Russian troops. The Red Army also took over several large cities in Poland, along with a concentration camp, liberating from Nazi rule.

Nazi Germany forces evacuated and destroyed some Lithuanian camps, deporting most of the remaining Jews to the Dachau concentration camp in Germany. Three weeks before the Soviet army arrived in Lithuania, the Germans burned the ghetto to the ground with grenades and dynamite, killing the inhabitants. Of the few Jewish survivors, some escaped to forests or bunkers.

In September 1944, the Allies continued to successfully liberate more European countries from German occupation. Germany surrendered Northern France to the Allies. By November, Hitler vacated his wartime headquarters, never to return, and stationed himself in a bunker in Berlin, Germany. Horrific crematoriums and gas chambers in several locations were dismantled and blown up by the Nazi's to destroy evidence of the mass murders of Jews.

***

Winter came to our camp in England with a vengeance. It was bone-chilling cold. The news from the front was encouraging with the Allies advancing against Germany, however, the cost was high with heavy casualties. In mid-December, 1944, something seemed wrong. Our hospital was almost completely cleared out. Then stark news arrived, telling us to prepare to receive immense numbers of casualties. Germany had broken through our lines and were advancing. The Battle of the Bulge was now in full force with mass bloodshed of troops on both sides.

Replacements from the States did not arrive fast enough, and a palpable tension hung in the air. We were out of time; this battle was expanding, urgently requiring more combat troops. The call to duty reflected on men's faces. We tried to support each other, but it was a devastating situation. Reassurance that we would not be called had ended, as combat units ordered replacements to be taken from our Station hospital personnel. Men from X-ray, ENT, the laboratory, were all summoned into battle.

As they departed, casualties poured in faster than we could manage. I dreaded the call for combat. I had no extensive combat training, and the others didn't either, plus my language skills were less than stellar. I expected the dark call every day, watching the bulletin board, and silently releasing a sigh of relief to not see my name on the list.

I asked the Major in charge of the dental clinic when they would call for replacements from the dental clinic? He responded that as far as he knew, the Dental Corps was within the Medical Corps, and he was quite sure that no one from Dental would be called. I hoped with all my heart that he was right.

A True Story of Surviving by Synchronicity

Less than three weeks after the emergency call for inexperienced personnel to enter combat from our hospital, some of our own men returned to the Station hospital as casualties. They didn't have a chance; they were not fighting soldiers. It was sickening to witness their arrival. I was not called, gratefully protected by my assignment in the Dental Corps.

***

The Battle of the Bulge started on December 16, 1944, when German troops launched a surprise attack on Allied forces in the forested Ardennes region in Belgium, Luxembourg, and France. The battle lasted until January 16, 1945, after the Allied counteroffensive forced German troops to withdraw. The battle was especially brutal with casualties on both sides. The U.S. suffered over 80,000 deaths. More than 23,000 American troops were captured as prisoners by the Germans. Germany's casualties were over 100,000 troops.

Additionally, it was remarkably cold at that time, with eight inches of snow on the ground and average temperature of 20 degrees Fahrenheit, causing weather-related ailments such as pneumonia and frostbite. Blizzards and freezing rain often reduced visibility to almost zero and frost covered much of the soldiers' equipment. Fuel supply was delayed and this especially affected Germany since they had intended to take over Allied fuel sources.

The location of the Battle of the Bulge, in the Ardennes region, was considered to be a minimal fighting area. Troops placed there were frequently inexperienced or had been moved there to rest if battle weary. With this knowledge, plus the debilitating winter complications, a surprise attack by approximately 200,000 German troops and 1,000 tanks temporarily weakened the Allied advance.

However, as soon as General George Patton had his marching orders, he made a fast trek to Belgium with his unit and within seven days rescued trapped Americans in Bastogne, defeating the Nazis. By the end of January 1945, American units had retaken all ground they had lost from this battle, and the full defeat of Germany was only a matter of time.

Bernard is second from Right in photo.

Chapter 9:
Surprise Meetings

The final war effort for an Allied victory was in full throttle in early 1945. Bernard remained at the 130th Station Hospital in Swindon, England, as casualties continued to flood into all wards. In his home country of Lithuania, Nazi Germany was forced out and Russia's Red Army took over with complete occupation. Germany was under attack from all sides by the Allies by March 1945.

The Soviets freed weak survivors of Auschwitz death camp in Poland, and, in April, Buchenwald and Dachau concentration camps in Germany were liberated by American forces. President Roosevelt, serving an unprecedented fourth term, died suddenly and Harry Truman became President. Hitler turned 56 years old while hiding in his Berlin bunker and was reported to be unhealthy, nervous, and depressed.

Nazi leader, Himmler, ignored Hitler and offered a secret surrender to the Allies, provided that the Soviet's Red Army was not involved. The offer was rejected by the Allies. When Hitler heard of the betrayal, he ordered Himmler to be shot.

On April 30, 1945, Hitler and his new wife committed suicide with a combination of poison and a gunshot. Before he died, he appointed Joseph Goebbels as Reich Chancellor. On May 1, Goebbels and his wife murdered their six children and committed suicide.

On May 2, 1945, Germany unconditionally surrendered the city of Berlin to the Soviet Union. May 6 marked the last day of fighting for American troops in Europe and on May 7, Germany surrendered unconditionally to the Allies. On May 8, a ceasefire took effect and was declared Victory in Europe Day. The Soviet Union officially pronounced May 9 as their Victory Day.

***

My unit was on the move in late spring 1945. We received orders for the 130th Station Hospital to depart England. We packed up everything, departed from Swindon and arrived in France at Camp Lucky Strike on May 25, 1945. The camp was a staging area for soldiers lucky enough to return home to America. My outfit served as a medical station and we also processed papers for the soldiers.

The war was officially over a couple weeks earlier, on May 8, and while we won against the inhumane Nazi's, the casualties and life-altering experiences were the high price for freedom against Germany. The Nazi mass destruction, horrific concentration camps, and murder of what we would later learn was millions of Jews and others, was beyond belief.

***

Camp Lucky Strike was located in St. Valery, France about 45 miles from the port of Le Havre, and named for a cigarette brand. It was the largest U.S. camp with a massive tent city for about 60,000 impatient American troops preparing to embark on the voyage home. The camp was primarily the chief assembly point for newly-liberated American prisoners of war, and they often arrived in rags, suffering severe issues with digestive system, malnourished, and weakness. To accommodate the soldiers, churches, PX-supply shops, souvenir depots, barbers, and movie auditoriums were built.

Intelligence was also gathered at Lucky Strike, where soldiers were questioned about their last mission before capture, as well as about treatment at the hands of captors. Information about crew members still missing in action was accumulated and some of these reports were used to locate remains or were used in court-martial or war crimes proceedings.

The Le Havre Port in northern France across the Channel from England, remained busy day and night with daily departures. It is estimated that three million American troops entered into the war or departed Europe through this port, with over 200,000 troops shipping out of Le Havre at the high point in June 1945, homeward bound. By the end of 1945, it was reported that over 70,000 soldiers were processed through Camp Lucky Strike. The camp was closed in 1946.

***

Our work helping the soldiers and processing paperwork at Lucky Strike continued, as well as leave passes. One of Aunt Leah's sons, Abe Simberg, and I had corresponded occasionally. He told me that he would be in La Harve when I was in France. One day, I was able to meet him at the port city and spend the day with his outfit. He was a kitchen mess Sergeant – what a deal he had!

My other French excursions included Rouen, outdoor cafes in Paris, and Dieppe, a seaside resort town. My brief duty in France lasted until the end of July, and as the mass return of war-weary soldiers continued home to America, my unit headed east to Germany.

We were traveling to Heidelberg, arriving on July 29, 1945. It was a long, uncomfortable ride, both physically covering 450 miles, and emotionally, passing through war-torn cities and towns completely destroyed by bombs and, obviously, the loss of many lives. The traumatic effect from war was on full display in piles of rubble. It tore your heart out to consider the panic, fear, and injuries.

Our unit took over a German headquarters near Heidelberg and transformed it into a hospital to serve the Seventh Army, which will become in command of the Army's European headquarters. I shared a room that was about six feet wide by fifteen feet long with another guy.

We had just enough space for two cots, but were grateful for the privacy. My roommate, Freddy, loved candy. I traded my candy for his cigarettes, which were worth $20 a carton.

The day we arrived in camp, walking around to check it out, I spotted a plum tree behind some warehouses. I ate plums until they came out of my ears, loving the taste of fresh fruit from that healthy tree. Food from the mess hall was terrible, making my stomach upset just being near that place.

With the hospital now in full service, I was given a small room to myself at the dental clinic with a female assistant. The clinic was on the first floor, and at the other end of the hall was hospital wards. We were told to be quiet and towels were placed around the door. I was doing teeth hygiene and developing x-rays. I got a kick out of the officers who came in to have their teeth cleaned. Since I was wearing a white smock, they would "sir" me to death. After I got through and removed the smock, there was my lonely little PFC stripe. The look on their faces was priceless.

In August 1945, the United States dropped two atomic bombs on Japan, resulting in their surrender and World War II was finally over. Even though our hospital was still busy in Germany, a temporary wave of lightheartedness filled the air with celebration, hopeful that there would be peace in the world now.

For the past two years, since 1943, I had been searching and writing anywhere I could think of for news about Lithuania. I even sent a letter occasionally to my family there, but it was always returned, bringing sadness and wonder. I kept writing to my sister in Palestine, but she knew nothing also. The military newspaper, *The Stars & Stripes,* started to print stories about millions murdered by the Nazi's. I couldn't imagine what that truly meant for my beloved family.

In late August 1945, I received a response to my letter from the Central Committee of Liberated Jews in Bavaria. It read:

My dear Mr. Rosenfeld,

Your inquiry regarding your family and friends has been forwarded to our offices here in Munich. You may rest assured that we shall do all that we possibly can to serve you and to serve those whose welfare is of interest to you.

You can help us. We have been receiving no assistance from the outside world for our 14,000 unfortunate brethren that we are currently helping. We are requesting the following:

1. *Packages that will contain only items of new clothing, soap, tooth brushes and paste, German English dictionary, Yiddish newspaper, modern Hebrew book, a religious object.*
2. *Propagandize the fact that as of this day without exception no material assistance has been given us by any of the major institutions.*
3. *The only solution for our problems is Palestine. Underscore this fact and bring it to the attention of those who may assist us.*

Sincerely,

Abraham J. Klausner, Jewish Champlain, US 9th Division

Another inquiry to the Displacement Center in Germany was responded to with a list of liberated Jews that was available at that time. I studied every single name on the list hoping for a hint of recognition.

One day, a name popped out from a page, my eyes grabbing it with my heart pounding. Here before me was a dear name of a person I actually knew. It was my brother-in-law's brother. Finally! I felt excitement and hope, immediately writing back for more information and to verify the name.

On October 10, 1945, I was able to obtain a leave pass to visit Munich and went straight to Feldafing, the camp for displaced persons. There were hundreds of people and I kept asking if anyone knew Yankel Ludgin. It is difficult to describe how those people looked. Some couldn't move, sitting as if made of stone. Some were laughing with eyes closed, others were crying unconsolably. They walked around as if in a daze. I kept asking the same question:

"Do you know a Yankale Ludgin? We were connected through my sister, Dvierke, as Yankele was the brother of her husband."

Finally, there stood Yankale Ludgin before me. We stared deeply into each other's eyes as tears flowed down our faces. Then hugging with all our might, we examined each other closely to make sure this was real. People watched, approaching us to ask questions, wanting to share their stories and family names.

Yankale didn't seem to be in reality or behave normally. What is normal after such a horrific ordeal as these people had suffered? At first, he joked and laughed as if nothing had happened. Is this the way they cope with horror and try to forget? Something wasn't right. I didn't know what it was or what to expect. What secret did these people hold? They must be protecting some painful secret, protecting their hearts and minds from shattering.

Slowly, he shared. Yankale had spent three long years in a German concentration camp, too terrible and unbelievable to go into detail. He was the only one of our family alive, as far as he knew. The news about other family members was beyond awful. As far as my sister, Dvierke, was concerned, Germans burst into their home, grabbed her baby, Nathan, from her arms. She screamed hysterically, begging shrilly for her child to be returned to her, but, of course, her pleas were dismissed. From that moment forward, she was emotionally destroyed, and never mentally the same.

A woman at Feldafing camp claimed she had been with Dveirke in Auschwitz concentration camp. We weren't sure if that was accurate. Yankele had been in the same ghetto as Dveirke in Sualai, Lithuania and heard she had died of a heart attack a few weeks before liberation.

"What about the rest of the family?" I asked hesitantly. He looked down, paused, and quietly replied, *"They were killing everyone in Raseiniai."*

I left the camp feeling empty, drained, walking in my own foggy daze. It was beyond comprehension to realize that I had just been with people who lived through a tortuous hell. How did they survive? I wanted to run, to shed the energy felt at the displacement camp. I wanted to run away and forget the pain that I had just seen and heard.

By the time I reached my camp, I was completely numb. I vowed to not think about the horrors I was told. I wanted to erase the images, sounds, feelings. One day, Yankale came to visit me at the hospital. We ate dinner in the mess hall and I kept watching him. He had enough food on his plate for three people. But he didn't eat the bread. I asked him why he didn't like the bread? *"I will save the cake for later."* Yankele had relatives in America, and a Jewish organization had already contacted them. He would go to America.

***

Feldafing, originally a summer camp for Hitler Youth, was 20 miles from Munich and the first all-Jewish displaced persons (DP) camp. For many of the Jews who survived the Holocaust, they could not or would not return to their former homelands. Options for legal immigration were limited. So, many created flourishing communities in these camps from 1945 to 1951.

In July 1945, American chaplain Abraham Klausner played a significant role in convincing authorities to empty the Feldafing camp of non-Jewish persons and replace them with the remaining Jewish survivors from another camp, Dachau. The Feldafing camp became a model for implementing a suggested policy toward Jewish survivors. Chaplain Klausner was the same man who had responded to Bernard's letter in August.

***

A rotation system was introduced for U.S. soldiers still in Europe. The men who had served overseas the longest would return to the States first. Everyone was getting excited by the thought of going home, with more relaxed joking and favorable moods. There was less and less to do at the hospital resulting in many guys receiving seven-day furloughs. I signed up for Switzerland when it was my turn.

On November 5, 1945, many of us left for Switzerland. We boarded a train and travelled first through eastern France, stopping in Mulhouse, France and changed to a Swiss train in Basel, just across the border. The next stop was in Beau-Rivage where we had our first truly delicious meal. I vividly recall how scrumptious the food was after eating too many blah meals from the mess hall.

Switzerland was nature's masterpiece, exquisitely beautiful and incredibly clean. The train moved quietly and fast, as my eyes stayed glued to the windows enjoying continuous breathtaking mountain views passing by. Mountain peaks were covered with snow, cascading down into pristine valleys. It was a clear, blue-sky day so we could delight in these views, seeing for miles in many directions.

Next stop was Bern, Switzerland. We were now way up high in elevation and the temperature dropped quickly. In fact, it was so cold that buildings were designed to hang over sidewalks, enclosing them from above, keeping snow and ice away. Streets were almost empty as our group of American Army guys walked around exploring the city.

We traveled further on the train, going higher and higher, stopping in Lucerne where it was freezing, causing us to seek indoor shelter for almost the whole visit. At the hotel we stayed at, I met a girl named Marta who worked there. I also met two Swiss men. The four of us talked about everything and drank together until the bar closed. We continued on to Marta's apartment and drank some more. It was so cold in her apartment that we kept our overcoats on. The only heat she had was a hot pad.

Lucerne was a unique compact city with many historical structures in medieval architecture, and an Old Town wall and bridge dating back hundreds of years. Marta was my tour guide to many sights, including a museum, and even bought some little gifts for me to take back.

Our Army tour group stayed in Geneva for two days, offering us time to shop, except I had no money. I quickly came up with the idea to sell my raincoat, with almost instant success. Then I was on a hunt for Swiss watches and walked around to a variety of jewelry stores. Finally decided, I purchased one nice watch for myself and five Mickey Mouse watches, with big faces that made lots of noise.

As we waited at the train station for our journey back to camp, I seized the moment to scout for customers. It didn't take long before my first client appeared - a Moroccan soldier. I showed him my good watch. He looked at it, placed it next to his ear, and shook his head, no, from side to side. He was not interested. I took back the good watch and pulled out a Mickey Mouse watch. His face lit up! It was a gem to him and he wanted all five for $20 each. With a cost of only $3 each, it appeared that my selling days were back in full swing!

By December 12, 1945, there was still no news for when I could return home to St. Louis. A few replacements arrived every week since some guys from our hospital had left for America, but the majority were still waiting to go home. We stopped rising early for roll call, and we went into town without a pass. We were a bad influence on the new solders.

I still worked at the dental clinic, but there wasn't much to do, so we sat around acting like we were busy. One morning around 10, all hell broke loose. Everyone was running around. Towels were being wrapped around door locks to keep doors from slamming. The camp Commander shouted orders to nurses and doctors. My heart raced when I was called on for urgent assistance to help move an incoming casualty. He must have been extremely important given the significant commotion going on.

We didn't have to wait long before discovering who this important person was. General George Patton had been in an accident and was enroute to our 130th Station Hospital! This was a huge ordeal, with excited anticipation circulating among all personnel.

When the ambulance arrived, energy pumped through my veins with heart pounding. I ran out to help move this mighty chief from the ambulance stretcher to a hospital bed. He was very large, tall, and heavy, with a shaved head. Reports of a jeep accident were overheard. Everyone was hustling around the famous leader, feeling the significance of this memorable moment.

Energy buzzed around the hospital throughout the night. The next day his wife arrived, while he remained in very bad shape. Reporters came from all over and the news spread like wildfire. Our small camp was the center of attention due to this incredibly important leader in America's war history.

On December 17th, most of us were moved out of the camp to a temporary staging area not far from Heidelberg. It was a small town called Eberbach. With the delay in returning home, some of the men made a racket and were a bit rebellious. So here we were with absolutely nothing to do except play cards and go to bars. Eberbach was a very picturesque historical town. When it began to snow, the town glowed even prettier. We went for long walks in the mountains with scenery that reminded me of a Christmas card. The Black Forest will stay in my mind forever with its magnificent peaceful beauty.

On December 21st, 1945, General Patton, the greatest general of our time, died at our hospital in Heidelberg.

***

The death of four-star General George Patton was a very important moment worldwide in late 1945. Here is one account from a free online historical library called erenow.net. The mention of Bernard's location is recounted:

> "130th Station Hospital, Heidelberg, Germany. George Patton's body is wheeled down to a makeshift morgue in the hospital basement. The room was a horse stall back in the days when this building was a German cavalry barracks. It might have made more sense simply to keep Patton in Room 110, where he died, but the humiliation of his body being stored in a stall is nothing compared to the grisly spectacle that will unfold if a photograph of the dead general's body is splashed across front pages of newspapers worldwide. Hiding Patton in the basement is the best way to avoid the horde of journalists that has descended upon this tiny military hospital. Patton's personal four-star flag is brought to the hospital, where it shields the general's body draped over his corpse.

> There will be no autopsy, at the demand of his wife, Beatrice Patton. The doctors quietly insist, but she will not bend on this issue. She mourns him by making plans for Patton's funeral. There are many issues that need to be confronted immediately. For instance, the hospital has no morticians, and thus no one capable of preparing the body for burial. There are also no caskets, so one will have to be flown in from London. Finally, there is the matter of where George Patton will be laid to rest.

Beatrice wants him buried at West Point, where he can be surrounded by soldiers for eternity. The army says no. Of all the thousands of Americans who have died on foreign soil during the Second World War, not a single man has been shipped home for burial, due to the cost. Vast cemeteries in Europe and Asia now hold the American dead. As distinguished as Patton might be, allowing him to be buried any place other than Europe would set a dangerous precedent.

"Of course he must be buried here," Beatrice Patton says when she is informed of this policy. "I know that George would want to lie beside the men of his army who have fallen."

He is laid to rest at the American Military Cemetery in Hamm, Luxembourg. Neither Gen. Dwight Eisenhower nor President Harry Truman attends. One German newspaper, writes eloquently about their former enemy's burial: "In spite of the pouring rain, thousands lined the streets from the railroad station along the tracks to the cemetery, in order to render this last homage to the dead general. Hundreds of people walked from the capital to attend the burial ceremonies. Representatives of nine countries and highest-ranking officers of the American troops stationed in Europe followed the coffin. A French battery fired a seventeen-round volley of salute. During the burial, a military band played the Third Army March. After a brief religious service, the coffin was lowered into the grave."

A True Story of Surviving by Synchronicity

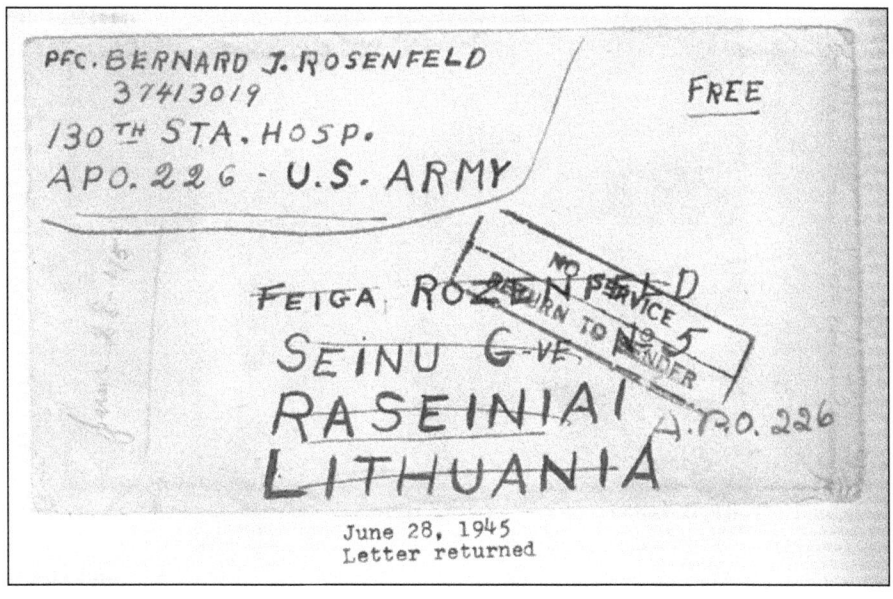

June 28, 1945
Letter returned

Dec. 17, 1945 moving to staging area, waiting to go home

Chapter 10:
Homeward Bound

Soldiers were beyond restless, constantly asking: *"How much longer until we get to go home?"* Our group that was waiting together for a ride home was moved again in January 1946, this time to temporary quarters in Bremerhaven, Germany. This port city was located on the north coast of Germany and was an outlet to the North Sea. The wait trudged on, every day feeling like forever. The bitterly cold winter winds kept us inside. Our U.S. Army living quarters were in a large warehouse with little heat and nothing to do.

Finally, on January 30, 1946, a smaller military cargo ship called the *Norwalk Victory* set sail with a thousand soldiers below deck, packed in like sardines. Many were seasick. The smell down there was horrible and you had to walk carefully so that you didn't step on someone. Winter seas were rough and anything not tied down was thrown around as the waves surged.

Our transport ship stopped after 2,000 miles from where we began in northern Germany. We were now in the middle of the North Atlantic Ocean, near the Azores island of Sao Miguel, about 1,000 miles west of mainland Portugal. Rumors circulated that there was engine trouble on the ship and it would be at least two days before we could sail again. The guys started to come up from below looking like hell. Natives came to our ship in little boats with all kinds of things, especially food. I ate a loaf of bread, sardines, and a dozen bananas. Soon the deck was covered with garbage as more and more men came up and took part in the exchange with islanders. I can imagine how we must have looked: unshaven, uncombed, and green from seasickness.

It was announced that half of the men would be allowed to go ashore, and the other half would go the next day. Well, by nightfall, there were reports from shore that soldiers had made a mess on the island. Soldiers in fights, drunk, in jail. No more shore leave. The island was off limits now.

The islands of the Azores were truly a magnificent sight. I stayed on deck both days and sketched the dark green mountains that touched clouds and hid churches within surprising nooks and crevices in the distance. *"I will paint this green island one day,"* I said to myself.

Our ship set sail once again and arrived in New York City on February 17, 1946 - my second time to come ashore to the United States from a foreign land. This time, I was arriving and welcomed as an American citizen and soldier, with seasoned Army duty overseas completed.

Loud celebratory music, blasting from a military band, played as our ship moved into the port. Red, white, and blue, "Welcome Back" signs hung from tall buildings. People waved excitedly, smiling, throwing kisses. Gazing out upon my new home country as the ship pulled into harbor, I wondered how many times the band played and how many times people waited for the arrival of a military ship. Some of the boys would not make the journey home.

After exit processes were completed, I was soon on a train to Jefferson Barracks, Missouri, where this Army duty began. It was a very long ride covering almost a thousand miles. The circumstances of this train trip in 1946 from New York were vastly different than when I arrived from Lithuania in 1939. I was in uniform and felt some familiarity as an American now. People on the train kept asking all kinds of questions and telling us how it was here in the States during the war and about all the shortages. When someone new sat next to me, it started all over again. But I didn't mind, it was good talking to people and responding to their curiosities.

I was officially discharged from the U.S. Army on March 2, 1946, after serving for three years. It was an eye-opening journey of experiences during that time, including becoming a U.S. citizen abroad, with orders as an artist and dental assistant in the Army, and colorful, as well as haunting, situations in new countries, cultures, and war. But one thing had not changed, my deep yearning to find family and friends from Raseiniai, and an unspoken fear of revelations that awaited me.

***

Bernard's original documents are held by his daughters, including becoming a citizen and an honorable discharge from the United States Army. As the Commander in charge promised in England, who was distraught over the painting of flags, Bernard never rose in rank beyond a PFC, private first class, a low rank. His military decorations included a Victory ribbon, European African Middle Eastern Theater ribbon, Good Conduct Medal, and four overseas service bars. His military occupation is listed as Artist, even though he was a dental technician for two of the three years served.

***

The train finally pulled into my station in Missouri, and my exit papers were stamped, marking the conclusion of my military service. I was officially out of the Army now! There to welcome me home was Aunt Leah and her son Jack, now Captain Jack Simberg, since he was still in uniform. With warm hugs eagerly exchanged, we were soon off to St. Louis. It felt good, like a welcome home reunion, with Bessie and Ben making an appearance. Cousin Ethel had matured a lot, becoming quite a beauty. The next few days were busy with meeting family, except for my uncles Isadore and Meyer, for they were in Mineral Wells, Texas taking hot baths.

I went to see my bosses and they were excited and happy to see me looking well. They were ready for me to return to work and I responded willingly, the sooner the better. But I wanted to have a little time to get re-adjusted to civilian life first. Also, my uncles requested that I travel to Mineral Wells to spend time with them. My bosses understood, I was free to choose when I returned to work.

St. Louis, in March 1946, held onto a wintry chill and appeared a bit worn. I wrote to my sister in Palestine sharing about my return to America and that I would resume my old job, earning $50 a week. I asked if she had any news about our family? She wrote back with somber news, a few of my friends had survived the war and concentration camps, but most died. Our town of Raseiniai lay in ruins. Stark to comprehend, my heart sank upon reading that no family members had survived.

More letters followed and more devastating information began to surface. I felt numb in response to this news. I just couldn't grasp the reality of such horrible stories. How could this inhumanity be true?

Little did I realize that the lasting effect of my emotional suppression would shadow my lifetime. I had no one to confide in, since there wasn't anyone in my circle in St. Louis who shared a connection to Lithuania during the time period I lived there. Days and weeks blurred by where I deliberately refused to think about it, begging my mind to dismiss it as unreal. When my uncles reminisced about home, it wasn't the familiar home or faces from my youth, instead, they were recollecting about their youth, 40 years earlier.

One difficult letter arrived from Henke; she had resided on the street adjacent to my family. She wasn't Jewish and now lived in Brooklyn, New York. She recounted, in horrible detail, what happened in Raseiniai when the Germans occupied the town. The Germans, with help from Lithuanian nationalists, seized most of the Jews and marched them out to the woods not far from my family's orchards. The Jews were forced to dig a large trench, and there met a tragic death amidst a hail of gunfire.

Henke continued, with more unwelcomed news, that the reports informed of Jews taken to a pit, mercilessly shot, falling on the spot where they would lay to die. Some who fell remained alive, yet were still buried in the pit, with other bodies on top of the living. Only a thin layer of dirt covered the mass of humans.

I couldn't finish reading Henke's letter, it was unbearable. Tearing it into pieces through angry sobs, I never replied to her. These stories and more that I will later learn haunted me for the rest of my life.

The sale of that radio spared me from the tragic fate of my family. The angel-like synchronicity, aligning actions that granted new travel documents and money for a new ship ticket out of Lithuania in October 1939, charted me on a different course. That was over six years ago, as I sat safely in St. Louis, reflecting on how swiftly time had passed. Three of those years were in the American Army in Europe.

How little we can see into the future of possibilities. Who would have ever envisioned that my life would unfold without my family and friends, often leaving me with a persistent sense of loneliness and sadness?

Never have I met someone, even as I write this today in 1987, whom I could say,

"Remember when we were kids and did such and such? Remember the frozen lake? Remember sitting around singing and drinking schnaps in the cold winter in our drafty house?"

Even my sister, Hedva, knew little about my youth and my life. When she left home in 1935 for Palestine, I was only 13 years old, and she hadn't lived with us at home much anyway, instead taking care of our grandparents.

What was making me start to think like this? I should be happy that I was home in America. But whose home? I thought I better cut it out and stop thinking these thoughts. I was preparing to see my uncles in

Mineral Wells, Texas, and felt sure that their warm reception would help shift these dark thoughts. Uncle Isadore, in particular, was such a wonderful, kind man. He looked like his mother, my Grandma Marcus.

After a comforting reunion with my uncles in Mineral Wells, together we drove back, stopping in Shreveport, Louisiana to visit a cousin, Lil Spitzer, and her husband. Shreveport looked beautiful in the sunshine of late March 1946. Everywhere you looked, fresh vibrant flowers adorned shrubs, especially in soft hues of pinks and whites, decorating lawns of houses and entrances to buildings. Lush green grass added to the city's pristine appearance. It was in stark contrast to the cold, grim landscape of St. Louis, where the view was dominated by endless apartments. I was amazed by all the single detached houses in Shreveport. They all looked something like Francis' nice home in University City.

Dinner was festive at the Spitzer's house and, as usual, when a relative met me for the first time, conversation quickly flew to the old country, Lithuania. Next, they asked what I was going to do now that my Army service was completed? My reply was ready, announcing proudly that my bosses were eager for me to resume my old job. Conversations inevitably came back to the same subject: *"Everyone is getting married now that the boys are coming home."* My response: *"I'm not planning to get married for a long time."* I thought it was ridiculous how everyone was running to the marriage altar. I was 23 years old.

From Shreveport, we had a five-hour drive to McGehee, Arkansas where Uncle Isadore lived. Once there, I could relax from all the questions. But not for too long, for I was soon on my way back to St. Louis, with my bosses awaiting my arrival.

Before I had left Germany to return home, I received a letter from Francis telling me that she had a big surprise waiting for me. No sooner had I returned to my room at Bessie's house after my trip with uncles, when the phone rang. It was Francis and she would be over in a few minutes. Sure enough, we heard the loud noise of a car horn. Francis had a new car!

But that wasn't the surprise. She had had a nose job! It was not healed yet so her face was swollen and she looked like hell. I told her she looked real good, and, with that, she was satisfied. We went for a long drive, and the whole time she talked nonstop, telling me about all sorts of things that happened while I was in Europe. This would continue to be my experience during my early weeks and months back from the Army.

I had several dates with different girls. There was the date with my boss' sister. She told me how much she liked the way I had changed. I guess she didn't like the last date we went on before I went into the Army. Francis would come by the house. We went out to a movie or just drove around in her new car. Francis had changed too. She wasn't all that shy anymore. She would stop the car, and we would talk and neck. She was fun to be with.

My cousin Ethel was attending a fine college, Washington University, in St. Louis. When I returned from McGehee, Arkansas with my uncles, she wanted to know if I would like to meet her friend from college. I had a new date for Saturday night – Jack Gentle and I were going on a hayride with girls – but Sunday would be fine. So Ethel invited this girl for dinner on Sunday.

I met Jack Gentle at the St. Louis YMHA. We were discharged from the army around the same time and quickly became good friends. He was a nice guy, upbeat and fun to be with. The girl I went to the hayride with was okay, but her hair was stiff as a board. You couldn't get close to her with that hair. But we had plenty of laughs and my return home to Bessie's house was in the early morning hours of Sunday, March 31, 1946.

My life was about to change again in the next few hours, in a very big way, in a very good way.

Chapter 11:
From the Depths of Love

Ethel announced we were leaving right away to pick up her friend and classmate, Dorothy Schwartzberg, at Washington University. She chided me: *"You better wake up since you were out so late."* It was around eleven in the morning on Sunday, March 31st.

We drove up to the dormitory and my gaze locked onto a statuesque girl wearing a beige suit, with lovely thick, dark reddish-brown hair adding to her allure. She instantly caught my attention, walking toward us in a way that I'll never forget.

"Is this her?"

"Yes," Ethel responded.

"Oh boy," I quietly murmured, knowing that I was in trouble with this one.

Dorothy was beautiful as she walked, standing tall with her head up, taking fast steps. I will forever remember this lovely sight. Ethel quickly introduced us, and off we drove, back to Aunt Leah's home for dinner, with my eyes straight ahead, heart pounding, and thoughts in disarray about this enchanting girl.

Dorothy and I sat in the living room, just the two of us, while dinner was being prepared. I mentioned my recent visit to her hometown of Shreveport, Louisiana, expressing how much I liked the city. There was a moment of hushed silence, with our eyes cast downward, but I stole a glance at her, well, glanced more at her legs crossed with the skirt just above one knee. There was an irresistible magnetism about her that caused my heart to race. Our eyes met for an instant, triggering a quick smile from both of us. Aunt Leah interrupted the gaze, calling everyone in for dinner.

Sunday dinner and small talk with family finished, but I didn't want my time with this girl to end. I suggested we call Jack and all go to the movies later. In the meantime, Dorothy, Ethel and I walked over to my place to view my paintings, since she was studying art in college. As we strolled from Aunt Leah's house to Bessie's, a small child came running after me crying, *"Daddy! Daddy!"* That was all I needed to impress Dorothy.

Jack arrived in the evening and, after introducing him to everyone, we climbed into his car for the drive downtown to see the movie, "Captain Kidd." The long line didn't matter because we were having fun talking and laughing. The movie was something else, not too good. Afterwards, spirits were still high so we walked nearby for coffee and pie, before driving everyone home.

The next day, I told the girl I was working with about my date and all that we had done in one day, ending with, *"I sure like this one."*

"Did you ask her if she'd like to go on another date?"

When I responded, no, her eyes shot open in surprise, *"What?! You like her. Why don't you call her and ask her for a date?"*

"Well... I don't know." There was something about Dorothy that told me that I wouldn't be able to just see her once or twice. I felt drawn to her like I had never felt to anyone else.

Tuesday evening, I called Dorothy. She was in the shower, but came running all wet to the phone anyway. When I heard her voice, I knew there was more to this than just saying hello. She had just celebrated her birthday yesterday, on April 1st, turning 19 years old, and we made plans to see each other again. Before I knew it, we were dating a lot.

Unfortunately, my boss wanted me to travel to Shelbyville, Tennessee to take care of a store for a week or so. The evening before I went to Shelbyville, Dorothy and I stayed out past her dorm curfew, late into the night. She was grounded for two weeks. When I returned from travel sooner than expected, Dorothy was still confined to the dormitory, but that didn't matter. Spending evenings in the sitting room together made me happy just to be with her.

Ethel and Jack Gentle were dating now also. After the two-week grounding was over, and Dorothy was free to go out, we double-dated with them, or sometimes with Dorothy's friends, Phyllis and Dick. But mostly, it was just the two of us and I always looked forward to that time.

On June 9, 1946, on a moonlit night in Forrest Park, a little over two months since my eyes locked onto her beauty approaching me from the dorm, I asked Dorothy to marry me. Thankfully, she said yes and, just like that, we were engaged!

Naturally, Dorothy wanted me to meet her parents, her younger brother, Stanley, and friends. I hoped this Lithuanian immigrant with an accent would be welcomed by them, especially after such a brief courtship. In July, the trip from St. Louis to Shreveport, Louisiana was deemed a success with a wedding date set for November 2, 1946.

After the trip, I suggested to Dorothy, *"Let's live in Shreveport!"*

Since I had no one in St. Louis except for a few relatives, Dorothy would want to live near her parents and friends, right? I don't think she was too thrilled with my idea, but she agreed anyway.

I moved to Shreveport soon after the trip and lived with my cousin, Lil Spitzer. Little had I known, that when I visited several months ago in March with my uncles, that I would soon return to temporarily move in with Lil.

I went to work for Dorothy's father who owned a small retail store, where they sold Levi jeans and hats, among other dry goods. The idea was that I would work for him a few months until I found a job. Those few months turned into 14 years.

Dorothy was a stunning young bride, wearing a stylish satin dress suit, befitting of the 1940s, with her rich auburn hair arranged under a matching satin cap. Our newlywed residence was Centenary Terrace apartments, paying $38 per month, a hefty sum for the time. Dorothy's father found a yellow convertible and purchased it for us as a gift, a rare accomplishment in 1946, since it was very difficult to acquire a car or even an apartment. Synchronicity seemed to weave connections, making us remarkably fortunate in both of these aspects of our lives.

How do I drive this classy yellow convertible, this generous gift from Dorothy's father? At age 25, driving was an extravagance I never had the luxury to learn, so my young new bride soon taught me.

My relationship with Dorothy's father was, unfortunately, limited. I feel there was a misunderstanding that involved Dorothy's mother telling me things that are unimportant now. I regret very much the years wasted by having such a cool relationship with him. Looking back, I am sure we actually liked each other and that he really was a nice and caring man. He loved his granddaughters, my girls, and demonstrated that throughout many years taking them to watermelon gardens, events at the Elks Lodge, and even lakeside fishing. He regularly showed up on Saturdays, gathering them for lunch at Pizza Hut or Griff's Burgers, and to sunbathe at his favorite summer spot, the local swimming pool.

In 1947, my three uncles and aunt, delighted me with a visit to Shreveport. I felt flattered that they drove all the way from St. Louis and Arkansas just to spend time with us in Louisiana.

The last time I saw Uncle Morris was in Raseiniai, Lithuania in 1923, when I was only one year old. The memory was captured in a tattered photograph, and rose vividly into my mind. I was a plump baby, sitting on Grandmother's lap, while Uncle Morris stood next to us in the horse-drawn wagon, dangling a fishing pole line into the river. Now, in 1947, we reminisced, mostly laughing and enjoying our intimate reunion!

There was a noticeable silence, however, about news or details of tragedies in Lithuania. I didn't push to find out more about my home or village, yet.

As you might imagine, I was somewhat distracted by my new married life and work in Shreveport. What a different culture living in the deep South was, a huge contrast from all that I had known before.

Our married years were never dull, that was for sure. I was grateful to Dorothy on many fronts. She was a sincere person and never did anything to harm another. She never complained about my wages. She was smart with numbers and managed our finances with care and good judgement. We were able to buy what we wanted and always had a savings account. That was important.

However, life is not always easy for married couples. There are moments when you say things that hurt the one you love. At times, you do things that hurt even more. It is hard to endure. But true love can weather such storms. To love another does not necessarily mean that you like them all the time.

My life, the way I grew up in the village of Raseiniai, my entire experience of fleeing suddenly, and having no contact from Lithuanian family since 1940, added an extra layer of complexity to adjust to during our married life. I never confronted the emotions of trauma, loneliness, or the weight of what's recognized as survivor's guilt. These feelings will cast a haunting shadow on me for decades.

It was a bumpy start for both of us, new to each other and marriage. I didn't know, at first, that Dorothy received little affection when she was growing up, this lack contributed to many misunderstandings between us. But we would find our way, with perseverance, stubborn determination, and many gifts of opportunity. That's how it was living in America, and I wanted to embrace it all.

My Love, your Mother

Chapter 12:
The American Dream

Dorothy had a deep desire for a child. Unfortunately, for one reason or another, the doctor cautioned us that we would physically be unable to conceive. This news left her disheartened, as she yearned to provide the love that she felt she didn't receive during her own upbringing.

In January 1951, we received a phone call from an attorney agent and were elated with the opportunity to adopt a beautiful baby girl, just a few days old. We named her Diane Faye, in honor of my sister, Dvierke, and mother, Feige. The moment I laid eyes on her, a sense of joy and awe swept over me. She was pink and perfect in every way. I couldn't help but marvel at my good fortune.

The doctor was wrong. Dorothy became pregnant, but sadly the baby, a boy, did not survive and was stillborn. I'm unsure if Dorothy knew the baby's gender. She didn't want to talk about it and I didn't know how to approach the delicate grieving, so I didn't push her to talk. That's the way it was with us. His gravestone marker is in the Agudath Achim Cemetery in Shreveport near Dorothy's grandparents. A small flat gray stone is engraved, *"Rosenfeld Infant 1955."*

At last, we found the right combination and Dorothy became pregnant once more. This time, she was watched closely by the doctor due to having high blood pressure. On September 10, 1956, Tina Marie (named for my sister, Taube) was born. Long and thin, she was early, and would grow up to be a beauty! Diane had a playmate now that she adored, and was becoming a good mama's little helper.

Just when we started to get some sleep at night with Tina, Dorothy became pregnant again. The new candidate was slow in coming, perhaps content in its own world, or not ready to face this one. We were planning on a new tax deduction in late 1958, but no way. It still was not ready by year-end. On January 16, 1959, Nancy Irene (named for my father) finally entered our world – a relatively larger baby for us at almost seven pounds. At least we could hold this one. Now Diane was really excited - two sisters to play with! At this point, with a family of five, the need for more space was evident. We were fortunate to be able to buy a red brick, one-story house at 2046 Shadywood Lane in Shreveport that year.

In late 1959, I felt it was time to look for different employment. Dorothy's brother, Stanley, was not intending to go to college and there wasn't enough income for all of us to earn from one little store. I accepted a job with Levine's, a large chain store, requiring that we move all the way to San Angelo, Texas, 450 miles away, a long drive with three young daughters in the car. We rented out our new house in Shreveport and headed southwest, where it was very hot and dry. Dorothy struggled to acclimate to such a small town, so far away from home. We lived there for 18 months, and then I was promoted and transferred north, to Arkansas!

Levine's had acquired a store that I was to manage. It looked very promising and I needed to get up there quickly. That meant I was on my own, at first, undertaking a two-day journey covering 500 miles to reach Fort Smith, Arkansas. The winter weather was wreaking havoc across the South. Unable to fly by plane out of San Angelo, or even Dallas, because of so much snow and ice, I slowly made it there by car. I was occupied getting the store ready amid persistent bad weather conditions, while Dorothy had the busy task of closing up our San Angelo house. She then had the challenging 500-mile drive to Fort Smith, with daughters ages 2, 5, and 11 years old, and our yellow lab dog, Tinkerbell. That was far from easy.

I worked very hard in my new position of managing the Levine's store and everything looked promising. We made friends and really liked Fort Smith. My employees were nice and people, in general, were friendly. The Jewish community was small, but there was a temple and a rabbi, and we participated in events, holidays, and services. Of course, being Jewish and from Lithuania, living in the southern U.S., is very different from the traditional religious community I grew up in. But this was my active and engaged American life now, and I liked it. The less I allowed feelings or questions about the past to emerge, the better off I was. Or so I thought.

Then a heartbreaking tragedy occurred. Dorothy's young brother, Stanley, was killed by accident on February 10, 1962. His close friend was working at a pawn shop and Stanley was there with him. His friend was in a small back room cleaning a gun that was empty of shells. Except it wasn't empty. As he was cleaning it, the gun fired and the bullet struck Stanley's chest, killing him. Dorothy received an urgent phone call to come to Shreveport immediately. Stanley was only 22 years old and Dorothy's mother would never be the same again. It was a sad and shocking time for the family and community.

Letters arrived regularly from my sister in Israel, and I replied, enclosing a few dollars once in a while. She lamented about her health and asked when I was coming to visit her? It was now 28 years since we had last seen each other in Lithuania, in 1935. I felt bad about that, however, the practicalities of supporting my family with a modest income, plus demands of my work, made such distant travel an unlikely possibility. So much time had passed that I hardly remembered her.

Dorothy started to feel poorly. She felt a lump in her throat and finally went to the doctor. He told her that she was a little pregnant. Well, that news shocked us! A tiny, four-pound girl was born October 7, 1965 in Arkansas. She was so small, but perfect. She looked more like a doll. Shelley (named after Stanley) had to remain in the hospital a while, being too little to bring home. Once she was home, all her big sisters doted on her, treating her like a little princess. Now we had four daughters - what a blessing, and an important, busy responsibility.

Soon, news arrived that Levine's wanted to transfer me to Austin, Texas. This time I said, no. The potential of frequent moves for a family of six, plus two beloved dogs, coupled with the temptation to try something new, steered me to resign from Levine's in January 1966. Here I was, with a large family and no job. Scared and anxious to find the right work quickly, was a huge understatement.

In the meantime, quietly resourceful, Dorothy's father discovered that a well-known boutique store was for sale in Shreveport. Southern Gift and Fashions was a reputable, locally-owned, ladies clothing and gift store, where brides registered their wish-lists and women of economic status selected well-crafted outfits, usually funded by the oil and gas industry.

The owners invited me to come to Shreveport to discuss this unbelievable opportunity. I didn't think much of the idea, since I knew that I couldn't possibly afford to buy that fancy store. Besides, I didn't know anything about a fine, high-priced, inventory such as they showcased.

On February 28, 1966, another stroke of blessing and good fortune allowed me to buy Southern Gift and Fashions. Dorothy's father helped with a downpayment and I worked out a purchase plan with the owners. They were genuinely happy to see me take their store to new possibilities of success. At 44 years old, I felt like the luckiest man! Angels were watching over me once again, following me since the day I innocently said goodbye to Lithuania in 1939.

The deep south of Shreveport, Louisiana, dressed in pink azaleas, became home once again by spring 1966. Now, with a larger family than when we left, we moved back into the original house purchased there in 1959. That modest, red brick, ranch-style house would eventually expand with renovations over many years, adding a large master bedroom with bathroom suite, and an enlarged family room. The new screened patio featured a hot tub jacuzzi that Dorothy loved to soak in.

Beneath the graceful branches of a sprawling weeping willow tree, my backyard garden was my favorite destination to relax. I grew delicious lettuce and tomatoes, and prepared rectangular patches of dirt for my girls to plant vibrant flower seeds. The familiarity of having my hands and body digging and kneading the soil, offered an emotionally soothing outlet, and a healthy physical release when worrisome thoughts darted around my mind.

Years later, my painting desire returned, and a small metal shed joined the backyard oasis. The exterior of the shed was transformed by an elegant landscape mural that I painted, and the interior provided me with a tiny artist's studio, well organized with brushes, paints, and canvases.

There was always work to be done - in my demanding boutique store, with the girls and Dorothy, fixing things in the house, creating outside in my garden or art studio, or taking leadership roles in the local Jewish community.

I was living the American dream, with a large, active family, owning a spacious four-bedroom home and two new automobiles, and enjoying the pride of growing an esteemed business to high reputation. The turmoil of Lithuania from decades past seemed a world away, like recalling hazy details from a long-forgotten movie.

Was it real? Did my mother, siblings, and many friends really face a brutal death? I stuffed the horrible thoughts deep into a hidden, locked place, not wanting to feel crushing pain or longing for answers to so many difficult questions.

I was living a contrasting life in a primarily conservative Southern Baptist city with few immigrants. How could anyone here truly understand? They had no connection to what I had lived. I guarded my past closely, confiding only occasionally in Dorothy or our rabbi - when emotions could not be contained, engulfing me, shattering my disguise. My daughters, Jewish friends, and broader community were aware only of my Lithuanian origins, my enduring Eastern European accent, and somber curiosity about my family perishing in the Holocaust. I staunchly wore an armor of silence, withholding details of personal history and terrible family tragedy.

A burning ember inside me, fueled by lives lost and post-war news, cast a shadow of sadness over the present moment. For decades, this flame smoldered, gathering energy for an eventual quest into the fate of my family and friends. Unbeknownst to me, I was biding time until the search was activated, not knowing if acceptance or reconciliation awaited me in this lifetime.

Yes, I had survived, grateful for blessings and angel-like protection saving me. But deep grief lingered in the shadows, knowing my loved ones not only perished, but met inhumane ends. How could true happiness coexist with knowing that they never had a chance?

***

People who experience feelings from tragedy, as described by Bernard, often suffer from Survivor's Guilt, the emotional trauma after surviving a calamity when others did not survive. It is considered a serious symptom of PTSD, post-traumatic stress disorder. While not everyone who endures a traumatic event will develop PTSD, some research estimates that as many as 90% of people who lived through events where others died, experience feelings of survivor's guilt. People living with this unease struggle to turn thoughts to anything else, further elevating anxiety that results in bodily reactions and ailments.

Survivors may question why they escaped death while others perished? They may also wonder whether there was something they could have done to prevent the traumatic event, to preserve a life. Symptoms can include flashbacks, obsessive thoughts, anger, feelings of helplessness and disconnection, insomnia, stomach issues, headaches, even thoughts of suicide.

Bernard experienced anxiety attacks that refused to relent - a racing heart, severe nausea, and escalating fear and panic from symptoms, often spiraling into an ambulance ride to the hospital Emergency Room.

Fueled by an obsessive need for organization, he felt an urgent drive to complete tasks promptly, finding calmness in being in control of his life. This need for control left him impatiently frustrated by delays, and his struggles resulted in restless nights with little sleep.

Decades of locking emotions deep inside, trying to hide from the pain of his family's plight, emerged in his body through a broken heart. Bernard had two quadruple bypasses, stents, and pacemaker. The cardiologist commented after surgery that opening Bernard's chest was like finding a jungle of wire, amazed at his strength to survive.

Bernard also suffered a severe case of pancreatitis in 1988, staying in Intensive Care on morphine for weeks. A spiritual meaning of this disease is associated with the inability to digest the sweetness of life, and is also associated emotionally with worry.

Bernard lacked both personal experience and specialized guidance to constructively navigate his emotions. This challenge was compounded by societal norms, where expectations for men discouraged emotional vulnerability. Living in the conservative deep South further complicated these hurdles, as conformity and concealing painful truths were more common than sharing and acceptance of others' wounds, resulting in living inauthentically.

Other survivors, who were more emotionally rehabilitated, often associated progress with living in a strong Jewish immigrant community, with trained individuals who helped with psychological healing. Also, Bernard kept himself distracted and busy, and possibly unaware of the correlation of repressed emotions to his physical heart ailments.

Self-therapy came later in his life, primarily through painting, beginning in the late-1980s. He remarked, "Painting is how I cope." His writing of this manuscript was also a cathartic act of healing. Gardening was fondly rooted in his past, and healthy, digging deep into the dirt. He was passionately devoted to serving the local synagogue, taking leadership roles, rolling up his sleeves to help, raising money, and participating in events. He donated money to the Jewish community, the arts, and others in need. He unquestionably felt it his duty to help others in these ways, all part of his self-healing.

But still, Bernard lacked professional psychological therapy and a community where he felt secure enough to be vulnerable. This highlights the importance of such resources to those who have survived tragedies. Seeking support and learning to express themselves constructively is a path to a healthier, more balanced life.

Living the American dream.

Chapter 13:
Search and Release

I couldn't shake the feeling that I must go to Israel – it was a relentless urge, impossible to deny. Traveling to reunite with my sister, Hedva, was long overdue. With my family and business stable, Dorothy and I made the lengthy journey from Shreveport, Louisiana to Tel Aviv, Israel, in 1970. With my own eyes, I saw my only living sibling for the first time in 35 years. Can you imagine the intense feelings of what closing that long void felt like?

Upon arrival, my heart beat rapidly and anxiously, as my mind drifted among old memories of life in Lithuania. Immediately, upon first sight at the airport, tight hugs wrapped each of us in comfort as tears streamed down our faces. We stared at one another with moist eyes and awestruck smiles, in disbelief, and then words began to flow, in Yiddish.

Soft words of both sorrow and gratitude filled our days. We reminisced for hours, and poor Dorothy couldn't understand any of our conversations since Hedva spoke no English. I was elated to spend time with my three strong adult nephews, who had previously served in the Israeli army. We toured parts of this important beautiful country, impressed by its grit, resilience, and stamina. There were also feelings of concern, from the constant threat of surrounding dangerous, conflicting countries. It was a trip of a lifetime, with many powerful emotions experienced daily. Yet, a deeper, unspoken, knowingness told me that this was the beginning of a new phase in my life.

I departed Israel with lingering questions about my family and an unfulfilled sense of closure in my heart. It was a complicated journey back to family roots within a changed world of 1970. I wasn't exactly sure what I expected after 35 years of separation from my older sister, especially since she had left Lithuania even before I did. What was I seeking? What did my heart need to find peace?

I would see my sister again in 1978, in America. We celebrated Shelley's Bat Mitzvah in Shreveport that year, an important rite of passage ceremony, which is celebrated at around 13 years old, after years of studying Hebrew prayers and reading from the sacred Torah. It was delightfully satisfying to witness my youngest daughter complete the rituals of our heritage. To share the momentous occasion with Hedva, her husband, and one of my nephews Rani, and his wife, traveling far from Israel to Shreveport, made the celebration extraordinarily special.

Family is sacred to me, the nearest path to comfort that I know.

In 1983, I made the long trip back to Israel alone, continuing the search for information about my family. I went from one place to another, between Tel Aviv and Jerusalem, that could possibly shed light on any names or places in Raseiniai. Nothing. Not one mention, as if they didn't even exist.

My mood sank in despair, my heart shattered. How could this be? I kept trying and trying, driven to find something, even a morsal of evidence of their lives. Hedva asked me with concern, *"Bernard, what are you looking for? There is no one left."* But that didn't stop me. I was determined, and kept on looking for something, anything.

One day, during my visit, my sister drove us an hour away to Jerusalem from her modest apartment in Tel Aviv, again with the purpose of satisfying my relentless quest to uncover any mention of our family or town. During that trip, I went to one place where an official came out to greet me with a briefcase and different book registers. One register was in Hebrew. Another was for important people. He told me that Germans, with help from Lithuanians, had murdered 99% of the

Jewish people in my town, leaving them in mass graves. The Germans had retained meticulous record books with numbers killed daily. This time, there was no escaping the truth. A wave of unease gripped my stomach, heart and mind, as I visually processed the profound meaning of his words.

With somber determination, I registered individual names of my family members at the heart-wrenching Holocaust museum in Israel, named Yad Vashem. This famous museum, with its historical records and walls covered in full-size photos of concentration camp victims, displayed nothing about my town or people. Frustration mounted within me, even churning with anger at times, as no recorded evidence of their existence was identified.

My final day there, I joined a walking tour through the Old Quarter of Jerusalem. Towering limestone walls, dating back to the 1500s, loomed at 40 feet tall and eight feet thick, enclosing the busy sector for over two miles. These ancient walls exuded a strong physical presence, serving as a protective buffer around the old city and its holy sites, including the revered Western Wall of the sacred Temple. Open-air stalls and colorful markets filled busy alleys, with merchants selling religious and Mid-Eastern items to anyone who glanced their way.

Somehow, I became separated from the tour group and was walking alone, ending up in the direction of Mount Zion. I wandered through a quiet historic area, away from the markets, often seeing no people and definitely no tourists. Stone walls framed the sides of every pathway, taking step after step through narrow alleys, turning right or left as instinct guided me. I was completely lost but not concerned, even though it was desert hot and at age 61, I had had quadruple bypass surgery not too long ago. I continued moving alone along the narrow, weathered stone paths.

Suddenly, I stopped, remaining motionless near an unexpected sight deep within the cave-like maze of stone. What was this curious place ahead of me?

My eyes searched for recognition, staring at what appeared to be an intimate and hidden outdoor museum, full of memorial plaques embedded into stone walls. The moment was eerily quiet. A sacredness hung in the air, demanding reverence. No one else was in sight. I stood there unmoving, all alone, with the thick stillness of the place matched only by the profound silence surrounding me.

Finally, the spell was broken when an elderly man emerged from inside the open-air walls, shuffling slowly to where I stood at the entrance. He motioned for me to follow him into the interior walls, quietly sharing that this was the location where holy Torah scrolls were first brought and saved from war-torn Europe, right after the Holocaust in the 1940s. He continued by noting that this was considered the first and original Holocaust museum. I silently gasped at the connection to my life, unsure what to expect, yet following him deeper inside.

The walls of this silent memorial were made of white marble, somewhat weathered being open to the climate, with engravings of names of places that suffered or were destroyed in the Holocaust. I softly asked, *"Raseiniai, Lithuania?"* He walked me over slowly to a far corner of the museum, and the world stopped for a moment.

There it was, written in Hebrew. I saw my town's name for the first time, etched into the old white marble wall as a memorial plaque, *"Raseiniai."* My hand instantly rose to the engraved stone, touching my town with trembling fingers, feeling a flood of memories, sadness, and grief envelop me. This was as close as I would ever get to a visible record of my people and town. My heart sank in despair by that thought, yet, gratitude for the privilege of touching this stone remained a cherished reward.

I stayed a while, staring entranced at the stone, and feeling its declaration in silence. After capturing photographs, thanking the elderly man, and offering a modest donation, I walked in a daze through the shadowy labyrinth of stone alleys, with not one other person in view.

I stopped walking to make sure this was not a dream, touching the stone wall of the alleyway, feeling its aged, solid warmth, acknowledging that this was real. I was buzzing with energy, marveling that I had just discovered by "accident," or incredible synchronicity, a hidden museum treasure containing the first sight of my town's name. This was very real, and I knew that my hunt for more information was far from over. Renewed with fresh hope, this felt like just the beginning.

***

Bernard's original manuscript, written and sent to his four daughters in the spring of 1987, ended here. But Bernard lived a long life and his story continues.

From here forward, one of Bernard's daughters, Nancy Rosenfeld, will share the remainder of his active life with you, including a search that reveals vivid discoveries. There will be requests by Bernard for accountability to the Lithuanian government, as well as, a momentous and emotional occasion to speak in Washington, D.C. at the U.S. Holocaust Museum; and finally, he meets someone from Raseiniai. Nancy also shares the strength and spirit of his final months of life and the angelic experience of his passing.

But first, Bernard added a closing to his 1987 manuscript, found below, that reflects the endless classic cry of Survivor's Guilt:

I never stop thinking about my family. I get emotional and cry in hiding. I can't watch a movie or television show about the Holocaust without choking on pain and tears. I see pictures of the bodies in my mind that will not go away. I can see non-Jewish Lithuanians taking delight in having a scapegoat of the Jews and applauding my family's atrocious death. Tears blur my vision as if to say, don't look!

The price of being alive is high. At times, I almost am glad to feel pain. I want to feel the pain that my loved ones endured. At other times, I feel very lonely. There is no one from the Old Country with whom to share all the good things which have come my way. Yet, I know I am blessed to have such a wonderful family of my own. I am thankful for having met my wife whom I have always loved. I am thankful for having four lovely daughters and six grandsons. God has given me more than I deserve.

The town I was born in and grew up in, I have left behind forever. My family lies in some field covered by dirt and grass, a field where I likely walked in my youth. I will forever think about them and cry for their sorrows and pain. I wish I could find peace within myself and let them rest in peace, for they only found peace in death.

Sister, Hedva, in Israel

Chapter 14:
A New Voice

Hello, this is Nancy writing now, Bernard's daughter. I feel privileged to share my father's story with you, hoping it serves as an inspiration for others to persevere amidst life's challenges, to believe in seizing opportunities that can arise as gifts from unexpected sources.

I'm the third of his four daughters. My interest in Judaism sparked in high school. I traveled often with a youth group known as United Synagogue Youth (USY), expanding knowledge and friendships beyond small Shreveport, to larger cities in the United States, culminating in a trip to Israel in 1977 where I met my Aunt Hedva and her three sons, my cousins.

My dad, Bernard, expressed his pride often for our academic, Judaic, creative, and career accomplishments, especially since he came from no formal education or financial means. I was lucky to share many spontaneous conversations with him in person, over the phone, and later through email, about mutual interests in art, gardening, business, and leadership. He was always happy to hear about my career in finance and consulting, and actually read some of my published books on personal growth, surprising me with his reflections on how they related to his own life experiences.

His unwavering desire to protect his wife and daughters was undeniable, and his genuine delight for six grandsons, and later great-grandchildren, never failed to bring a smile of contentment to his face. Even when silent, his presence commanded the room, his energy filling every corner with strength and care.

It is a true honor to continue his story, weaving together the threads of both struggle and magic that define it.

***

In 1983, Bernard returned to Shreveport from Israel, feeling energized and rewarded. His solitary journey proved serendipitous when he stumbled upon a hidden, open-air museum, witnessing for the first time, his town's name engraved in an old stone wall, which nurtured deep wounds in his heart.

He soon began making plans to sell his beloved, but demanding, fine clothing and gift store. None of the four daughters desired to settle in Shreveport, and he didn't cause any feelings of guilt or obligation to continue the thriving business that he had lovingly developed since 1966. There was no need for discussion because he knew we were happily forging our own paths in Texas, Florida, and Pennsylvania.

In 1984, he sold the highly-reputable store, with his usual attention to detail, valuing each inventory and fixture item. He agreed to continue managing the business for several more years, to train new owners how to purchase merchandise and operate within a boutique local presence.

During the 1980s, a surge of curiosity suddenly burst open regarding my father's life. I guess there was finally realization about how little I truly knew about him. Recently a college graduate, my financial work in a bank would abruptly be interrupted, as a question appeared out of nowhere, demanding a phone call to him right then or later that evening.

"What did your father do for a living? What did you do when not in school? What was it like living in bitter cold winters? Did your family have cars back then? How are we related to Uncle Isadore?"

One surprising thought at a time gave rise to a question, and he would matter-of-factly respond. I sensed from the warmth in his voice over the phone a genuine enjoyment in the questions posed, an appreciation that someone, his daughter, was interested in his life, his family, his past. I don't know if he had encountered such specific inquiries before, since he shunned curiosities as a way to avoid revisiting the painful times.

We continued this spirited game of my inquisitiveness receiving his thoughtful replies for several years. He never told me more than I asked. He never expanded on details of tragedy or horror. We knew his family died, except for his sister Hedva, but we didn't know how they died. He later told me that he and his sister wrote at least once per month for 57 years, until 1997, when she died in Israel. He eventually traveled to Israel a third time, in 1987.

As Jewish children attending religious Sunday school, even in the Christian small town of Shreveport, we received an education about the Holocaust. Documentary films depicted the horrors of concentration camps and gas chambers. Information emphasized the significance of remembering this dark chapter in history to help prevent its recurrence. We were instilled with the understanding that awareness was crucial, to be empowered to speak up and take action, ensuring that atrocities never happen again.

In spring of 1987, he called to say that I should be on the look-out for a large brown envelope in the mail, I didn't give it much thought, having no idea what to expect. All he said was that he was mailing each of the daughters the same item.

I lived in Florida at the time and visited Shreveport for brief stays, two or three times per year. He never mentioned that he was working on a collection of photos and timeline of his early years. I do recall glimpses of him in the back office of the clothing and gift store, engrossed with a task of manually typing a page filled with single-space sentences, reaching for liquid white-out to make corrections. I can still visualize his large-framed body hunched over the vintage typewriter. First, there was an antique-looking black manual machine sounding the distinct click-click of sticking keys, as he progressed using two fingers. Later, an electric typewriter appeared, faster since the letter keys didn't stick, but still operating with two fingers and liquid white-out.

On a Friday afternoon during that spring of 1987, I arrived home from my job at a Ft. Lauderdale, Florida financial institution, walked over to check the mail, and discovered a substantial brown envelop with his characteristic print handwriting. Still in my banker's clothes, a grey skirt and white blouse from my father's clothing store, I opened the weighty package with curiosity. My heart skipped a beat as I extracted a thick stack of typed pages, feeling stunned as I read the cover page: "*50 Cents for a Life*."

It was unimaginable that he had written this manuscript, full of photos and copies of documents carefully inserted into specific sections. Settling onto the sofa, eager to read, my mind was innocent from knowing the painful significance about to unfold. The manuscript's beginning delved into the lives of his sisters, mother and brother, who had met tragic ends - a horrifying and shocking revelation. My heart ached at the thought of him carrying the weight of this silent tragedy for all these years. Overwhelming sadness washed over me for the grandmother, aunts, uncle, and cousins who suffered, and whom I never had the chance to meet, living foreign lives in an old-world country.

The emotional force of his narrative held me in a trance. I was absorbed by the manuscript, urgently wanted to unravel more, yet sickened by the intense images painted from his raw words. Sobs choked from my throat and tears streamed down my cheeks, as I grabbed tissues until the entire box lay emptied.

The descriptions were vividly effective, as if he wanted to excruciatingly regurgitate and expel it one last time from his mind. It was the beginning of a catharsis, with the intention of passing his family's story on to the next generation.

His writing was raw, unexpectedly abrupt, and painfully informative. Hours later, laying spellbound on the sofa, with only a lamp illuminating the now darkened room, I was still wearing my work clothes. Through the night, I continued reading, absorbed by his words as tears fell. This was my family. This was his mom, siblings, friends, who were humiliated, tortured, deprived, and killed.

The following day, having finally finished reading, I felt a pressing need to telephone him. Unsure how to articulate the overwhelming emotions stirred by his manuscript, I realized it was a moment and conversation that we had never experienced, both being so vulnerable. Gratitude filled me for his courage to lay bare such intimate and intense pain, and I was in awe of his story-telling ability that communicated feelings and images with clarity. I could see and sense what his words described. So that's what I shared with him, how incredible it was to receive this gift, honoring his family, and recognizing the immense pain he had bravely relived.

A hushed stillness lingered on the phone, at first. Then he spoke, barely above a whisper.

"I appreciate that you value the manuscript. It's important for all my daughters to know what happened to their family. The manuscript is not intended to be shared with others or put on a table as a showcase. This is just for family to know the truth."

"Of course," I replied.

At this point, in 1987, my dad chose to share the complete story solely with his daughters and wife through the manuscript. Others in the Jewish community knew that his family had been killed in Lithuania, but details remained undisclosed. He was known to participate in annual Holocaust memorial ceremonies in our small Jewish community, somberly lighting a candle and reciting Hebrew blessings.

Otherwise, he was fairly quiet about what he was thinking and doing, as his daughters' lives unfolded in diverse corners of the country, absorbed in careers and families, occasionally celebrating together for happy reunions and holidays. Meanwhile, what he was doing in his newly retired existence was painting profusely and actively serving in Jewish leadership roles in Shreveport. Silently, he still persisted in scouring the globe for any trace or mention of his family or town.

And then, in 1990, Lithuania was declared free from the grip of the Soviet Union. That dynamic freshly awakened his questions and search. With stubborn determination igniting his spirit, he was primed to continue the quest for truth.

Chapter 15:
Hello, Are You There Lithuania?

As Bernard's search for truth unfolds, historical context helps to frame the Lithuanian response that complicated his painstaking efforts.

Since mid-1945, when the Allies succeeded in ending Hitler's terror reign, Russia continued to occupy and rule Lithuania. Early on, Jewish communal and religious life was severely restricted by Soviets. Communist authorities downplayed the Jewish aspect of the Holocaust, for they were guilty of shipping Jews to Siberia and mistreating others at home.

In 1953, with the death of Stalin, who led the Soviet Union, mass arrests diminished and some freeing of the culture was restored. In the mid-1970s, opposition to the Soviets became louder, including in the Catholic Church, both openly and underground. Several thousand Jews were allowed to emigrate, mainly to Israel.

In 1987, Soviet leader Gorbachev permitted Lithuania greater freedom of expression, and a push for independence of the country became more widespread.

In 1989, Gorbachev allowed elections in Lithuania to take place and the non-communist Lithuanian nationalists won. Huge, non-violent independence celebrations rejoiced in this newfound freedom.

In 1990, Lithuania declared independence from the Soviet Union and became the Republic of Lithuania, and was admitted into the United Nations in 1991. By 1995, corruption and unemployment were out of control, and inflation was reported as high as 1000%. In that year, the Lithuanian President traveled to Israel to apologize for his country's role in the Holocaust, thus acknowledging that they helped the Germans conduct horrid massacres and destruction. In return, Israel honored almost 900 Lithuanians for helping to hide or save Jews during World War II.

However, the sincerity of Lithuanian nationalists was in question for decades. In 2017, some publishers destroyed documents and books that discussed Lithuanian collaboration and accountability in the Holocaust. This revealed and validated that harsh feelings and antisemitic beliefs remained within some country loyalists all this time, and intentions offered by the Lithuanian government were not necessarily implemented, as Bernard would discover.

Back in Shreveport, during the 1980s, life was comfortable for my father, transitioning away from running the boutique retail store six days a week. All four daughters had moved out of Louisiana, either studying in college or starting careers or busy with new families. With a new abundance of time, Bernard's energetic pace focused on rekindling two heart-felt passions: painting and searching for his Lithuanian family and town.

He began his quest by storing clippings from newspaper and magazine articles into file folders. Never one to be idle, every possible connection was examined; he even asking the local rabbi to translate communications written in Hebrew.

He was haunted by a compelling determination, fueled by heartbreak and anger, to engage in this continued search for names and data. The obsession was growing, not dwindling, with time. He refused to forget about his family and their suffering, which became his nightmare. The unspoken goal engulfed him, to validate and honor the existence of their lives and community of Raseiniai.

In 1990, when Lithuania finally gained independence from Russia, Bernard fired up with renewed appetite. News was spreading that property claims were being made to the newly freed country. In

November 1991, Bernard wrote to the Lithuanian Embassy in Washington, DC., opening with:

"Gentlemen: I would like to take this opportunity to congratulate Lithuania on her new found freedom and independence."

He continued in his letter to the Embassy to describe his family property, to which he was making a claim, stating that one half belonged to his father, Nathan Rozenfeld, and the other half to Nathan's sister. Dates of his father's death and his own departure to America, were provided, noting that there was one other surviving family member, Hedva, living in Israel. He drew with colored pencils the layout of the property, with structures and land areas identified, noting proximity of side roads and main streets. His hope and effort received no reward, as the Lithuanian Embassy remained silent to his letter.

A new tactic was devised. With his sister in Israel and one of her sons, they decided to commence the property claim by retaining legal representation. Bernard rebuffed any notion of giving up. The property was the last thread connecting him to his family and childhood.

In April 1992, Bernard wrote a letter to a Mr. Spazierer in Tel Aviv, with the following request:

At my request, my nephew, Mr. Yossi Sada, obtained a copy from your office regarding property in Raseiniai, Lithuania. My sister who lives in Tel Aviv and I wish to engage your company to represent us in seeking reparation from the Lithuanian government for property which belonged to our family.

I would like for you to send me an agreement form with your company's heading and a questionnaire to give you all the information that you may need. This will help your representative in Lithuania to make inquiries and come to a prompt conclusion whether or not we have a claim to the property.

Please make it quite clear as to the power of attorney, stating that it pertains to the property in Raseiniai only. As soon as I receive the official agreement and other forms, I will have my attorney look it over.

Bernard felt pleased when he received a reply to his letter on Hebrew letterhead ten days later, saying that Mr. Spazierer returned from Lithuania three weeks ago, where he met with lawyers. The work must start as soon as possible. Information requested included a family-tree listing ownership of the property, and all members of the family, alive or dead, and their children. Street address and property description, including if near shops or apartments, and any photocopies would be helpful. A registration fee of $99 was required, and papers to sign in front of a notary would be provided.

Not one to waste a minute, Bernard responded with all the requests in May 1992. Months trickled by. Hearing nothing, Bernard followed up in September 1992, writing impatiently:

I am not accustomed to procrastination. Four months should be enough for you to find time to reply to my letter from May 1992. I sincerely hope that you are not in the habit of dragging out a case for untold months.

In November 1992, Mr. Spazierer finally responded with papers, written in the Lithuanian language. Undeterred, Bernard searched for help in translating the documents into English. The Lithuanian embassy refused his request. Ultimately, an organization in Chicago was identified to translate.

A year later, by the end of 1993, Bernard's frustration and grief for a property that represented much more - his family's suffering - was vented onto this claim and lawyer. In December 1993, Bernard wrote:

I am very much concerned about this matter and am wondering if you are giving it your full attention. I would greatly appreciate some proof that our claim is being taken care of. I especially want some pictures of the property. I plan to write to the Raseiniai Administration and inquire about the status of claiming property.

In January 1994, a response was received from Mr. Spazierer, in Israel:

I'm giving your claim full attention, as we are to all 5,000 claims in eleven countries. There is no news from Lithuania about their passing a law to pay claims. I'm sorry, but no one will go special for you to Raseiniai to take pictures of the property. If you want to go there yourself, it can be welcomed and I'll give you some information. But, dear Mr. Rosenfeld, you must understand that we waited 50 years for this new situation, and we should understand it will take a little more time as expected.

Bernard tried to be patient, hearing nothing more during 1994, and most of 1995. Attempting to find any means of progress, his energy released into more letter-writing and research. In October 1995, his patience was worn thin, writing to Mr. Spazierer:

I last heard from you in January 1994. Surely by now you must have some information. I am surprised and concerned that I have not heard from you. From what I have read in the Jerusalem Post, some Lithuanian government officials have visited Israel and stated that they will honor claims from survivors. Please bring me up to date regarding our claim. I am particularly interested to know if the house and other buildings are still there. I have read that 93% of the Jewish population have been murdered. It is urgent that I know something regarding the claim. I am 73 years old and have had two quadruple heart bypasses. I thank you in advance for your prompt reply.

Ten days later, Bernard received a letter saying that a response had been mailed months ago, in May 1995, to his sister, Hedva, in Israel, asking her to relay the information to Bernard. In the letter to Bernard in late 1995, the information was repeated for him:

> *The news is not good. There is still no agreement with Lithuania regarding return of property. There is a further problem with obtaining copies of land records from Lithuania. The authorities there are demanding high fees that we are unwilling to pay and unwilling to set a precedent even if clients want to pay the high fees. It would be a good idea for you to write the Knesset President, Dr. Shevach Weiss, asking him to intervene in this matter. You may mention our office since he knows us and our work.*

The Knesset is the supreme state body and has complete control of Israel's government. It is the legislative authority with a house of representatives. I don't know if my father actually wrote to the Knesset President.

More than a year passed, and in spring 1997, Mr. Spazierer wrote to my father:

> *No law has come in force in Lithuania, but we are hopeful that eventually this is going to happen one day. All the claims are ready to be submitted for the minute a law comes in force. The agreement to retain our company is for four years only and those years have passed since you signed in November 1992. An endorsement to the agreement has to be signed now by you and your sister.*

Bernard signed the agreement for himself with a notary and, by this time, his sister Hedva had died in Israel, turning the matter over to her sons. The new agreement would be for five more years.

A couple years later, in 1999, another revision arrived to sign, extending the agreement to represent the property claim in Lithuania until the end of 2005. Request to notify heirs in case of death of claimant was highlighted, knowing that the claimant population was aging. The cover letter included: *"The whole operation is free, with no payment."*

Bernard, now 77 years old, signed and returned the documents with a list of heirs. Being relentless and fastidious, he inquired: *"I was wondering why I could not find your organization through the Tel Aviv Bar Association? I wanted to find your Email address. Please send it to me as soon as possible."*

In early 2000, Bernard received a form letter from the International Commission on Holocaust Era Insurance Claims (ICHEIC), describing the claim process and official participants, including Chairman Lawrence Eagleburger, former United States Secretary of State, and U.S. insurance regulators, representatives from Israel and survivor organizations, as well as European insurance companies. After dedicating nine years of effort to the property claim process, Bernard now had to start completely fresh, following their instructions. Several months later, in June 2000, he received confirmation that his claim had been received.

Finally, in August 2005, Bernard received a response from the ICHEIC. Parts of the letter are extracted below:

We have concluded that the individual named in the claim possibly held some form of insurance. As a result, ICHEIC would like to acknowledge this likelihood with a humanitarian award. In recognition that some claims cannot be validated due to the ravages of war and passage of time, ICHEIC created a broader humanitarian award category. We fully recognize that no amount of money could compensate for the painful suffering and historic injustices of the Holocaust. Nonetheless, I sincerely hope that you will regard this as a small acknowledgement of those injustices.

In October, 2005, Bernard closed his weighty file for the property claim. With a heavy heart, he reluctantly accepted the harsh reality, recognizing that the painstaking time, angst, and sorrow for a family lost, was the best he could offer. He finally laid the effort to rest.

With that act, he also closed the door on any remaining hope of uncovering further information from Lithuania. Enduring 14 years of persistent, and at times, emotionally-charged correspondence, asking for any shred of evidence, pleading for something tangible to validate his memories and the lives lost; he had to let go.

Case closed. The check from ICHEIC for the humanitarian award arrived. It was in the amount of $1,000.

Chapter 16:
Momentous Milestones

In the late 1990s, as my father was following any lead to recover information about Raseiniai or family property, I was living in Washington, DC. My financial career had evolved into becoming a strategy consultant to leadership teams, and often included dining with clients to discuss casual or formal issues.

One client I was working with in 1998 produced multifaceted event-planning services for large organizations, such as coordinating complex conventions or large-scale corporate meetings. During lunch together one day, my client mentioned that they were researching potential speakers for a gathering in Washington, DC, uniting a vast international group known as Young Presidents Organization (YPO). YPO members were under age 45, with the title of CEO or President, and categories of revenue in the millions. During YPO's upcoming gathering in Washington DC, there would be field trips to distinguished places with private speakers and guides. One such place was the impressive U.S. Holocaust Museum, which had opened in 1993.

We chatted about this prestigious gathering of the YPO organization, and my client unexpectedly revealed a dilemma. They were on the lookout for one more distinctive speaker, someone with personal or unconventional insights, for the Holocaust Museum field trip.

My fork remained suspended in mid-air, as a whirlwind of thoughts darted through my mind, contemplating, *"Do I speak up?"* Up until then, my own personal story had never been divulged to any client, but this felt mysteriously different, like an "in my face" sign to speak.

"Well, my father was not in a concentration camp. He escaped from Lithuania in 1939. Yet, his family suffered horrifically in the Holocaust. As a result, my dad suffers from what is known as Survivor's Guilt. He's never spoken about this to anyone outside of family, and lives in Louisiana. If you're interested, I could ask him if he would be willing to share his story with YPO?"

My client's eyes lit up, astounded, *"Yes! That's exactly the kind of speaker we want! A personal story that is unique, revealing, and touching."*

I called my father in Louisiana that night, carefully explaining the speaking opportunity, and who the YPO audience was. Assuring him that I'd be there every step of the way, if he chose to do this, I emphasized that the decision rested completely with him. I also shared that expenses for him and my mom to travel to Washington, DC would be covered, along with a modest honorarium.

He listened quietly, commenting on the distinguished audience, and profound significance of the U.S. Holocaust Museum. This unexpected opportunity surprised us both, emerging like a chosen assignment for him. With complete autonomy to decide, he was at a crossroads of sharing his personal narrative in public for the first time. This was a coveted opportunity, to lend his voice and story to the most esteemed Holocaust memorial and education center in the United States. He softly chose.

"Yes, I will do it."

Conference calls, emails, and back-and-forth reviews of speech content, commenced. Soon, my parents were ready to fly to Washington, DC in mid-October 1999. Having relocated to Orlando, Florida, I, along with my seven-year-old son and then-husband, also traveled to the nation's capital, joined by two of my sisters, united in anticipation to provide family support and celebration. He appeared honored and humbled by it all, hushed, somber, revealing a hint of disbelief, that this incredible milestone in his life was about to be real.

Coincidentally, or serendipitously, prior to this important occasion, he had contacted the U.S. Holocaust Museum on his own, in 1998, writing a letter to the Director of Survivor Affairs. With the opening of this new auspicious museum a few years earlier, he added it to his lengthy search list, mailing in names of family members who perished in the Holocaust decades ago.

In his letter to the Director, he wrote about discovering the hidden museum in Old Jerusalem, seeing marble plaques representing entire towns that were destroyed, witnessing for the first time his own town's name etched in stone. Information about his home and family were included, and he pleaded once more, to please inform him if any records of names from Raseiniai surface at the U.S. Holocaust Museum. He added that he was donating to the museum a copy of his personal story manuscript.

I'm not sure if it was truly coincidence, sacred synchronicity, or triggered by my father's upcoming speaking engagement, but, in early October 1999, less than two weeks prior to his trip, a letter arrived in Shreveport from the Assistant for Registry of Holocaust Survivors at the museum in Washington, DC.

The letter stated that his correspondence from 1998 had been received, and after searching their official Registry, six survivors from Raseiniai had been discovered, for whom they had a current address. The names were included, one being Berelis Rozenfeldas, or Bernard Rosenfeld. For privacy reasons, the museum could not disclose address information, however in some cases, they agreed to serve as a Third Party, to forward information on the requestor's behalf.

Bernard was instructed to fill out a form and return it to the U.S. Holocaust Museum. A decision would be made whether to seek approval from the Raseiniai survivors to share their contact information. From there, the onus would shift to the survivors, allowing them the autonomy to decide if they wished to establish direct contact with my father.

Never one to procrastinate, he eagerly returned the form. A decision was quickly reached to forward Bernard's request for contact, along with his accompanying message, to the other survivors. Wheels were set in motion, propelling the potential to fulfill a life-long yearning, to connect around a beloved shared hometown that had disappeared in a destructive history.

The profound significance of identifying these matching hometown survivors was broadcast by my dad in incredulous tones, in complete astonishment and disbelief: *"It's been 60 years of waiting and hoping!"*

The timing of such good fortune, however, was somewhat eclipsed by the equally extraordinary event looming on the horizon - his sharing, for the first time in public, at the most important Holocaust institution in our country.

So, returning to when we arrived in Washington, DC, I was quickly reminded of the powerful effect from this museum - capable of instigating a transformative experience in visitors. Having toured it years ago, I recalled how it fostered new awareness through informative event timelines and compelling multi-media presentations.

The impressive modern building stood adjacent to the National Mall and Smithsonian museums in downtown Washington, DC. Made from limestone and brick, the Holocaust museum's design allowed for natural light through windows, casting somber and hopeful moving shadows, against etchings of victim names in the glass. Housed within its walls was an eternal flame, a six-sided dome ceiling, and multiple levels amid almost 300,000 square feet of educational and emotional space holding documents, stories, and history.

Upon entering the tour, I vividly recalled the immediate unease as visitors were handed a "passport," adopting a victim's identity. We were then silently crowded into a freight elevator, with tall, dark, worn steel walls, feeling a tiny trace of anxious emotions, to hint at what victims experienced. The elevator jerked abruptly, then lifted us up a few floors to exit, and quietly begin the chronological journey that described what led to the horrors, global involvement, massacres at camps, and breath-taking liberations. There were hundreds of videos, photos, documents, clothing, shoes, artifacts, and story recordings, meticulously researched, immersing visitors into an unforgettable experience.

The most disturbing gasp of sorrow from me was in seeing a massive horizontal clay sculpture, standing only inches tall, stretching across an entire section of one floor. The viewer walked along the display's edge, witnessing the sequence of events at an extermination camp, ending at the gas chambers. Even on tiny clay bodies and faces, I could sense their hopelessness, fear, then horror. That display impacted me greatly, even to this present day, permeating into the emotions of terror-filled victims.

The museum fulfilled its mission extraordinarily well:

"To advance and disseminate knowledge about this unprecedented tragedy, to preserve the memory of those who suffered, and to encourage its visitors to reflect upon the moral and spiritual questions raised by the events of the Holocaust as well as their own responsibilities as citizens of a democracy."

Now, back to the grand occasion in that museum, on October 15, 1999! The significance of the date, 60 years ago to the month, resonated deeply with my dad. The pivotal month brought forth memories of when he swiftly sold his prize radio, securing enough funds to escape from Lithuania. His destiny was forever transformed, and the memories contrasted wildly from where he stood in the present moment.

Approximately two hundred YPO executive leaders filled the theater-style hall, eager to be captivated. Soon, a gentle Eastern European accent would weave through the air, accompanied by a spellbinding narrative delivered with a blend of endearing humility, unapologetic candor, and confident dignity.

Nine members of the family had traveled to rally for this moment - three daughters, three grandsons, and three sons-in-law, plus Dorothy, all seated together towards the front of the vast modern auditorium. I anxiously locked my eyes on him as he was introduced and silently walked forward. My heart raced, adrenaline pumping, staring up at the stage. At 77 years old, my thoughts were of concern- would he be able to make the speech? Would he breakdown in tears? Would his physical heart be too anxious, resulting in a panic attack?

He strode up to the stage with a subdued and serious expression, appearing tall at almost six feet. His silver-hair looked regal, and, dressed in a tailored suit, he stood as a lone figure on the large barren stage behind a speaker's podium in the Meyerhoff Auditorium. A sea of eyes stared at this man. The room plunged into such an intense silence; you could have heard a pin drop.

Waiting anxiously for his first words to part his mouth, there was a long pause instead. Finally, he spoke. His accent sounded magnified through the microphone. *"Good morning,"* the uneven voice began, softly, a little unsure, likely nervous, with spaces to breathe. Soon, he bonded with his purpose and his voice strengthened. He declared his story, describing Lithuania in the 1930s, the miraculous events allowing the escape, the emotional pain of searching, and a lifetime of remembering tragic loss.

He shared details of the political circumstances, such as the Lithuanian National Guard taking revenge on the Jews for being friendly to Russia, and how the nationalists helped the Germans butcher without mercy. He courageously entered vulnerable places, emotionally whispering:

> *"I never had anyone with whom to share my pain, not finding anyone from Raseiniai. At times, I feel lonely and empty, tears come easily. Sometimes I think suffering and pain bring me closer to them. I became obsessed with wanting to feel what they felt. In 60 years, I have forgotten many names, but their faces are always in front of me. I wrote a manuscript to share with my family, but could not ever read it after it was written. Events have a strange way of happening. Once again, I ask myself, was it a coincidence or was it my fate to survive?"*

The audience was mesmerized into an entranced silence throughout the entire 45-minute speech. The only movement was reaching for tissues to wipe away tears streaming from eyes, as they sat among business colleagues. Individuals remarked, awestruck, of being transformed, taken on a journey that was unimaginable, until now. Together, the family released a collective sigh of relief - he did it!

With pride, we stood by his side offering support and smiles, as he fielded one-on-one questions. Then everyone was escorted to buses for a large lunch gathering, including my father and the family, where more questions and congratulations were celebrated.

This momentous experience launched an emotional release and a new chapter in my father's life, which continued upon his return to Shreveport. It was as if a pressure-filled balloon was now floating through air, bouncing with lightness, his energy refreshed by unloading the weight and burden of his story.

Before his speech, the curator of the museum had escorted him privately into a room of archive computers, displaying for him the matched names from Raseiniai. He returned home hopeful that connections and responses from these survivors would arrive soon. On October 22, 1999, he followed-up by mailing to the Assistant of

Registry of Holocaust Survivors, at the museum, three letters for individuals from his town, along with copies of photographs of his family as they looked prior to 1939, praying there might be recognition.

Needless to say, it was an astonishing moment, on October 28, 1999, precisely 60 years to the week since first setting foot in America, that he answered a phone call, hearing a softly accented female voice, who had originated from Raseiniai!

The voice belonged to Chana, and she exclaimed, *"Of course I remember you and your family!"* A long conversation ensued, jettisoning Bernard to a different time and place in the old country. He didn't recall as much as she did, and Chana promised to write and email more information, and, importantly, connections to people from their town.

Chana's first letter soon arrived, identifying the street of his family's residence, asking: *"Didn't you live deep inside a walkway?"* referring to the scary alley. Chana provided six more names, and warmly invited my dad to visit at her homes in Philadelphia and Palm Beach, Florida.

Pure elation surged through him! After 60 years of waiting and searching, a journey laced with deep frustration and despair, cheer burst open like a child's, leaving him feeling giddy by this good fortune.

The very next day, on October 29, 1999, another phone call was received, this one from Rella, who had also lived in his town. He also spoke to Rella's brother, who recalled Bernard. Stories unfolded - Rella had immigrated to America, a mere two months after, and settled in Michigan in December 1939. However, with that difference in destination, Rella's family found solace within a large supportive Jewish immigrant community. It presented a stark contrast to Bernard's experience, isolated in the deep South, where the absence of shared stories left him with no one to relate to or understand his personal journey.

Rella now lived in Orlando, Florida, the very city that I called home! Warmth enveloped me when I spoke with her on the phone several times, and even visited at her house. As we sat surrounded by her family photos, chatting about the different life experiences, it highlighted the profound impact of lack of like community, coupled with emotional pain, versus the resilience found in a community where many were literally in the same boat. They could hold and support each other, and they did.

Later, in December 1999, Bernard happily spoke to another Raseiniai friend, Philip Kagen in Australia, identified from Chana's connections. In 1941, Philip and a friend jumped a train from Lithuania to join the Russian army, a better alternative than the certain cruelties imparted by Nazi's. In 1945, when Bernard went to Munich to visit the Displaced Persons camp and found Yankele, Philip was living at that same camp! Philip was told an American soldier, originally from Raseiniai, was there at the camp. Unfortunately, by the time of that revelation, Bernard had already left to return to the 130th Station Hospital. It was a poignant twist of fate, paths intersecting over 50 years ago, and only identified today.

Soon, it was time for face-to-face reunions, a lifelong desire finally rewarded, to meet others from Raseiniai in person! Bernard and Dorothy traveled to Pennsylvania to visit the oldest daughter, Diane, for Thanksgiving. While there, they drove to meet Chana and her husband for an afternoon, with my dad excited beyond words. Still reeling in disbelief from all of these simchas (celebrations), all of this joy had occurred in less than a month since marveling over that first phone call.

The grand reunion was now in the works. In February 2000, Chana would be in Palm Beach, so we planned a special gathering at my Orlando home, with Chana and her husband, Rella and her husband, and my parents, who flew in from Shreveport. Thrilled and eager for my father, I busily prepared a festive meal for the Raseiniai tribe, anticipating with curiosity, ready to witness what would unfold.

As they entered my house, a wave of ecstatic energy filled the air! Hugging and laughing, I could honestly say that I've never seen my father exude such incredible happiness and light-heartedness. He exhibited a radiance, with a beaming smile and delighted eyes lighting up his face, shedding sixty years of pent-up angst. In that moment, at age 78, he embodied a joyful man, celebrating in satisfaction, infused with a fun-loving, youthful spirit. He was visibly embracing present blessings, relishing the profound human connection to his early life and experiences. The room echoed with lively conversation, punctuated by boisterous laughter, then hushed quiet, as they delved into a tapestry of names, news, and enthralling or saddening stories.

After dinner, Rella brought out a thin, rectangular white dress box, delicately lifting the top, to expose an overflowing jumble of photographs. They each pulled out random photos, chuckling, reminiscing, and sharing stories inspired by the images.

Suddenly, I heard an audible gasp released from my father, halting any movements or voices, commanding everyone's attention. The photo that he had extracted from Rella's trove of old images captured a gathering of girls standing together. Scrutinizing each face closely, a sudden realization struck him. There, amidst the frozen image of past time, he recognized one of the girls. It was his sister.

That discovery hung in the air, buzzing with electricity. The shock in seeing the familiar face of a long-ago sibling, with her name escaping his lips in despair, released tears from his grieving downcast eyes. The sacred moment held the room in silence, as everyone honored the depth of his emotions. Sensing the need for understanding, Rella, who knew his sister, gently shared more details about the friends - just teenagers enjoying life in their small town, with his sister woven into the fabric of the friendly social group.

A True Story of Surviving by Synchronicity

It was quite a profound reunion, filled with emotions, cherished memories, and the birth of enduring friendships to treasure for the rest of their lives.

Over the next decade, the bonds forged among the newfound Raseiniai friends remained strong. Connections grew through letters, emails, phone calls, and exchanging photos and Jewish New Year cards. My father gifted a painting each to Chana and Rella. His artwork reflected vivid memories of Jewish life in their village during the holidays of Sukkot and Passover. The ladies loved the meaningful gift created by my dad, and he cherished their openness to connect. The relationships were a precious healing gift that offered him evidence of his childhood life, something he had longed to share for 60 years.

***

While the unforgettable occasion to speak at the U.S. Holocaust Museum in Washington, DC, and to unite with matched survivors from Raseiniai in 2000, soared to the top of the list for significant life moments, there was one more "chance" encounter that left a priceless legacy.

By 2009, my parents had moved from Shreveport, Louisiana to Orlando, Florida, where I lived. One evening, attending a social event, I was chatting with an intelligent woman whom I had never met. Somehow, the topic of my dad's story was relevant to our conversation and her eyes focused intensely, absorbing with genuine interest when I shared a few details. She wanted to know more, and offered a little about her career background. After asking my father if it was okay to share, a few days later a copy of his manuscript was given to her.

The woman, Debbie Walters, called me after reading the manuscript, and calmly stated that she would like to make a filmed documentary about Bernard's special story of survival. The film, which required funding and sponsors, would illuminate the incredible synchronicities that saved him. The theme would build on hope and perseverance during desperate times, as if angels mysteriously surrounded him with protection.

Debbie was an experienced television and film producer, especially favoring documentaries. Because my father was already in his eighties, she wanted to film an interview as soon as possible, concerned about later difficulties due to his age or health. It was thrilling to imagine his story being professionally filmed and shared with a wide audience, and he said, yes; he was interested!

A written agreement was drafted reflecting Debbie's intention to create an outreach package to support funding of either a PBS television production and/or to enter into film festivals. Maybe even a trip to Lithuania could be funded, she hoped! That was a No. We quickly clarified that Bernard would not travel there for emotional and physical reasons, so it would be me and possibly my sister, if a trip manifested.

On my father's 87th birthday, August 4, 2009, the agreement was signed. We were all eager to begin! The interview was only step one of a lengthy technical and creative process.

During two long consecutive days, the interview was conducted at my home, with a professional camera and sound assistant, along with Debbie. My living room transformed into a small stage set. Rearranging furniture, they strategically positioned a large camera, microphones on poles overhead, and light filters, into place. The mood during set-up shifted into quiet professional movements, providing a tender calmness in the air, respectful of the forthcoming emotional story and my father's age.

Everything was ready and the interview began gently. My father sat on the sofa with his overstuffed photo album on the coffee table in front of him, next to a black mug filled with cold water. Debbie sat across from him in a comfortable living room chair, inspecting the camera's view, moving plants in the background, and adjusting Bernard's collar.

She softly asked the first question: *"Is it okay to share your story with the public?"*

He nodded his head and replied, *"Yes, it is okay."*

I stayed out of the way, yet within listening range. My father's memory at age 87 was incredible, as he shared vivid stories and thoughtfully responded to Debbie's many questions, which were not in sequential order of his life.

He stated clearly for the camera, *"This is my story up to this point. What happens next is for my daughters to make it their story. From here on, you write and do whatever you want with it."*

The string of inquiries, responses, pauses for a sip of water, or to rest for a moment, continued until late afternoon. I was simply amazed by his tough stamina and far-reaching memory. Debbie's patience with his softly accented voice, sometimes barely above a whisper, showed compassion. Her preparedness to capture on camera specific messages and events was impressive. It was a long and successful first day.

The following morning, I drove to my parents' apartment to bring him back to my home to continue the process. By this time, he was in the flow, and ready to give Debbie what she wanted – emotional details that would enhance understanding of horrors inflicted upon his family, and examples of survivor's guilt that he experienced. Permanent scars were obviously woven into his broken heart. Saving graces that he was blessed to receive still mystified him. All of this was shared through his expressive voice during vulnerable story-telling.

Late during the second day of interviewing, tears finally shed from his watery eyes and filming stopped. Debbie and the cameraman cast their gaze downward in respect, remaining silent and giving him space for emotions to release. He took a deep breath, pausing after the painful memory. Soon, he softly murmured that he was ready to continue, and the interview wrapped up with final questions and clarifications.

Sunlight had shifted its shadows into late afternoon, completing another full day. Now, at age 87, his story was documented in his manuscript and captured through many hours of filmed interview. Debbie's short name for the project was *Lithuanian Legacy*. Bernard had indeed preserved a legacy gift for both those living and for those who tragically perished in the Holocaust.

***

Over a decade later, during summer of 2022, I finally listened and watched the five-hour recorded interview that Debbie had given to me in 2010.

Life happened, and she was pulled into other projects, unable to devote the time for funding *Lithuanian Legacy*. We parted on mutually appreciative terms. I was ecstatic to receive a professionally filmed interview, capturing forever his revealing face, soft voice laced with accent, and emotive damp eyes locking the viewer to the screen.

For many years, I didn't feel prepared to listen to the interview. Life was being lived in the present moment, which felt appropriate for me, and cheered on by my dad. Moving cross-country after divorce, rallying during my son's college years, enjoying a new career, exciting travel - all of this wanted to be lived.

Yet, I knew with certainty that one day I would pause and listen. A yearning to do something with his story and plentiful photos and documents was always near the surface.

In August 2022, one hundred years since my father's birth, thirteen years after the interview, a gripping desire and curiosity to know more converged. That insistence demanded my attention to begin the process of birthing this book, by first listening to the interview.

Accompanying the urgency to begin, was clear internal direction to enter his story from a place of appreciation, not heaviness or burden.

I was not going to work on this memoir project under a weight of obligation to bring his words forward. I had written other personalized books over the past two decades and knew that I must write when fueled by positive desire, not guilt.

So, with that instruction to myself, I carried my laptop in August 2022 to the car, drove a short distance, and parked at my favorite place, next to the rolling turquoise waves of an expansive ocean. I was blessed to be living on the paradise island of Maui, Hawaii. Stunning nature scenery easily reminded me to appreciate the gift of present moments, especially when I was working on this emotional story of the past.

With car windows down and doors flung open, a warm salty breeze refreshed my mind, spirit, and body. Sitting comfortably in the shaded open vehicle, I could listen and see without sun glare or flying sand, yet, still enjoy breathing outdoor freshness, with a cheerful tropical view. Soon, the sound of my dad's low voice and the sight of his somber face filled the laptop screen.

My heart skipped a beat. Vision registered. This was the first moment in a long time to see this important human in physical form. He had passed prior to 2022. That will unfold in the chapters ahead.

Viewing his facial features on the computer, alive and in motion, initially felt uncomfortable, eerie. After a while, I became accustomed, and even comforted, by seeing him. He was physically right there talking to me in the car, like in a hologram. Observing his movements and hearing his soft raspy voice seemed completely real in the present, even though he was not alive. I sensed an energy, telling me that he was really happy that we were finally working on this book together. He was patient, and ready whenever I was.

While viewing the filmed conversation, the laptop's *Pause* button was pressed often, stopping to take notes or provide space for spontaneous tears to shed. I watched portions of the interview over many weeks, and only when fueled by positive desire. Finally, after a couple of months, the five-hour filmed interview was complete. A long exhale escaped from my mouth. Whew, that was a lot to embrace, to re-live, to feel, to grasp his very much alive spirit and story.

Closing the laptop in my car, hearing soft ocean waves rush to shore over and over again, I contemplated on this first step of a very long process. Internal guidance remained clear: Enter the story only when feeling inspired with love and appreciation. Thank you, Debbie, for the momentous legacy of filming this interview and nurturing this story forward.

Bernard smiling between Chana and her husband

Chapter 17:
Passions of the Soul

Bernard was a focused energetic man who was all-in! Whatever captured his attention, due to desire or needing his help, there was no stopping him from quick action.

During his career years, significant time was devoted to his retail store in Shreveport, open six days a week, managing a small staff in sales and administration. I recall every month, our family gathered together stuffing envelopes and mailing bills to customers. Every holiday season, fancy giftwrapping was in demand, and I loved using colorful ribbons and unique paper to create special surprise packages. My dad traveled to Dallas, Texas several times during the year, buying fine inventory from vast wholesale markets and galleries, carefully selecting clothing, gifts, jewelry, and décor. Owning that retail store was a demanding responsibility.

Family was an obvious priority. Sundays found him enjoying gardening or completing endless small home repair projects. He trimmed his daughters' bangs after lifting them up to the kitchen counter, and along with Dorothy, attended dance recitals, drove carpool, and applauded school projects and creative activities.

Evenings found him in the backyard, perfectly grilling the juiciest medium-rare steaks, marinated overnight with Good Seasons salad dressing. Special occasions called for all-day smoking of turkeys or ribs using fragrant mesquite wood.

Traveling involved driving vacations with all of us packed into the car. He liked to depart from home in the dark hours of the morning, heading west to Six Flags Over Texas amusement park, or east to Panama City Beach, Florida, earning a sunburn on the famous white-sand beaches. While living in Fort Smith, Arkansas in the 1960s, the Rambler station wagon was filled with family adventuring to eastern Oklahoma, bouncing on unpaved dry rocky roads far into barren land. The destination was an Indian Pow Wow, where we watched into the darkened night, mesmerized by bonfires and traditional costumes and dancing, a trance-like vision that I still recall, despite being only four years old at the time.

My parents enjoyed traveling further distances alone, mostly in the 1970s and 1980s, arranging for a sitter at the house with the girls. There were cruises to Alaska, Norway, and the Caribbean. They enjoyed Tauck Tours in Europe, several trips to Acapulco, Mexico, and as far away as Russia, with Bernard adamant that he still had no desire to visit Lithuania, which carried too much emotional pain.

After the girls left Louisiana, one by one, there were visits to see them in their home states as they moved around, traveling to the mountains of Pennsylvania, San Francisco hills, Florida beaches, Texas, Virginia, Washington, DC, and New Jersey, with a visit to New York's Statue of Liberty.

However, two passions, after family and career, engulfed my father with rich soulful connections. One passion was his commitment to the Jewish community. Always engaged and at the forefront of his heart, he was forever reading global articles and watching documentaries on TV. Financial contributions were willingly sent to the Israel Ambulance fund, Hadassah organization, Jewish Federation, and many other Jewish charitable organizations.

One place, in particular, persevered with an unbreakable bond, and that was the small traditional synagogue in Shreveport. The best way to convey his meticulous and relentless efforts to keep the synagogue alive, financially and physically, is to share messages from the grateful community. In 2004, he was honored with the highest award of recognition for exceptional contributions. First, his thoughts are below, followed by excerpts from synagogue leaders:

> *"I've always wondered why I have been so obsessed with the synagogue for so many years. I am not that observant or even religious and, yet, the synagogue has been my life. I could never understand why until lately it came to me.*
>
> *It's not the prayers or the beautiful sanctuary. It's the sounds. The sound of chanting melodies of prayers that take me back to a small synagogue far away that is no longer. The sound of prayer, prayer from the heart, pleading with G-d for good health, a long life, and forgiveness for any wrongdoing. I sit here and listen to the Rabbi's voice, but I hear the sound of men who are no more." Bernard, 2004*
>
> *"Bernard Rosenfeld is to be honored March 12, 2004, a very worthy recipient. There is not an item in the synagogue that does not bear the imprint of Bernard. He knows every brick and bush, rule and regulation, dues and debts, members past, present and potential, fridge and freezer, kitchen and cooking utensil, heater, humidifier and air conditioner, light and lamp-post. His oil paintings adorn the walls, and he serves at times as the religious kohen on Sabbath mornings and festivals. He has occupied every executive position on the Board and now officially leads "House and Grounds." Nothing escapes his attention. How fortunate we are. The synagogue is very much part of his being. The aging building and the diminishing membership disturbs and frustrates Bernard. He always hangs on and we are eternally grateful for his almost full-time involvement to the congregation." Agudath Achim President, Aubrey Lurie, MD.*
>
> *"You may wonder what more can be said about Bernard Rosenfeld's contributions. There is no way to convey what Bernard*

has meant to this congregation. He has been willing and able to do what no one else has been willing to do, including indispensable and thankless service inherent in house and grounds, and the task of negotiating dues with members and collecting on those dues. He always saw what needed to be done and did it, without being asked. He has no equal here. I have not known anyone who has given more of himself than Bernard. It would be incomplete not to praise another person who played an indispensable role of service, and that is to Dorothy. She has held many leadership positions in the Sisterhood and is active in events. She provides to Bernard moral support, patience, understanding, that enabled Bernard to devote so much of his time. Thank you, Dorothy." Past President, Arnold Lincove*

During his active years of involvement, from the 1970s to early 2000s, he dismissed negative sighs about declining membership, determined to persevere, no matter what, in keeping that synagogue alive. He supervised every inch of design and construction of a new synagogue building, raising sufficient funds to pay cash, in order to have no mortgage debt for the future. The spiritual warmth and clean design were thoughtfully imagined, and it offered a holding place to appreciate many of his Judaica paintings. Walls of memorial plaques included his family members by name and birthdate.

Still, he was adamant about not sharing painful details of his past. He ignored any connection between his deep personal loss and his selfless service to the synagogue. Even though he had spoken to an audience of strangers at the U.S. Holocaust Museum in Washington, DC in 1999, the vulnerability of speaking truth within his beloved local Jewish community was too much to ask. When one leader wanted to honor Bernard's early years in Lithuania, during the 2004 tribute, he responded:

"Dear Richard, I hope I can find the right words to try to tell you how painful it is for me to talk about my family - seventeen members

of my family were murdered during the Holocaust. The fact that I waited until my children were grown to write a book in 1987, in hopes that they will understand more about their father and where I came from, is proof of how painful it is for me even to talk about it to my children.

Richard, I have the greatest respect for you and I understand your interest in my story is sincere. I hope that you will understand how impossible and emotional it is for me to talk about it. I am asking you not to speak about this. I am being honored for what I have done for the Synagogue and it doesn't have anything to do with my personal life. I consider you a friend and admire you and your family, how much you have contributed and participated. As ever, Bernard."

***

This quiet selfless service to the Jewish community was a complicated legacy for him. In stark contrast, was a vibrant man, sparkling, visible, and inviting, when he was enveloped by his second passion - that of artistic creation.

When I was preparing his biography for the 1999 speaking engagement at the U.S. Holocaust Museum, I asked what he wanted to emphasize?

"What do you most want to be known for, Daddy? Since the audience is the Young Professionals Organization, do you want to emphasize your business ownership success, starting from zero means and no formal education? Or maybe, your leadership in the Jewish community? Or, the miraculous journey with synchronicity and determination, escaping dangerous Eastern Europe?"

His simple response surprised me: *"I want to be known as an artist."*

He confirmed this clear choice of soulful passion when printing his business cards after selling and retiring from his retail store. In the place of *"Business Owner"* was one word, *"Artist."*

The strong urge to go to his canvas and paint comforted his heart and mind during times of loneliness, grief, and hopelessness. Expressing through painting didn't fully blossom until the 1990s, after daughters and business responsibilities eased.

Rooted back to early days arriving in the United States in 1939, it was there he first observed painting classes at the Young Men's Hebrew Association (YMHA) in St. Louis. Wandering through libraries and museums, fascinated his attraction to detailed paintings. Dollars he earned from months at low wage jobs, allowed the purchase of art supplies. Collecting discarded magazines with images he admired inspired the lure of trying his hand at the skill.

It was a distinguished photo in a Life magazine, of a bald and bearded statesman in a business suit, with twinkling eyes, that captivated and challenged Bernard to try his hand at creating. He loved blending oil paints and later said that this first painting, in 1941, of *The Senator,* was his best. Fine, realistic details in facial features and clothing, with contrasting light and shading, effectively captured a delighted laughing expression. This painting would be remarkable for any artist, yet, even more so for a first painting as difficult as a portrait.

During that same year of 1941, still in St. Louis, he painted turbulent ocean waves bouncing a small boat fighting for survival amidst rolling whitecaps. Men rowed frantically with oars, tossed in rough, dark blue seas, panicked to escape from a larger ship nearby, which was sinking and billowing in deadly orange and black flames. It was not until I wrote the previous sentence and viewed the art again, in 2023, that I connected the dots to his personal journey, declaring: *Oh! That's what it means...* To me, the painting depicted a survivor's tale -

anxious and afraid on an endangered lifeboat, fleeing the certain tragic destiny of the sinking, blazing ship that was once home.

At this time, he was experimenting with art, yet, also quietly feeling his own turmoil as concern for Lithuanian family increased. In 1942, a more complex painting was completed of Moses, his body being held up by two men at his side, and titled *"Forsake Us Not, O Lord."* This painting was also reflective of inner pleading, as family letters were returned, with no future responses ever received.

Bernard was shipped off to the U.S. Army in 1943 and soon painted a small canvas of a darkened open tent with soldiers inside, titled *"130th Station Hospital."* This was followed by months of special assignments painting portraits of officers' wives from photographs, and five murals in the Officer's Club in England, using acrylic paints for the first time. One of the murals was reported to be exhibited in London among artwork from several other artists.

War years trudged along and his time was diverted to the dental clinic, however, Bernard did paint the image of the Heidelberg Castle in Germany, captivated by its structure and beauty. After he was honorably discharged, sailing home to America in 1946, his vision was entranced by the stunning green mountains of the Azores, with lush St. Miguel Island imprinted in his mind, promising to one day paint the mountainous scene. This magnificent nature-rich painting was finished by the end of that same year, remaining as one of his largest works at 30 inches by 40 inches. Later, the framed painting hung in the family living room for decades.

Bernard's artistic passion was sidetracked for over twenty years with a long pause for marriage, four daughters, and a rising business career. In 1969, three meaningful portraits were suddenly created. The first was a portrait of himself at age four in Lithuania, standing upon a brown woven chair, wearing a dark full-length heavy winter coat, with a fur hat, entitled, *"Scared."* This is one of his best-known paintings, in beautiful soft oils, with impeccable attention to detail, weaving the chair with tiny brush strokes, texturizing the fur down the front edge of the coat, and mastering a concerned child's facial expression. Bernard employed unusual tools to create textures, such as a feather, toothbrush, and sticks. The original photograph that inspired the painting *"Scared"* graces the front cover of this book.

The remaining two portraits completed in 1969 were of Dorothy and himself, at his then-current 47 years of age. He referred to formal professional photographs to paint from, offering a distinguished remembrance of their appearance during prime adult years.

Still busy with daughters, business and community life, his passion was again placed on hold until 1975. During a warm and light-hearted family vacation to Panama City Beach, Florida, he experimented with pastels from the hotel room balcony. Calm ocean views were captured with one version transforming the balcony into a broken railing mess, titled, *"After the Storm."*

His four daughters reached independent adulthood, and he sold the retail boutique store in 1984, continuing to manage the business for a few more years. Feeling released from great responsibility, his passion celebrated more attention, welcoming the creation of 12 paintings in 1988 and 1989.

This was the decade of the 1980s, when his youngest two daughters graduated college, two daughters had weddings, he visited Israel twice, traveled elsewhere with Dorothy, underwent quadruple bypass heart surgery, suffered a critical pancreatitis attack landing him in the hospital for weeks, and he manually typed his over 100-page manuscript, shedding the secrecy of his painful past. Even with all these transformative life events, his soul called, demanding that it was time to paint.

Receiving photographs from his daughters for subject matter in paintings was always treasured, and featured their houses and dogs, his six grandsons, and especially images from their travels. In 1988, I fell in love with Switzerland's pristine green mountainside, crowned with snowcaps, and dotted with meadows and picturesque farmhouses. Many photos later, my father impressively cut and pieced together five photographs producing a perfect Swiss mountain village composition, with the famous Matterhorn rising in the background. I could hear cow bells and touch overflowing geranium flowerboxes under cottage windows every time I walked by that painting in my house.

Other subject matter, among the dozen paintings of 1988 and 1989, included serene landscapes, colorful surprising abstracts, and traditional Jewish religious scenes. Two especially important paintings were created during this time.

One featured Bernard's old synagogue in Raseiniai, with bearded orthodox rabbis dressed in long black coats overlayed with white prayer shawls. They clutched the heavy sacred torah scrolls near their hearts, next to an altar draped in burgundy-colored velvet fabric. This captivating memory painting recalled chanted prayers that comforted his longing for the familiar place of long ago. The painting was gifted to his synagogue in Shreveport.

The second important painting illustrated the activities of his early years in rural Lithuania, with a lone horse and wagon crossing a dark shallow river in 1924 Raseiniai. Sitting in the simple wood wagon was baby Bernard, accompanying his grandparents and Uncle, who was visiting from England. He painted this touching real-life memory from a photograph that still remains with his daughters.

Creative explorations with unrestrained emotions poured out, releasing 39 paintings in only three years, from 1992 to 1994. There were peaceful colorful landscapes with titles: *Serenity, The Village, Lonely Lighthouse, Autumn Morning,* and *America the Beautiful,* all reflecting nature's heartwarming majesty. His appreciation for eye-catching landscapes offered an objective observer style, with a vast appetite and vision, illuminating picturesque scenes from snowy Colorado, blue Hawaii, an Oregon lighthouse, the behemoth Redwood trees, traditional Lancaster, Pennsylvania, and the green English countryside. His colors flowed into New Orleans, Garden of the Gods trail, Butchart Gardens, Pikes Peak, a high-rise night-sky, and Virginia horse-country. Upon visiting Shreveport, we didn't know where to look first in astonishment, with household walls covered in his new artistic passion.

A particular talent emerged in painting structures, such as his daughters' houses, countryside barns, and village or city storefronts. He used a ruler and masking tape to keep lines straight, and drew erasable angles between objects to configure proper placement and perspective.

Judaica and stoic memory paintings prominently jumped out of his collection. Ethereal *Jacob's Dream* displayed a slanted upright ladder leading to puffy clouds and heaven above. Another offered a Chassidic Jew praying in solitude at the massive ancient Western Wall in Jerusalem. Symbols of Jewish life revealed the blowing of the shofar, a ram's horn., and several brightly lit stunning gold-leaf menorah candelabras. A quieter mood spoke through snowy winter scenes in Lithuania, and images from European towns quickly visited during Army years.

Playful and light-hearted, real-life subjects of animals and Bernard's growing family were expressed with obvious joy. When painting a human, he carefully drew lines of a matrix on the photograph and the canvas, matching sections to know what part of the body or face to paint in each square.

Lively creations danced from the canvas, showing a colorful horse carousel, a smiling scarecrow, and, himself holding youngest grandson, baby Ryan. His art captured a happy daughter, Shelley, sitting on a horse, and, an accidentally triple-exposed photo of a grandson blowing out candles, entitled *Birthday Fantasy*. These family-oriented paintings in the early 1990's reflected a man contented with a colorful, successful life.

Hanging in my living room today is my most favorite painting, a delight of curiosity. Created during his prolific year of 1994, the mysterious Victorian house is actually located in Eureka, California, known as the historic Carson Mansion built in 1885. Whimsical flowing lines meet in a convergence of roof elevations, framing intricate trim details as the house rises four stories, crowned by a cupola. Shaded gray tones ooze haunting intrigue, yet humorous quirkiness is the result. It reminds me of the unnerving Addams Family house from old movies, and always stops visitors in their tracks!

In 1995, at age 73, my father's heart was failing requiring a second quadruple heart bypass surgery. Long incisions healed slowly as gradual strength regained under attentive medical care. Determined as always to return to his passions, he diligently followed doctor's orders with diet and regular rehabilitation exercises. Soon he was back to easels and oils.

From 1995 to 1999, thirty-four more paintings were finished. There were scenic tranquil lakes and green mountains, vibrant sunflowers, and detailed houses lived in by his daughters. Two paintings startled us, with broken glass, of a shattered flower vase and a window.

His most replicated painting, titled *Magazine Street,* featured a manicured New Orleans courtyard filled with colorful houses and lush plants. It was first displayed and sold at an exhibit in the Shreveport airport. He then painted the same elaborate composition again, at least three times, only changing the color of houses. Tina and I each happily requested and received one of the large 36-inch square paintings, and the other was commissioned and sold.

By far, most of my father's paintings during the late 1990's featured Judaica subjects. Among the thirty-four paintings completed in a few years, there were six shiny gold-leaf menorahs with rough raised texture, producing a 3-D effect. Images of men praying or blowing the shofar or dancing with Torahs poured from his heart. Women blessed Sabbath candles, children played Passover games and prayed inside Sukkot outdoor huts. These latter two works were gifted to Chana and Rella from Lithuania.

Scenes from modern Jerusalem, and a memory painting of his Rabbi studying Hebrew with a boy, maybe him, were revealed. As several of his grandsons studied for Bar Mitzvah ceremonies, he poignantly painted traditional items that memorialized their personal rite of passage, such as specific prayer shawls or synagogue arks holding Torah's to be read and celebrated.

In 2000, he decorated the backyard in Shreveport by transforming the dull metal work-shed into an elegant canvas. Imagining a refined scene, he painted a black iron fence framing a glassy lake, with surrounding mature trees, overhanging heavy lush branches. Distinguished red brick pillars supported sturdy rails, creating an air of sophistication. In the mural's background, formal upper-class houses peeked through, completing the artistic touch of style in a simple backyard.

There were so many paintings! And, where were they kept? In 2002, with my father's permission and blessing, we rallied the family to help create a catalog to list each painting with its year, title, description, medium used, size, and location. By year-end, after many months of collaborative effort, we made copies of the catalog inventory list and his painting images, which my father had captured and retained all these years. At a Thanksgiving family reunion, together we assembled large notebooks filled with data and photos documenting over 100 paintings completed as of 2002. History was being recorded!

His portfolio expanded after 2002, with a series of colorful underwater paintings featuring Australia's Great Barrier Reef, photographed during Tina's two years living there with her family. In 2007, my parents had finally moved from Shreveport, and new window views from different senior facility homes were, of course, painted - featuring landscapes, autumn trees, and blue swimming pools. Family dogs joined the portfolio that eventually graced us with over 125 paintings in all.

With so many paintings, he began to actively participate in local art shows, solo exhibits, and special events. In the mid-1990s, at over age 70, you could count on his presence at the lively downtown Shreveport *Neon Saturday Nights* summer festival. Proudly displaying colorful artwork on easels, he chatted easily with visitors and local residents strolling among the creative booths, with many locals remembering him as owner of the fine boutique store, *Southern Gift and Fashions.*

He entered a painting at the Shreveport airport's *Artport* event for many years, often selling his creation. His exhibits brightened walls at a bank, local theater, the synagogue, libraries, and later, the retirement living reception halls.

In 1995, Shreveport's distinguished *Barnwell Art Center* featured some of his unique works. And in 1997, the first time for this southern art institution, seventeen of his Judaica paintings were featured, in addition to nine landscapes, which was a milestone given the conservative Baptist demographic of the region.

The local Shreveport newspaper wrote articles about his many exhibits. As a self-taught artist, his style was described as a mixture of objective realism to a more naïve charm. In 1997, descriptions of the Judaica paintings, along with quotes from this unusual Lithuanian man living in the South, were written:

"I want people to look inside these paintings and see what's in them. Look at the faces. I want people to get an education. People who know the Bible will appreciate it. I am very emotional about

my past, and this is a way to express myself. It's much easier to put on canvas than it is to talk about."

The article stated that *"Bernard's paintings are brushed with deep emotions,"* sharing briefly some of his story.

The local rabbi was also quoted in articles about Bernard's gifts: *"His art does something to you emotionally and visually. You see what a synagogue looks like where Bernard grew up. You get a better feeling for what was there."*

Bernard's dogged focus was quoted, with him saying, *"My paintings deal with my memories. I want to be authentic. I usually get ideas at night and then it eats at me until I paint it. Once I start, I don't stop. Everything else goes to the side."*

The Rosenfeld house, and later senior living apartments, doubled as a museum showcasing his evolving artwork that lavishly adorned walls. Dorothy, with her background in college art studies, served as a knowledgeable museum docent in the community and avid supporter of performing arts, adding to the rich culture of their lives.

It wasn't surprising that all four daughters absorbed the atmosphere that encouraged creativity and experimenting with different mediums.

Diane mastered the art of sewing custom doll clothing, with impeccable detail and finishings that she created for American Dolls. Tina immersed herself in a variety of crafts, from stained cut glass and intricate mosaics to colorful crochet and beautiful quilts. Shelley created needlepoints and studied Marketing in college, delving into creative copywriting, video, and graphic design. Both Shelley and I shared a passion for dance classes, performing in modern dance and tap, until age 17 for me and adulthood for Shelley. Shelley even traveled from her home in California to New York City to perform in Macy's Thanksgiving Day Parade as a tap-dancing Christmas tree!

I was the only daughter who ventured into painting, spurred on by encouragement from high school teachers, my parents' interest, and curiosity to experiment. In just a couple of years, I found myself representing my high school by earning a spot in a weekly regional program funded by the state. This initiative aimed to nurture the talents of emerging local artists by teaching a variety of mediums.

Painting in the shadow of my talented father felt a bit daunting initially, but he generously provided me with space and positive feedback to develop my own style. I loved creating realistic images that popped forth from practiced brush strokes. Unfortunately, I let the talent sleep for decades while my business career blossomed.

My father painted until his last year of life, aged into his 90s. One of his final pieces depicted my small Brussels Griffon, an Ewok-like dog, perched regally on the sunlit grass, staring out into the ocean near the edge of a rocky cliff on San Diego's coast. Despite fading eyesight and strength, he was determined to paint the scene. When he presented to me the completed canvas, I saw a stark departure from his detailed works of the past. The dog's basic body shape and shadow upon the ground were a strong foundation, but the remainder was incomplete, without shading, texture or facial or body definition. I silently thought, *"One day, I'll finish this painting and it will be our first collaboration."*

For five years, that painting lingered in my closet, making the journey from San Diego, California to Maui, Hawaii. One day, living on the island, I felt called to take the canvas from the shadows, placing it in the warm light, and propped it against a pillow on a loveseat. Staring at the rough image of the dog, I could visualize my dad's large, strong hands loosely holding a brush and applying color. Unknowingly, inspiration had just leapt into my heart.

The next day, I located paintbrushes from his art supplies that I had preserved. Tiny, wet strokes of acrylic paint slowly brought the dog to life, adjusting facial features and body proportions. Playing with fur texture until strands of hair emerged, you could visually feel the softness and gentle wave of her light brown coat.

I couldn't believe the realism that I was creating and there was no stopping the flow! After twenty-five intense hours spread over the following days, I was all smiles, charged with energy and a profound sense of fulfillment, the result of a magical collaboration of artistry.

Stepping back after completing the painting, I was left in awe. Never had I achieved such striking realism in my artwork. Experimenting boldly with shadows and contrast, I felt his spiritual hand overlaying my hand, guiding, instructing: *"Be bolder, try this color, or that shadow."* The realistic effect surpassed my imagination and previous experience. Together, we had breathed life into that puppy dog, against a newly vibrant Hawaii background of black lava, blue ocean, and green palm trees. The only words I could speak were, *"Wow, thank you Daddy."*

"Magazine Street" in New Orleans, 36x36

Chapter 18:
Life Moves

My father and I often exchanged thoughts, feelings, and projects through long email messages rather than phone conversations. This preference stemmed partly from his gradual decline in hearing. However, more likely, writing allowed each of us space to share free-flowing, meandering ideas in a thoughtful manner. There were a few emails that were so special and revealing that I felt compelled to print and save them - I'm very grateful that I did.

The first email below focused on my new book, titled, ***A Left-Brain Thinker On a Right-Brain Journey.*** I gave copies of my books to my parents, not expecting them to read, just simply as a gift from their child acknowledging the feat of having a book published. So, I was quite surprised to receive the email, indicating that not only did my father read at least part of the book, but applied it to his life.

An early chapter in the book described the importance of identifying the root cause that could ignite a desire for significant change. A root cause usually stemmed from pain, trauma, or subconscious messaging, and often shaped how one lived life. A significant event was often required to create awareness and readiness to consider alternatives to what is.

August 9, 2005: From Bernard to Nancy. Subject: ROOTS, CHOICES and CHANGE

"Chapter three really hits you. It is strange that I was wondering for many years why I am the way I am and the way I think of myself. The cause of most problems does go back to roots. I know my roots

and why it has been almost impossible to make changes. I have known my situation for many years. Thanks to your mother, I kept and still keep to myself. She made it easier for me to accept it and just go on. But it bothers me a lot and this is why I don't let myself get in a situation which I could not handle. Now that I have given up the Synagogue leadership, my root cause is more present and I fear most should something happen to mother, that I would become a hermit. She is an outgoing person, makes and has a lot of friends while I am the opposite. It all started when I left home. I was alone and at the beginning in St. Louis, I was more alone than ever. A change in my life could have happened had my relatives sent me to school instead of the work I did. It made me feel more alone. End of chapter three.

Your book is a good learning instrument and I am sure it will be accepted with appreciation.

Love you, Daddy"

Another email exchange occurred after one of many discourses between my parents regarding my father's intense focus on his projects, causing my mother to feel angst due to his distraction. Her frustration with his busyness associated his overzealous drive with obsessiveness.

September 20, 2005: From Bernard to Nancy

"Good morning, Last night I was thinking about the question of, what is being happy? I am content and satisfied with my life. I only hope that all of you, my daughters, are content and if you are, are you happy with your life? I think if a person is contented that means he/she is satisfied, but does that mean they are happy?

You may be wondering why the above. Most nights when I am awake, I think and think about each one of you.

You get satisfaction for achieving the result even if you work very long and hard at it. As long as the result has been achieved and you are content with it, that should make you happy. That is the way I am. The problem is that most people will only see how hard you work and that must make you unhappy. Mama is not contented and is unhappy.

You may be thinking that I am going nuts. Far from it.

Have a contented weekend, love you, Daddy"

The next email saved was received a few weeks before my son, Ryan, celebrated his Bar Mitzvah ceremony, a very important and studious rite of passage for a Jewish boy or girl around age 13. Although my husband was not Jewish, his support and involvement were always appreciated, especially with the approaching ceremony.

Marrying someone non-Jewish stung my father painfully. He was devastated at the time of my engagement. I had grown up close to my dad and it was tormenting to know that I was responsible for his sadness due to my choice. I promised him at the time of my marriage in 1987, that should there be children, they would be raised Jewish. He was going to have to trust me on keeping that promise. My father stayed mostly silent but respectful towards his intelligent, Catholic son-in-law, hailing from a large Irish-descended family. Over the 20 years of my marriage, my dad's respect deepened, along with his fondness for my father-in-law and the loving foundation of their large family.

January 7, 2006: From Bernard to Nancy. Subject: Thank You

"Dear Nancy, We are very lucky (that may not be the proper word to describe) how proud all of us are of Ryan's Bar Mitzvah. You and Mike came a long way in fulfilling every parent's dream to see their son Bar Mitzvah. You and Ryan have given me more than I have ever dreamed.

Mike, I haven't said much to you. I want you to know we have the highest respect and admiration not just for you, but for your entire family. Your understanding and help you have given Nancy in raising a son in a way which made us very proud to have a son-in-law who has given it all to bring us to the moment we are waiting for.

Ryan's Bar Mitzvah means so much to me because I never had a full Bar Mitzvah since my father died when I was 5 years old, on the sixth candle of Chanukah. I remember his last words to me as I slept across from him as he was dying. His passing left a terrible void in my life which never left me. I wish I had a father to teach me and guide me as I was growing up. I am telling you this in hopes that you will understand how important it is for me to see Ryan be a Bar Mitzvah. Mama and I thank you for giving us this moment. We love you and wish you Mazel Tov, Shalom, Daddy."

Dorothy, my mother, was of concern to my dad. Her physical and emotional wellness were declining, with chronic depression and heart issues. Life in her birthplace of Shreveport had been festive and dynamic, renowned as the instigator of social gatherings, seeker of knowledge, bridge-playing Silver Life Master, art patron, participant at Mardi Gras parties, and volunteer at the Miss America Pageant.

In earlier years, they had gathered with friends every Saturday night for dining out or enjoying a house party, often poker nights where she was a lively card shark. Now, friends had aged or died or moved to be near children. In 2006, he was 84 years old and she was 79. He shared an email with the four daughters, who were spread far from Louisiana, living in California, Pennsylvania, Florida, and Australia:

April 6, 2006: From Bernard to Shelley, Diane, Nancy, and Tina,

"To my very dear daughters, I am staying busy cooking, planting flowers, painting, and have little time to sit down for a chat. A person who does not have anything to do must be lonely and unhappy.

I am very proud of my life, a person who came to this country with ten cents in his pocket and not speaking a word of English and raised four beautiful daughters should be proud. Now, married 60 years, we are both very proud of you.

Life wasn't always easy. There was a time when I was making only fifty dollars a week. We had a house, two cars, four daughters and two dogs, all on fifty dollars a week. Your mother was a good manager and never complained and we never got into debt to this day.

The problem we face (not yet) is what should we do? Mother is unhappy, why? The question is, will she be happy someplace else?

I don't want you to worry about us. When the time comes, we will be ready to decide what to do. I am contented with my life. I may not be happy all the time, but I'm staying busy and enjoying it too. But what about mother? So, my children, thank you for caring, but don't worry (yet). Love, Daddy"

By the end of 2006, discussions focused more specifically on finding a new residence closer to one of their daughters. Given his age, managing household tasks along with caring for my mom became challenging and concerning for my father. We started exploring assisted living senior facilities. The daughters took charge, creating spreadsheets comparing offerings, location, and costs. Finally, in early 2007, the process of letting go of Bernard and Dorothy's lifelong home began. Owned since 1959, it was crowded with furniture, clothes, paintings, and memories, making the task a major ordeal. The daughters made multiple trips home, and ultimately, hired an estate sale company to disperse of the contents.

They chose to move near me in Orlando, Florida, after Tina packed and escorted them on the plane. In April 2007, the emotional milestone moment arrived, moving from their familiar red brick ranch-style home, downsizing to a two-bedroom apartment with meals, activities and transportation provided. My father loved it. My mother hated it.

They arrived to an upscale senior community that resembled a nice multi-story stucco Florida mansion on the exterior. The residents were elders at various stages of life, some vibrant, many not. My father quickly became president of the Resident's Council and my mother organized poker games, complaining that the men didn't welcome her at the card table because she won too often.

Her reputation as a Silver Life Master in bridge spread, leading to invitations to play at the offsite bridge house. Enthusiastic partners eagerly chauffeured her, making for stimulating extended days away.

I clearly and adamantly declared that they not get a car. Driving at their age, with reflexes, strength, and vision unstable was downright dangerous. Continuous grumbling ensued, wishing for the freedom of a car. My mom desired to dine out with better food, and he valued autonomy for his own errands and grocery shopping. With no Florida driver's license, the issue was closed.

One week in July 2007, I traveled out-of-town, returning home to discover they had purchased a car! My immediate reaction was one of shock, coupled with a sense of horror and fear for their safety and the safety of others on the heavily trafficked roads near their residence.

My father was single-minded, and sly at age 85, knowing that I was away. Not much had changed from over 60 years earlier when a young, non-U.S. citizen, was determined to enlist into the Army after a head injury, choosing his timing to register when he knew his doctor was away. It worked then, why wouldn't it work now?

Furious with the car dealer, I called to admonish him for selling a vehicle to an elderly person who didn't even have a driver's license. The salesman innocently responded that a license had been provided. Barely able to breathe, I questioned my father about his cagy actions.

Ever resourceful, he had asked another elderly resident, who had a car, to drive him to obtain a license. When he didn't pass the vision exam, he ingeniously informed the DMV employee about upcoming cataract surgery. The Florida DMV issued him a license!

Terrified every time he took the wheel, I never dared to join him in the car, refusing to allow my son to do so as well. The breaking point came when, upon returning home to the senior community one day and parking, he fell onto the concrete while getting out of the car. Lacking strength to get up, staff rushed to the scene, requiring help from several to lift his heavy frame of almost six feet and nearly 200 pounds back to a standing position with the aid of his cane. That was the end of the car. Fearing the possibility of future falls, especially when alone, and considering his heart ailments, we convinced him to surrender the keys. He quietly sold the car.

For the first time in their lengthy married relationship, it was my father who shined brightly in social activity within the new senior residence. He smiled, greeted others, sat for personal or worldly conversations, and invited couples to join their table for meals. The staff adored him, admired his artwork, and appreciated his taking on of leadership roles.

My mother, on the other hand, was sour on most everything, especially disliking the food, saying *"It's not like Louisiana."* Her spunky comments were as hot as the Tabasco sauce she carried to meals.

Sweet friendships evolved with a few other men and my dad, surprising my sisters and me, since we never witnessed such ease before. One elderly man created a woodcraft shop in his tiny apartment. My father visited, watching, helping, and talking for hours. His painting passion returned also, transforming the second bedroom into an office studio crowded with art supplies. His artwork even graced the facility's welcoming reception area, providing him exposure and conversation with new friends. He was certainly not a hermit.

In 2008, about a year into their Florida move, I dropped unexpected news on them during our weekly restaurant outing. I solemnly revealed that my marriage was coming to an end. Immediately quiet, their eyes cast downward to soak in the weight of the somber news. No one in our family had been divorced and their concern for our well-being was palpable.

Disappointment visibly covered their faces, yet they thoughtfully asked how their youngest grandson, Ryan, was doing and how I was coping. I shared how our paths of interests and life perspectives had widened. My parents softly nodded, saying that they cared about Mike and agreed he was a good father to Ryan. Gentle, loving words of support were generously spoken, as my father murmured, *"We trust your decision."* I couldn't have asked for more understanding parents, not questioning or doubting me.

A few years later, in 2011, Ryan was happily gearing up for high school graduation. Another serious conversation with my parents was in order. I expressed my wish to leave Orlando once Ryan headed off to college in June. Although unanticipated, they were once again considerate of my desire for a fresh start elsewhere, declaring that they would stay in Orlando after I departed. On a comforting note, my sister Tina and her husband, now residing in Virginia, had purchased a condominium in Orlando for quarterly visits, ensuring a continued family presence.

With a conflicted heart, I knew it was time for my other sisters to take the lead. Feeling melancholy about departing, after four rare years of getting to know them as an adult, I was also exuberant about moving to San Diego, California in July 2011.

My parents didn't wait long after I left. By November 2011, they were on a plane to California, moving as far away from Florida as possible, to be near youngest daughter Shelley. After living in one place, Louisiana, for over 50 years of marriage, residing a few early years in nearby Texas and Arkansas, they had made a big change by moving to Florida for four years. Now, at ages 84 and 89 years old, they were crossing the country into the unknown, 2,500 miles away.

Walnut Creek, in northern California, was their destination. Tina and Shelley moved them into a charming, cedar-shingled, cottage-style senior living facility. Onsite gardens overflowed with a colorful variety of flowers found in cooler climates. For healthy fresh meals, staff picked tasty herbs from the garden, served in a lively bistro-style dining room with beautiful stain-glass windows.

Compared to their Florida experience, residents seemed more vibrant, independent, and intellectual, with frequent stimulating lectures and field trips, along with the usual bridge-playing and musical entertainment. My father, once again, transformed the second bedroom into an office and artist studio. He paid to have the small open-air balcony enclosed with glass windows, for extra work space in all seasons, with refreshing natural light warming their new home. But they weren't really progressive Californians, instead, more homey down-to-earth Southerners.

After four years in Walnut Creek, they moved once again. In May 2015, at ages 93 and 88, with increased needs for physical assistance, they departed for Houston, Texas, to be near Tina who had relocated there. Tina had more time flexibility, plus costs for care were less than California. With physical mobility at risk, Shelley carefully accompanied them on the plane. Unfortunately, the anxiety of packing, moving, and traveling proved too much for my father's fragile heart. Upon landing at the Houston airport, Tina rushed them straight to the hospital emergency room concerned about the pain of his stressed heart.

Their life resumed and steadied, happily feeling familiarity in Texas near Southern roots. The twangy accents, soul food, and neighborly cordiality, helped them settle in quickly. Painting filled my father's time and bridge-playing for my mom. Tina indulged their love for dining out, with special treats of soft-serve vanilla ice cream dipped in chocolate at country-style Dairy Queen.

With his wife happier and more stabilized, my father focused on his many projects, from repairing things to creating new art to reading the Jerusalem Post. However, he was slowing down and his balance was a challenge. He reluctantly used a walker and sometimes a motorized scooter. Pride and determination often pushed him to dangerously walk independent of support, declaring with frustration: *"I don't know why my knees won't support me?!"*

In August 2017, we all planned to gather in Houston to celebrate his 95th birthday! I was delighted that my son, Ryan, would join us from Florida, Shelley was traveling from Northern California, and my route was from San Diego.

Regrettably, just days before our arrival, he was rushed to the hospital, feeling weak and unwell, staying there in bed during our entire visit for his birthday. Medical professionals monitored him but couldn't pinpoint an exact diagnosis beyond his strained heart history and age. They were not hopeful for a full regaining of strength. Our sad disbelief edged higher as he was referred for hospice coordination and round-the-clock private care, until hopefully he improved somewhat.

He always bounced back! We were stunned by the prognosis. After multiple heart surgeries, pancreatitis, chronic cellulitis hospitalizations, we had often called him a cat with nine lives. When the hospice coordinator privately commented to Tina that our dad would likely only live for six more months, the abruptness of that thought rudely stabbed reality. Refusing to accept those words, Tina promptly requested a different hospice coordinator.

The thought that he might not bounce back this time shocked us to the core. Despite his weakened body, he still retained a tough presence at close to six feet tall and 190 pounds. Medical staff consistently applauded his vitality, acknowledging that he appeared much younger than his age and health history. His survival always felt surrounded by a touch of magic, defying odds time and again, bouncing back under any circumstances. Now, at age 95, the question lingered: Would the magic endure?

Bernard and Dorothy

Chapter 19:
Visions of Transition

Never one to stop surprising me, another mysterious experience awaited my father.

It was my last day visiting in Houston in August 2017, before returning home to San Diego. I stood next to my dad's hospital bed to offer a loving hug and a tender goodbye. Tina and Shelley sat nearby on a small sofa in the private hospital room, whispering sisterly chatter. My mom sat quietly on a vinyl recliner in subdued expression, obviously concerned for her husband's fragile prognosis.

As I drew near him to lightly kiss his cheek goodbye, he whispered a startling message in a raspy, weak voice, speaking in breathless bewilderment: *"I had the strangest dream last night!"* His eyes popped wide open, recounting the dream with child-like wonder in a hushed voice.

"I tried to leave the hospital and was waiting outside, waiting and waiting. Finally, a nurse came outside and made me return inside. I really, really wanted to go but they would not let me and brought me back in. It was so strange. I can see it clearly."

My gut instinct told me that this was something more than a dream, so I encouraged him to continue, gently asking a few questions, grateful that he was talking, remembering, sharing. Intrigued by his "dream," I wanted to know more.

He continued sharing the visualization, exclaiming with awe: *"When I returned inside the hospital, escorted by the nurse, two small boys were in the reception area, singing with the most beautiful clear voices I've ever heard! Their voices were absolutely like nothing I've heard before, so pure and clear."*

His eyes were still open wide, appearing incredulous about this dream memory. His weak, hoarse voice and pale, tired body told a different story – a tale of a man who had glimpsed a vision, a vision of transition.

Suddenly, recognizing that this was likely not a dream, but an out-of-body or near-death experience, my mind immediately began analyzing clues for meaning. He referred to trying to leave and go outside (of his living body), yet he was escorted back inside (into his living body) by a nurse (or angel spirit?) He really, really wanted to go (his body was tired, weak, and ready to pass.) The pure, incredible voices of the boys singing. (Cherubic angels or childhood friends welcoming him?)

I glanced quickly away from his awestruck face seeking eye contact with Tina and Shelley, to validate if they had heard his dream story and connected the dots for what this might represent. When my vision met their moist, red eyes staring at me with tears flowing, my heart skipped a beat. They heard everything and came to the same conclusion as I.

He had had a vision of transitioning, yet on his 95th birthday in August 2017, it was not his time to go.

Four months passed as he rested at home in a hospice bed with 24/7 care. Weak and immobile, he relied on a wheelchair, a task demanding two strong people to lift his large frame from the bed. During my December visit for Hanukah, I witnessed him in the wheelchair - pale and visibly frustrated with the limitations of his body. Two months later, an unexpected and significant change occurred.

On February 12, 2018, I arrived at my parent's small, pleasant, new space in the assisted living facility. A substantial announcement had recently been uttered from his lips – that he would last two more years, regardless of being with hospice. We not only acquiesced; we believed him.

This declaration motivated Tina to coordinate their move from the independent-living side of the property to assisted living. Round-the-clock private care was costing a fortune. They needed to move to the other side where access to help was available with regular check-ins, and it was much less costly than private caregivers. My duty for a few days focused on unpacking boxes, hanging paintings, and setting-up the small apartment.

Lack of strength to walk since leaving the hospital months ago frustrated the heck out of him. Adamant to take steps again, he repeatedly pleaded to me over the phone, *"I don't know what's wrong with my legs? Why won't my knees support me?"* Attempting to help him find peace, I offered: *"Your legs are tired – they served you well for 95 years, walking to many places!"*

Of course, that response was ridiculously ignored. Stubborn and determined to desperately regain independence, a renewed feisty resolve was born with an unyielding goal.

Slowly, over the previous two months, he doggedly exerted all the energy he could muster and astonishingly increased muscle ability to sit up on his own in bed. With that prized accomplishment, he pushed support away and gradually built strength to transfer himself from the hospice bed to a waiting chair with only a little help. Staff looked on in amazement, letting him persist, knowing it was only recently that two people were required for movement assistance.

When I arrived, he defied expectations by rising from a chair on his own, reaching for a walker placed in front of him, reigning in every muscle memory forged from years of physical rehabilitation therapy. In just two months, I was astounded to witness his power and progress. Against all odds, he was resolute, demanding to walk again. Everyone dismissed this as impossible. But he persevered and accomplished his goal, despite what anyone else thought or said. This was the defining story of his life - determination and perseverance.

One morning during that brief visit to Houston in February, I arrived at their new space to hang his paintings on the walls. He sat in his remote-controlled comfy recliner, with my mom relaxing next to him in her recliner. I smiled thinking that they reminded me of Archie and Edith Bunker in the TV show, *"All in the Family."*

Retrieving the paintings from a closet, I presented them one by one, seeking his approval for display. With each painting, he would gently instruct - a little to the left, a touch to the right, or motion with his hand - until the perfect balance was achieved, and the nail was hammered into the wall. This decorating game extended to placing favorite objects on shelves and tabletops, each location considered through his artist's perspective and sense of spatial quality. This playfulness was a delight and his strength, clarity of thought, and upbeat mood demonstrated his most robust health in years.

After decorating was complete, he asked to visit his storage room at the far end of the building. With deliberate effort, he slowly pulled his aged body up from the comfy recliner, reaching for the strategically placed walker placed in front of him. Shuffling a few steps, he climbed onto a motorized scooter. Skillfully reversing out of the apartment's narrow doorway into the hallway, he accelerated so fast that I had to jog to keep up with him. A hint of a smile revealed his amusement by the speed, yet his face remained reserved, as if deeply secrets thoughts lay hidden in silence. Racing down the hallway, I called out, *"Slow down!"* Clearly, he was on a mission to reach that storage room.

Seated tall and upright, gripping the scooter's handlebars, he maneuvered past the reception area and other gathering spaces, until we reached the small storage rooms. Turning the key to unlock the door, I stepped aside, allowing him to roll the front wheels of the scooter into the compact space. His eyes scanned the room, taking in boxes high on shelves and items stacked against the walls. The boxes shouted with heavy black marker: *"Holidays." "Lithuania." "Art Supplies." "Photo Albums.*" It felt like a journey down his lifelong memory lane.

I gently pointed upwards, commenting where his blank canvases and paint supplies were stored. Several wood easels stood folded, propped against the entrance doorway next to him. He continued gazing around the small room in silence, reviewing and registering beloved items in his mind and heart. Finally, he nodded peacefully, with soft resigned eyes, looking upwards to where I had pointed. His somber face acknowledged that his paint supplies were safe and accounted for.

Preparing to reverse out of the room on his scooter, his large, aged, hands patted the wood easels near the doorway. The touch was tender, loving, as if stroking them in friendship, thanking them for their generous role in his life. It felt like a contented acknowledgement, recognizing their contribution as a healing gift - supporting his artistic passions and helping him to express emotional wounds.

Then he quietly whispered a curious pronouncement.

"I don't think I'll be painting anymore."

What? I was confused by his statement, knowing that painting was his inspiration since selling the retail business in the 1980s. Painting was the foundation to emotionally survive early lonely years in America, while painfully missing his family so far away. Yet in that telling moment, I let his comment pass, attributing it to being tired and still recovering.

From the small storage space, we exited the building to enjoy bright sunshine and crisp fresh air. Pausing in the gardens, I wanted to photograph his appearance of strength on the scooter, yet his eyes revealed that he was thinking about something beyond that moment.

He gazed directly at me but saw something else, with his eyes communicating an unknown message in silent sign language.

I attempted to lighten the moment, motioning with a smile for him to give me a thumbs-up for the photo. Still silent and solemnly looking at me, he barely shook his head, indicating No. I let the request go, respecting his soundless solitude, and snapped a photo of him sitting in sunlight against a beautiful clear blue sky, still gazing beyond, with thoughts unknown.

We continued to roll purposefully through the bare winter gardens without voices or words, feeling the life-giving freshness of a sunny cool day. The physical closeness and solemn energy shared during those moments carried overwhelming feelings of gratitude. Strolling together in silence, he on the scooter, me walking next to him, I felt powerfully interconnected to my father in everything that was not said.

He was so involved in being present in life and also preparing for the future - a future that now meant, at age 95, the end of life. During my last three visits to Houston within the previous six months, he had pulled me aside, quietly asking: *"You know about Shreveport, right?"* Responding calmly, with a reassuring smile: *"Yes, we know about the plots purchased for you and Mama in Shreveport at the Jewish cemetery."*

This visit in February brought a shocker of a surprising question. Back in the apartment, he quietly asked me to follow him into the other room, slowly shuffling his feet and tired body, using the walker for support, then sitting down on the edge of the bed. We were alone and he peered into my eyes with curiosity, asking in a hushed voice so my mother wouldn't hear in the next room:

"How am I going to get to Shreveport?"

Stunned by that question, I swiftly processed how incredulous this conversation was. Coherent and objective, he exhibited no fear or sadness in asking me how his body remains would be transported from Houston to Shreveport immediately after his death. This final journey of over 200 miles must happen fast, for a Jewish burial was needed within 48 hours of passing. Embalming and cremation were forbidden in traditional Jewish laws. Ashes to ashes, dust to dust, as quickly as possible naturally, was the custom.

Unbelievable. Who asks how their body will be transported, without displaying any anxiety or despair, just pure curiosity with, possibly, a little micro-management and control?

I smiled at his unexpected question, trying to exude loving warmth and reassurance.

"No worries, Daddy. Tina did the research. We coordinated with Shreveport contacts and it's all taken care of, under control."

His inquisitive soft eyes were child-like, looking up at me for information and comfort. Nodding his head in understanding, he accepted my response. With no further questions, he pulled himself up holding onto the walker and shuffled back into the living room, sitting in his recliner chair next to my mom. I, on the other hand, was still reeling over his chutzpah to ask about his body's journey to its final resting place.

On my final day visiting their apartment in February, they were both sitting in their pillowed recliners when I leaned in to give them each a hug and kiss goodbye. The atmosphere was quiet, peaceful and calm as we studied each other one more time.

"Thank you for hanging my paintings."

I grinned in appreciation. *"It was my pleasure."*

He countered with a twinkle in his eyes, *"It was a pleasure."*

Even though he appeared to be at his healthiest, I felt compelled to say something of lasting significance and connection. Staring directly into his eyes, I gently spoke, *"I have your writings and I'm going to do something with them."*

He returned the direct gaze, smiled, nodded, and softly said, *"Yes, okay."*

I sensed a mutual understanding of importance that he attached to his manuscript and paintings, as his enduring legacy. He wanted them shared with a broader audience, to educate, honor, and remember. His gaze and words communicated that he recognized my comprehension of his desire.

The light-hearted moments of playfulness and meaningful connections during that visit remain a forever cherished memory. My heart is filled with gratitude for the privilege of such soulful experiences.

In the weeks that followed, his robust desire for physical independence propelled him to move too quickly, resulting in a loss of balance, causing three abrupt and injuring falls. The toll of these incidents proved too much for his fragile heart, prompting doctor's orders to rest. My sisters and I felt cautious, aware that his aged body couldn't sustain this game of fall and recover forever.

Chapter 20:
The Final Chapter

It was a light-hearted Friday for me, taking a day off from work in San Diego, smiling as I pedaled my old yellow beach-cruiser bicycle. It was a warmish morning on March 2, 2018. The thick tires glided easily along miles of flat, oceanfront boardwalk, then my legs pushed harder up to a grassy hill overlooking rolling Pacific Ocean waves.

I climbed off the bike, loving the smell of moist, salty ocean air, pausing to breathe it in deeply. Sitting on the soft green grass, I gently allowed my eyes to close. Hearing ocean waves, feeling a light breeze touch my skin, my shut eyes invited a relaxed breathing meditation. Inhale slowly and exhale fully. Quiet the mind. No thoughts are needed. Just breathe in stillness. After about ten minutes, my eyes opened slowly. Not losing a second, my hand reached for a pen to write in a waiting journal, capturing highlights of the meditative experience:

> *"A visual image illuminated eyes looking up. It was my father's eyes seeing the other dimension. A message came: The veil is lifted for him; he is in and out. He still feels some pain here. Encourage him to focus on the sweetness."*

A few hours later, refreshed back at home, I gently spoke to my father on the phone. It was difficult to understand him, his soft voice was faint, weak, tired. In a hoarse whisper, he thanked me for hanging his paintings and photographs:

> *"You did an excellent job. You did it just like I would, placed them just where I would."*

I smiled and asked: *"Do you see the photograph of your parents straight ahead from your bed?"*

It was a beautiful professional photo from the early 1900s of his parents dressed in finery, not smiling, but elegant. He laughed delicately at my question.

"Yes, I see the picture."

I had hung it strategically there so he could see it from bed.

"They are with you always and are taking care of you always."

He paused silently, then quietly agreed, *"Yes."*

I cherished this moment, and complimented him on being a wonderful father, always doing a great job for the family.

He replied, *"Thank you. Where are you?"*

"San Diego."

"Oh, that is far."

He sounded tired, needing rest, so I told him I was going to take my dog, Ali, for a walk.

"Ahh, that is nice," came the reply, sprinkled with a smile in his faint voice, always a dog lover.

I felt the urgency of dwindling moments and tenderly said, *"I have your manuscript and I want to work on getting it published."*

He responded with acceptance and stoic finality. *"Yes, okay."*

We traded goodbyes and I love you.

As the call ended, tears streamed down my face without interference. This was a different conversation. He was very weak. The preparations that we had researched needed to be activated.

I called Tina in Houston and she agreed. Shelley was scheduled to fly in Sunday, and hospice was present with him now. Tina requested that I contact the funeral home in Louisiana, informing them that the family was "on call," as hospice workers explained signs of final days. Daddy could pass at any time due to weakness in his heart and body. The coordinator at the funeral home was gentle, professional, and knew just what to say and do.

Feeling focused with energy and a need for purposefulness, an urge descended to write a worthy obituary while my thoughts were clear and emotions calm. The surreal moment was so close now. Words flowed from fingertips on the keyboard, followed by emailing the obituary to Tina. I sighed in appreciative relief and comfort when she responded that it was "incredible."

I spoke on the phone several times with the religious leader of the synagogue in Shreveport, the Cantor. We discussed the four-hour mortuary transport drive, from Houston to Shreveport, which was required immediately after he passed, and the Jewish rituals of preparation for burial. We had to move efficiently due to the limited 48-hour custom, from time of death until the funeral. The family needed to gather in Shreveport from both coasts of the country during that time also.

Having these conversations with the Cantor felt dreamlike – I was on automatic pilot for logistics preparations, a role often completed in my career. But preparing for death was unsettling, like tip-toeing on unstable ground. It was my father, the hero in my life, my biggest supporter. By the end of Friday, I felt numb by the reality of the moment. My mind couldn't focus. It was a waiting game now.

Saturday, March 3, 2018

Family members in Pennsylvania were making arrangements to fly to Shreveport, waiting for the signal to depart. I felt conflicted with moving too fast with burial and travel arrangements, or wait until we knew more. We didn't know how long this final phase would last. Would he live for weeks, days, or hours? My utmost intention was to honor him, yet I knew he respected being prepared. He was always incredibly organized and prepared.

A lot of details and decisions were necessary requiring communication. I floated through Saturday without focusing on much, other than getting my San Diego house and pet care in order and looking at my suitcase. Hospice nurses at his apartment in Houston continued to monitor failing signs of our larger-than-life father. Should I travel to Houston, or go to Shreveport to make final arrangements, which the Cantor requested?

Sunday, March 4, 2018

During the night, he had declined further, and was out of consciousness most of Sunday, on morphine and oxygen. His frail body weakened and signs of passing were clear. In recent days, the nurse reported that he had begun looking upwards, talking or staring above into the blank air. Startled by this validation of my oceanside meditation, just two days earlier, I had witnessed his eyes focusing upwards, as I sat in stillness 1,500 miles away from him.

He picked at his clothes, ate less. She said these were distinct signs that passing was near. Today, his skin color was becoming mottled and, later, it would turn greyish. So much life had been seized and lived by this man, and now his body pronounced it's almost time to let go.

Shelley arrived in Houston from Oakland, California. She called, speaking in a hushed tone, describing his coloring turning grey and his colder skin when she reached to hold his weak hand. I decided to be prepared to depart Monday, not exactly sure where I was going, since this could continue for days. Packing clothes and researching flights on my laptop filled solemn, anxious, evening hours.

Talking to my son Ryan in Florida helped. He knew that we were "on call," unsure if the flight would be to Houston, to be with his grandfather, or to Shreveport, to make arrangements with the funeral home and Cantor. The decision would be made in the moment, just be prepared to depart. How far apart we all were, stretched from coast to coast, needing to gather in the middle, in a small town with a small airport for a big purpose.

Monday, March 5, 2018

Shelley texted me around 3:30am (my Pacific time.) She and Tina were called by the hospice nurse to come now, to my parents assisted living apartment. My next text was to Ryan, before he headed to work on the east coast, to coordinate potential flights. He needed to drive two hours to Orlando to catch a decent flight. *"Start driving,"* I said. His travel destination, Texas or Louisiana, would be known by the time he reached the Orlando airport.

The hospice nurse reported that, based on signs of his greyish coloring, strained breathing and cool skin, it would be very soon, minutes to hours. I called Ryan, who was almost at the Orlando airport, confirming a flight plan to Shreveport.

Boarding the plane in San Diego, around 11 in the morning Pacific time, somberness blurred all thoughts. As the giant airliner taxied out onto the runway, my hearing instantly became fixated on mechanical sounds, which I had never paid attention to before. The whir of wheels rolling heavily on concrete and massive engines noisily raising volume, sucked me into their movement. Paralyzed in alertness, my attention was struck by sound intensity, building to a crescendo. The rush, rush, rushing forward felt significantly important, emphasizing incredible technical skill and finesse.

My head and body instinctively pressed against the window so my ears were closer, begging to hear the sounds. I was startled and puzzled by this captivation, staring into nothingness to concentrate, fully entranced by blaring engines. The airplane's mighty wheels accelerated, with the runway view racing by through the window. Engines thundered into peak vibration. This behemoth metal structure gracefully lifted from the ground, nose tilting upwards, front wheels free from grounded friction. Keen awareness of the heavy weight of the Boeing 737, left me in awe of the magnificent feat of its rising.

The plane's nose lifted higher as its enormous wheels left the runway, immediately causing me to gasp. Energy surged through my heart and body. I was lifting upwards also, vibrationally, feeling a buzzing radiate from my heart. This was combined with intense mental alertness and a rigid body with zero movement except for breath. I was lifting up, spirit to spirit, soul to soul, with my father. A message instantly emerged from my mind and heart in a silent rushing whisper:

"Daddy, I'm going to soar with you, we'll do this together. I'll get you started and then you can continue to soar beyond, if you are ready."

It was a tearful, melancholy, three-hour flight. Visions of my father's healthy face flashed in my mind. When the plane landed in Dallas for a layover, I immediately turned on my phone. A text pinged in from my sister.

It read simply: *"He is gone."*

He had continued to soar. He had chosen to fly on to a higher dimension. Tears streamed down my face as I turned my head towards the window sobbing, waiting to deplane. Thoughts rushed into my mind, disbelief; he was really gone. We elevated together, and his spirit finally let go of the body, to soar freely beyond.

Ryan met me in Dallas at the airplane gate, incoming from Florida and connecting to the same flight to Shreveport. My heart felt overwhelming relief upon seeing him. Through tears and sobs, I whispered the news and we paused for a long, caring hug.

Ryan had texted me last year with the message: *"I always knew Grandpa would be okay as long as he wanted to paint."* God, Ryan's insight was so significantly accurate. I had missed that connection in February in the storage room. I hadn't shared with Ryan, that only weeks previously, his Grandpa said he was finished with painting. We quietly reflected on that foresight while waiting for our connecting flight to Louisiana.

Landing at the Shreveport airport, we walked through the terminal hallway and a memory struck me of my father's paintings proudly displayed on these walls during the *Artport* exhibit decades earlier. His energy was everywhere in my thoughts.

Driving in our rental car, I noticed that Shreveport's southern charm had escaped dramatically with the arrival of casino gambling boats moored on the Red River. New establishments of chain restaurants and strip shopping centers replaced much of what had been cotton acreage, dairy farmland, long-time family-owned stores, and open land with thick swamp vegetation.

Wheels were in motion for funeral arrangements. The mortuary transportation service was in progress, carefully and respectfully driving his body from Houston to Shreveport. I made an appointment to meet the funeral director the next morning, before the rest of the family arrived.

As I tried to sleep that night, Shelley's descriptions of the atmosphere and events in the small apartment during his final hours, swirled through my mind. Tina, Shelley, and my mom stood next to his bed, along with a medical assistant and caregivers who had grown fond of this strong, Eastern European, artistic survivor. There were nine women holding an unspoken vigil around his hospice bed, honoring him with sacred respect.

His personality had been opinionated and demanding, yet he could be an empathetic gentle giant. Shelley had lifted her phone, playing soft classical music, near his ears. He had hung on, eight hours after they thought it would be any moment. Shelley's tender hands touched his chilled forehead, as she lay on my mom's twin bed next to his hospice bed. The nurse believed it was his pacemaker that was keeping his body alive; they were not allowed to interfere with a pacemaker.

He hadn't been awake since the previous day. The nurse suggested that the caring women in the small bedroom talk to him - he could still hear. They took turns quietly speaking and expressing love for him, thanking and saying goodbye. We knew he was still the patriarch until his last breath, wanting to survive and protect those he loved.

After he took that final breath, with sobs and tears from those surrounding him, Tina repeated how beautiful it was with nine women encircling his bed holding sacred space. He was so loved, cared for, and protected, even until the very last moment.

After he exhaled for the last time, his body remained in their apartment in the hospital bed until hours later when the mortuary service arrived. Shelley shared her raw experience with me:

> *"His body was left in the bedroom to wait for the transport van. I looked at him through the open door, feeling it was all surreal. This larger-than-life figure in my world was gone. It seemed as if he should just wake up and be okay again. How could such a once strong and powerful man die? That was my Daddy. I could feel across the apartment how cold the bedroom was with his body lying there. Not refrigerator cold, but freezer cold."*

Tina's community rabbi happened to appear just after my father's passing - a final synchronistic moment bringing reminders of the many blessings woven into his long and vibrant life. With utmost respect, the rabbi quietly closed the bedroom door, chanted prayers, and covered my father with a white sheet.

A solemn procession unfolded in the assisted living facility's lobby, where staff members, from the director to nurse aids to the chef, formed a ceremonial line. They stood in silent tribute as my father's body was wheeled on a gurney to the waiting transport vehicle. In a compassionate gesture, the staff gently presented Tina with flowers, leaving her touched by the sensitivity of the whole experience.

He departed his body in the same way that he lived - with dignity, respect, and love.

Tuesday, March 6, 2018

On Tuesday morning after breakfast, Ryan and I drove to a familiar park where I wanted to sit in silence, relax, and find the words that I had never wanted to pen – crafting of the eulogy. The nature-filled Louisiana scene displayed towering shady trees sprinkled throughout the expanse, alongside a meandering, narrow, brown bayou, stretching endlessly. Locals called it the "duck pond park" because of the plentitude of ducks. We observed beautiful mallards, their necks adorned with a dark, satiny green sheen, elegant white ducks, and unexpectedly, a solitary, striking black duck. Its presence evoked the sturdy, masculine spirit of my father, emerging wherever I might be.

Ryan sat on a separate bench nearby, silently gazing at the brown bayou and overhanging trees on this crisp, sunny, blue-sky, spring morning. I opened my laptop, inhaled deeply, and began the task of capturing my dad's essence in words.

Fingers typed urgently, transcribing thoughts and memories pouring from my heart. At times, my chest tightened, as tears spilled down my face. Sobs alternated with smiles, reflecting on distinctive characteristics. He always said that he had four "only children." His desire to treat us equally with attention and care, recognizing our uniqueness. He was intuitive like that, about understanding people, something that I didn't appreciate until later in life.

With the emotional script completed, I gave a silent nod to Ryan that it was time to depart. Our next duty was at Rose-Neath funeral home. Many details needed review for the funeral and death certificate. After numerous forms were signed, the funeral coordinator escorted us into a serene chapel-like carpeted room to view the light-color, natural-finish, pinewood casket, traditional for Jewish funerals.

My father was not yet inside the casket, but just the sight of it made me gasp – a stark reality that left me sobbing, overcome with heavy emotions. Turning away, I quickly exited that hushed room. This was too incredibly final and undeniably real. He was actually physically gone from this world that we still stood in.

A Jewish funeral and burial emphasize the spiritual over the physical. Desecration of the body is not allowed, prohibiting autopsy, cremation, embalming. Earthly belongings, including jewelry, are removed as part of the sacred process.

However, an exception was made for my father with one item. He had designed a special gold pendant that he always wore on a chain around his neck – the shape of two open palms raised, with thumbs touching, symbolizing his lineage from the Kohen, the high priests, inherited through the paternal line. This cherished pendant, of great significance to him, was to be placed separately, off the body, in the plain, pinewood casket.

Ryan and I walked out into the bright sunshine, breathing in fresh springtime air - a stark departure from the sterile and formal funeral home. Few words interrupted the silence as we individually absorbed the unique experience of the last hour, sharing a few fragments of what we were processing.

A contrast of energy awaited us at the hotel where arriving family was full of smiles, with undertones of heavy hearts due to the occasion. My oldest sister Diane and three nephews, bound in from Pennsylvania, were lively after the long flight. Tina, her husband, my sister Shelley and my mom, had driven four hours from Houston and were happy to stretch legs, moving about. I hadn't seen some of my nephews in years, so it was sweet to reconnect, even under the circumstances, and for Ryan to reunite with cousins he rarely saw.

Four of my parent's six grandsons had traveled to Shreveport, ages 20's to 40's, and soon they piled into a rental car to pick up pizza, salads, beer, Hickory Stick barbeque, and sinfully delicious Southern Maid donuts. The rest of us met with the Cantor, the religious leader, since Shreveport's synagogue didn't have a Rabbi at the time. Prompting family stories and fond memories, he sprinkled us with questions in preparation for the momentous occasion arriving tomorrow, the funeral.

Later, the intimate family group gathered in a private hospitality suite around a long, white-draped banquet table, relishing local food and rare family time together. Jazzy music from the 1940s softly played from a grandson's phone, thoughtfully considering what might bring a smile from their tired grandmother who sat silent with distant eyes. Laughter lightened a heavy mood as entertaining storytelling began, diffusing a healthy release of energy for why we were here. My eyes floated from one person to the next, observing. The spontaneous reunion felt especially loving, coming together from far distances with only a day or two notice.

Abruptly, I felt my father witnessing the scene.

His energy was sensed a short distance from the table, alone, with a broad smile gracing his happy face. He was delighted to see his beloved family together, celebrating within an atmosphere of lightness and care amidst a solemn purpose. Endless detours could have occurred in his 95 years that may have resulted in this family not existing, or bringing this inevitable moment of his passing much sooner.

His dominant, physical presence at every large family gathering was powerfully absent. Soberly feeling like a blank canvas barren of rich colors, the picture now was a little less vibrant.

Wednesday, March 7, 2018

We assembled outside the hotel, stepping into rental cars, and drove to the nearby conservative Jewish synagogue, Agudath Achim. The land and building were of unique significance to us. Our father had painstakingly raised funds to purchase the property with cash so the membership was not burdened with debt. His leadership of this small Jewish community had appreciatively spanned almost five decades. The passion he demonstrated for protecting the survival of the synagogue was well known, even to congregants he never met after departing Shreveport in 2007.

Opening the heavy front doors to the contemporary building, erected with sand-colored vertical brick stones, I sensed his watchful eyes again, observing the family's entrance. Over 30 years earlier, he had helped design and oversee almost every brick laid that created this light-filled house of worship and learning. Inside, his Judaica paintings jumped into view throughout the religious structure. Colorful acrylics and oil paintings happily adorned the social hall, classrooms, and private sanctuary, whispering a breath of life, history and culture into the space.

The Cantor escorted us into an inviting private chapel where we silently waited to begin traditional rituals. Each family member received a customary black ribbon, cut and pinned on outer clothing, worn on the left side over the heart. According to Jewish tradition, this black ribbon was to be visible on clothing for seven days, completing and honoring the first week of mourning known as "shiva," which was the Hebrew word for seven.

The small chapel prominently displayed rich ruby red velvet curtains that veiled an ark, which contained Torah scrolls dressed in embroidered velvet covers. These old adornments were carried over from the previous synagogue structure, which we grew up worshipping in during its final days. Memories flashed by of an old drafty place where I attended Sunday school, Hebrew school, celebrated a Bat Mitzvah, and many other events.

My eyes continued surveying the small chapel space. I halted suddenly when observing the wall right next to me, unexpectedly gazing at an important painting by my father.

The image was distinctively appropriate here, lovingly whispering of his past. A dark interior of a traditional, old-world synagogue beckoned, with long-bearded rabbis dressed in black, holding heavy Torah scrolls at the holy altar draped in ruby red velvet cloth. The feeling of a familiar scene stared back into my surprised eyes from the painting. A release of a knowing smile spread on my face.

We were sitting in the aura of a memory painting of his own sacred house of worship in Raseiniai, Lithuania, while being in the present day surrounded by similar décor in his final house of worship.

My stomach tensed as the Cantor guided us to the large main sanctuary. Bright sunlight and blue skies beamed through tall vertical windows. The inevitable moment had arrived.

Most of the people dispersed throughout rows of wood pews were strangers to us. Plenty of empty space made the sanctuary feel cavernous. The man who was instrumental in saving the congregation through fundraising and leadership had outlived his friends and peers that he served with.

Silently, we walked down the center aisle, smiling at or acknowledging the kind people who expressed condolences through their eyes.

Suddenly, I looked ahead down the center aisle, and there it was.

It felt like a punch to the gut, as shoulders sank and tears welled in my eyes. I was overcome with emotion by the finality of the casket.

Like a solemn soldier in rigid posture, attracting undeniable attention, demanding respect, rested the closed pinewood casket. Stately, solid, and elegantly simple, in a natural light color with no decoration, it was regally draped with a dark velvet cloth. The American flag, folded in a triangle, placed on top, honored the Army veteran of World War II.

My three sisters, mom, and I filed into the front row pew on the left side of the aisle. The four grandsons and Tina's husband sat in the row behind. Sunlight danced into the space, gushing through brightly colored stain-glass windows in the front of the large sanctuary. The wood altar, centered in front on stage, contained the holy Torah scrolls. I felt like I was inside nature's woods, so lovingly and carefully co-designed by my father to capture natural qualities.

The traditional Jewish service chanted by the Cantor was brief with Hebrew and English prayers. Soon, I heard my name called, rising towards the podium to speak on behalf of the family.

My heartbeat pounded as I silently walked past the velvet-draped casket, eyes seized by its commanding presence of strength. The energy emanating from that holding vessel was powerful and dignified. Though the body inside had struggled with survivor's guilt, he had been able to thrive with perseverance and magical support from life circumstances.

At the podium microphone, I gazed out into the sanctuary seeing 30 to 40 people patiently waiting for me to speak, deeply appreciating their compassion in that moment.

Beginning the eulogy was unexpectedly difficult. Trying to get my voice out of my throat was a surprising challenge. Speaking in public usually came quite easily, but today was obviously very different.

Emotions and darting thoughts swirled through my heart and head. My eyes cast down to focus on gaining composure and stillness within.

Breathing deeply, a profound peacefulness overcame me, shedding the frenetic energy like a snake slithering out from its skin. I became an observer to this scene from afar. Finally, I shifted my gaze to the velvet-draped casket a few steps away.

With eyes fastened on the casket, I softly uttered one word, "*Daddy.*"

Speaking directly to him as if no one else was present, my eyes were shielded by blinders to anything else – this message was to him.

Once speaking began, words flowed effortlessly and my voice grew stronger and more animated. My vision lifted from the casket to family seated in front rows, sharing memories that prompted smiles. He was an alpha male with a loving heart, and even the Doberman Pinschers bowed to him.

Suddenly, my ability to speak choked with emotion and halted. The memory I was about to share felt raw and palpable.

Taking a breath, regaining momentum, an uneven voice softly described his aged hands lovingly patting easels in the storage room only three weeks earlier. His surprising declaration in that moment - announcing that he didn't want to paint anymore - was followed by absorbing silence, emphasizing the gravity of that telling message. The eulogy was complete.

Sunlight again flooded lively beams of color into the space. It was a scene for his canvas, with contrasting shadows and treasured family in a sanctuary he helped to design and create.

Two black limousines awaited us, solemnly transporting, leading a twenty-minute caravan ride to the cemetery. Flashing lights from police escorts jolted us to the present. Remaining silent, each of us processed the moment in our own way.

A quaint, old, Jewish cemetery appeared soon, painted with a cheerful blue sky and fresh green grass, a joyful contrast to our black clothing of mourning. Grandsons paraded in silently escorting the casket through cemetery gates, followed by the Cantor walking slowly, chanting prayers. We were seated in folding chairs under a white tent canopy, facing the stark, freshly dug open grave, with no headstone.

My parents had purchased side-by-side cemetery plots decades ago, across a center aisle from my mom's parents and her brother's final resting place. For my father's family, killed in the Holocaust, there were no graves or remnants as a memorial.

The clean pinewood casket was placed atop two wide rope ties. Carefully and silently, his final remains were lowered into the freshly dug earth by two cemetery staff. This was the part that horrified me as a child, when my grandfather's casket was lowered into the open ground. Terror gripped me at the thought of bodily decay. Now, with more awareness, I felt comforted by beliefs that the body was a temporary vessel and the soul lived on into eternity, in another dimension of energy. Many metaphysical experiences had solidified my beliefs, which science could not explain.

Sitting in the front row close to the grave, my mom looked chilled, shaking a bit in the early springtime air. I reached over turning the coat collar up around her neck, hoping to provide some warmth. Faint tears in her eyes appeared, even though she always said she couldn't cry about anything.

The Cantor respectfully led a brief service in Hebrew and English, then reached for a waiting shovel, scooping up fresh dirt near the side of the open grave. He bent over to place the rich brown earth on top of the casket deep below. Instinctively, I stood, wanting to touch a physical aspect of my father one last time, for closure in this life.

Walking silently to the grave, taking the shovel, I lifted dirt and carefully placed it atop the casket below, feeling love, grief, and ritual duty. His loved ones were here to say goodbye to what was, and this was part of the process. My sisters followed, then the grandsons, and others in attendance. It felt sad and complete. I sensed he was watching, solemnly and peacefully.

The limousine returned us to the synagogue, this time holding soft murmurs of conversation. Still a family union, we continued on to celebrate life and memories at a local colorful Italian eatery, Monjunis. Amid light banter and tasty food, a marked contrast existed in the attention given to my mom from everyone. She was the matriarch now. Demure and quiet, she gazed at the family, passively involved, likely exhausted at age 90 from the ordeal of travel and burying her mate and partner of 71 years.

Thursday, March 8, 2018

The next morning, I hugged Ryan warmly goodbye, grateful for his presence and support, then off he went for his flight back to Florida. Other family members departed earlier for Pennsylvania. Climbing into Tina's car for the four-hour road trip back to Houston, we were joined by Shelley and our mom.

It was a sunny, brisk, blue-sky day. With Tina navigating country backroads, we leisurely traveled past grazing cows and horses, rolling green hills, old wooden structures with hand-painted signs, and splashes of spring wildflowers decorating the roadside. Many miles stretched our journey without sight of another car.

I felt my father's energy with us, guiding his girls safely home. We passed Inspiration Village and diverse spiritual structures in rural East Texas, coloring our route with touching amusement. The drive together welcomed a release of tightness we didn't realize we were holding, enjoying warm relaxed vibes, soft moments of emotion and memories, and fluid chatter among sisters and mother. We knew what awaited us.

Coming days would be filled with traditional Jewish mourning rituals following a death, involving prayers with the Rabbi, visitors at Tina's house bringing food and care, and candles lit all day and night. Later, we would sort through belongings and support our mom's fragile body, mind and spirit.

Sunday, March 11, 2018

Finally, homeward bound to San Diego, I exhaled a sigh of relief for the completion of the past eventful week. Taking my seat on the plane, out came a worn journal and pen, ready to write whatever flowed from my heart.

Daddy has transitioned behind the veil where I cannot see him. Yet, I know his spirit continues.

He is with his family and those in his life who have passed. It is a joyful reunion. He is at peace, yet still transitioning. He struggled towards the end of his days, resisting, not wanting to let go of his family here.

A new chapter begins: Life without Daddy.

My dad was a nomad of sorts, in 1939 at age 17, boarding a ship alone to a land far away, with a foreign language and culture. His desire for something better fueled his courage. There were many risks of the unknown but the alternative of status quo was unacceptable. He is a role model subconsciously in my quest for the best life possible. Taking risks. Traveling. What's to lose? Go for it! There is a whole life out there waiting to be experienced with joy and wonder.

Love, peace, and Namaste.

Chapter 21:
Unveiling

As the calendar pages turned, a year unfolded through the rhythm of birthdays, holidays, travel adventures, phone conversations, and visits to see my mom. I often forgot that my father was no longer physically present, for his essence lingered as tangible as life itself. He was quietly above my shoulder, smiling, nodding, watching. Sometimes I even spoke to him, asking a question or thanking him or sharing a beautiful nature view, reflecting: *"You would love to paint this, right?"*

In late March 2019, I had just wrapped up an adventurous eight-month travel journey and returned to Houston, Texas for an important milestone celebration. In Jewish tradition, one year after death, the engraved headstone is unveiled, with family honoring the deceased and ceremoniously marking the time since passing.

A couple of months earlier, in January, my sisters and mom collaborated with me in thoughtfully choosing words for the gravestone. When the religious leader in Shreveport suggested adding a small flat stone next to my father's stately upright headstone, to honor family members perished in the Holocaust, I was thrilled by the deeply touching tribute! Though unconventional to place a stone without bodies, it felt so perfectly right. With no grave or ceremony marking their lives and deaths, we would honor them now, seven decades later.

The small flat stone, made from the same beautiful granite as my father's marbled reddish gravestone, was inscribed with first names of five beloved family members:

Rosenfeld

Feige, Taube, Devorah, Mottel, Bayla

Perished in the Holocaust

The memorial celebrations began in Houston by first attending a special legacy event involving a Torah, at a small synagogue my parents had attended. A Torah scroll was among the holiest objects and symbols of Judaism, written in the Hebrew language on one continuous roll of parchment paper, hand-scribed using inked calligraphy. A portion of the Torah's holy scripture was read every Sabbath and on special holidays. The heavy scrolls were held upright in ornate arks, dressed in velvet covers and shielded by elaborate wood doors or curtains.

Through my mom's spry initiative, she recently uncovered that her father had donated a Torah to the Shreveport synagogue decades ago. Still in use in 2019, the Torah needed repairs. Given their expense, we recognized that this gift was significant for my modest-living grandfather in the 1960s. The donation likely honored Stanley, my mom's only sibling, who had passed tragically in an accident at an early age. Since my mother now lived in Houston, she asked if the Torah could be brought to the synagogue that she and Tina's family attended.

Upon approval from Shreveport, the sacred Torah was carefully shipped from Louisiana to New York City, where a trained scribe repaired portions of its 300,000 letters and inspected the quality of ink and seams of the parchment. After its return to Shreveport, a blessing ceremony honored the sacred scroll for its service to the local Jewish community. Tina's husband then drove the Torah four hours from Louisiana to its new home in Houston. My mother, meanwhile, had been busy ordering an elegant velvet Torah cover, embroidered in memory of Bernard.

The newly arrived Torah was welcomed with cheers during a traditional Orthodox religious ceremony in Houston. Women sat separately from men, so Tina, Shelley, my mom, and I silently and proudly observed this incredible honor bestowed upon my father's life. Smiling and laughing, the male congregants paraded in song in front of the holy ark, singing prayers within the festive and intimate circle.

Holding the honoree up high for all to see, the donated Torah seemed to radiate energy of old origins and fresh loving care. The heavy scroll was tenderly placed into waiting arms of the next man in the circle, igniting fresh jubilant songs and blessings. Sparkling brightly by sunrays dancing through windows, the new creamy-white velvet cover glowed with embroidered gold thread, with Hebrew and English words, *"In honor of Bernard Rosenfeld."* The whole scene felt like a mystical spirit was shining down onto the celebration.

Suddenly, I felt jolted awake by remembering a painting he had created two decades ago. Religious-garbed men danced in celebration, joyfully holding a beautiful Torah scroll dressed in a velvet cover. It was like the painting had come to life! Eerily surreal, I pondered if his soul knew that this moment would one day arise. His legacy was sealed as the Torah lives on.

After that momentous day, it was time for the four-hour backroads drive from Houston to Shreveport, once again. We were retracing that humble route for the one-year anniversary ceremony to unveil the gravestone. My mom, at almost 92 years old, declined making the trip, simply stating in her unfiltered candid style, *"I already said goodbye."* The travel and memories were not something she wished to revisit. With our oldest sister, Diane, unable to join, Shelley, Tina, and I set off on a sisterly milestone endeavor.

Shreveport shouted that it was in full spring bloom. Famous for shades of pink azaleas popping open to colorfully dress the city, showy shrubs femininely decorated expansive lawns of southern homes and public parks. It was a beautiful, softer season that I loved. Bees were busy and birds happily chirped, as warmer weather gave a nod it was here to stay.

Our overnight accommodations featured an eclectically elegant bed and breakfast inn, Fairfield Place, tucked within a well-groomed historic neighborhood. Lawns stretched wide and deep from the street, leaving us begging to know owners' identities and designs of interiors.

At Fairfield Place, it was a visual party for the senses. Imagine entering into each guest room to reveal uniquely themed décor in color and "over-the-top" accessories. Our three dramatic rooms were a "random selection" by the inn's host, yet it felt as if we each opened a door into our perfectly appointed home!

Shelley, who loved musician Freddie Mercury of the band Queen, chose her key and slowly walked into her private room, mouth dropping open in amazement! A glittering, bejeweled, three-foot round queen's crown dazzled above the bed! The theme: royal majesty, of course. Boy, we had a good laugh about that queenly "coincidence."

My room was next door. Sliding in the old metal key, fiddling with the lock until it turned, I carefully opened the door in anticipation. What met my eyes filled me with absolute delight! Welcome to a melody of serenity, a Zen space, offering calming Asian décor, with images of soft flowers, painted in orange silks and green bamboo leaves. Gold fabric curtains glistened, generously draping from ceiling to floor to conceal an oversized jacuzzi tub right inside the bedroom. Fluffy white towels, aromatic oil choices, and antique poetry books expanded the relaxed effect. How perfect! A luxurious soak that night and rising early in the morning for another, indulged the grateful yogi in me.

Tina's spacious room featured rich burgundy-colored walls with a sophisticated dark wood King-size four-post bed. The elegant bathroom was ornately dressed in white marble and gold-framed mirrors. Solid and regal, the dwelling spoke of security and classy comfort, well-deserved following a long period of parental care. Such perfect synchronicity had matched us each to amusingly appropriate rooms at the inn.

A scrumptious breakfast on formal settings was devoured the next morning, created by John, the colorful owner, chef, and innkeeper. Gourmet grits, quiche, blackberries, and buttery biscuits reminded us we were in the South. Stomachs full and hearts light, it was soon time to fulfill our purpose here.

Quietly walking through the old cemetery gates, we were welcomed by a clear blue sky, warm sunshine, and the sweet fragrance of fresh springtime grass. Here and there, colorful flowers waved silently, reminding me that new life goes on, even in cemeteries.

It was intentional that the ceremony be intimate, to embrace this sacred time alone with our father. At the entrance to the cemetery, a large aged ceramic bowl full of small white rocks greeted us. Jewish tradition invites laying pebbles on top of a headstone, as a physical connection that you touched the gravestone by your visit and lasting memories together.

I felt a palpable energy emanating from headstones as I paused before graves of family members, placing rocks on top, personally honoring and thanking them. My mom's parents and brother were buried there, as well as a small gravestone for "Rosenfeld Infant," our older stillborn brother who we never knew.

We tenderly placed fresh yellow daisies next to the white rocks and silently walked a few more steps to a large headstone draped by a pure white cloth. The stark blank canvas of fabric appeared regal, like a billboard proclaiming the special importance of this spot on this day.

At the foot of his earthen grave site, the small flat stone honoring his family was also covered under a clean white cloth. Relatives with personalities and talents, who we never met due to their fate in the

Holocaust, were finally honored with a visible memory that they had existed, resting next to our father, their sibling or son.

The religious leader, the Cantor, chanted prayers in Hebrew, sprinkling old-world sounds throughout the cemetery. He gently invited us to remove the white cloths, welcoming sunshine to illuminate the handsome marbled dark-reddish granite headstone, engraved in English and Hebrew:

Bernard Joe Rosenfeld, Cherished and Devoted to Family. August 4, 1922 – March 5, 2018.

We silently unveiled the smaller matching stone, simply etched with the first names of his mother and four siblings, void of known dates of death.

Emotions swept over me as I viewed his name carved deeply and permanently into the magnificent stone. The heavy, solid material felt strong and powerful, just like his spirit. My fingertips lightly skimmed the smooth cool stone, feeling its surface, wanting to connect, wanting to touch his hand one more time.

His presence observed the scene. He was pleased with the honor of the unveiling ceremony, especially with his girls gathered together for the tribute. We remained hushed and then I spoke from the heart, unrehearsed, trusting that whatever I said would flow. The message whispered out, simple and brief, a daughter speaking to her dad.

"Thank you, Daddy, you did your job very well. We are okay. We miss you and love you. You can join your family now, you deserve it, enjoy what is next."

A year ago, I had wished for his freedom to soar from an aged body, as my flight lifted off from San Diego. Today, my heart wished for his letting go of this realm in order to ascend to the radiance of his next magnificent chapter.

A True Story of Surviving by Synchronicity

***

The soul promise to write this book with my father is now complete. His life illuminated a path weathered by determination, persistence, and a compelling drive to express himself without spoken words. Being an artist provided the calming salve to a troubled mind and pained heart. The magical synchronicities, seemingly guided by vigilant angels, appeared unexpectedly, opening opportunities that saved and shielded him throughout his life.

He left a generous legacy inspiring hope and possibility. Hard work, with diligent purposefulness, revealed an appreciation for taking life seriously to protect loved ones and engage in passions your heart desires.

Fill your life with single moments of joy, find a way to do that, whatever it takes, was his way. Live life fulfilling duty and joy, and then, as Bernard said, *"you'll feel contented, satisfied, and happy."*

I am forever thankful to the boys who gave Bernard a 50-cent raffle ticket, and to the gatekeepers who opened the path for his safety and long life to survive fate.

Nancy Rosenfeld, daughter of Bernard and Dorothy* Rosenfeld

---

*Dorothy Rosenfeld, Bernard's wife of 71 years, passed on December 4, 2021, at age 94, in Texas. When the Covid pandemic forced isolation in March 2020 at her senior living facility, this very social, intelligent, and Life Master bridge player, suddenly developed accelerated dementia after three months of isolation. Her previous vibrancy affected us all with a zest for life and laughter. Her headstone, adjoining Bernard's, was fittingly engraved: "Bright, Loved, Queen of Fun."

Chapter 22:
Favorite Mystical Connections

Mystical events seemed to surround my dad, and for my sister, Shelley, and I, we were doused with our share, as well. The effect of these events provided clear inspiration to push forward, expanding possibilities and transformations with positive power. Three events, in particular, were magical in the legacy of my father and imprinted significantly on my life.

First, in 2008, curious about a unique program offered on energetic releases and healings, I couldn't resist delving in to learn more about the process and outcomes. Thoughts rolled through my mind. *What was this about, and what really could happen?*

In Orlando, Florida, where I was living, a practitioner in the alternative healing field traveled there to speak and demonstrate a technique that had shown evidence of numerous life-altering positive outcomes for clients, encompassing both physical and emotional well-being. The method centered around complete stillness, with a tranquil mind, striving for no thoughts, sitting in deep silence just softly breathing for approximately 45 minutes. A partner stood beside you, placing one hand on your forehead and another hand behind your neck.

It is known that energy meridians ripple throughout the body and connect to the conscious mind as well as the subconscious, so I was understanding the process so far. Curious to what might happen for me with this technique, if anything, I signed up with no expectations or life issues defined. At the time, I wasn't thinking about or immersed in my father's history.

So there I was, eager yet cautious, to participate in the unknown experience among a dozen equally curious strangers, each paired up with another individual. It was time to begin, with half of the group sitting and the other half standing next to their paired partner.

I sat on a cushioned folding chair, feet flat on the ground, back straight, in comfortable silence with eyes closed. My focus was on inhaling down to my stomach and blowing out the exhale fully through my mouth. A young man, who I didn't know, was my partner for this exercise. He placed one hand lightly on my forehead and the other on the back of my neck. Continuing to breathe silently, it wasn't too long before a clear image popped into my quiet mind.

I was a slim, petite, young woman with short soft black hair, standing in a hushed, single-file line that stretched as far as I could see in front and behind of me. There was nothing else to view except this long, slow, sad line of people, shuffling forward silently with eyes cast downward. The identical clothing that we all wore was a plain grey cotton smock, similar to a hospital gown but closed in the back.

The only object for my eyes to focus upon in that somber line was my black, ballet-style slippers, as one foot stepped in front of the other. The atmosphere was beyond dismal. And heavy with hopelessness. Our slow-moving line of grey smocks was inside of a shadowy, cavernous, institutional building with walls too far away to know where this hell ended.

The horrific destination for this profound despair led to a torturous exterminating gas chamber, a nightmarish realm under the rule of heartless Nazi's.

Stern-faced soldiers stood mercilessly on each side of our sorrowful trek, armed with rifles to prod or push those too slow. Numbing sadness and helplessness enveloped me, my head folded down, shoulders drooped, as I reluctantly continued shuffling forward in the death march line. Tears moistened my eyes, muting the surreal scene.

Silently I cried in my mind: *"Please! I don't want to die. I don't want to be suffocated from living the life I choose. I feel paralyzed with sadness and helplessness."*

The horror march continued, one step at a time, one last breath at a time.

Abruptly, my family, my ancestors who had been murdered in the Holocaust in Lithuania, crowded into a blurry distant view behind me!

Huddled together in their heavy old-world clothing, they called out to me, waving for my attention, shouting forcefully:

"Stand up! Rise up! You don't have to carry this burden for us, we've already suffered. You don't have to carry our burden or sadness. We get great joy from watching you! You are doing so many wonderful things and enjoying life. Keep doing that, we love watching you! We see the wonderful things you have done. We see how you have helped others. We know. We want you to be happy and celebrate in this life. You do not have to be burdened by our suffering and deaths!"

A dozen of them stood there, startling me - short, tall, men, women, old and young adults, dressed in worn woolen clothing with weathered faces, joyful, smiling, happy that I saw them! They desperately wanted to save me from this emotional fate. It didn't have to be my story. My destiny was for me to choose. Burst forward, free from burden of guilt, free from re-living others' emotional pain, including my father's pain.

I was free to create my own story. Their message echoed loudly - my potential for vibrancy and inspiration in this life was boundless, achieved by embracing a path of authentic joy and positivity.

That was it. That was all it took. Something happened to my mind and internal compass that day. It was like a reprogramming occurred. From that simple forty-five minute experiment in 2008, in my 40s, my life perspective dramatically changed.

I didn't have to carry life's burdens or shoulder burdens belonging to others. My purpose was simply to authentically enjoy life, and that was more than enough. What a wonderful mission! In return, I not only brought joy to myself but also to my ancestors, who cheered my playful and happy shenanigans of life. Plus, I was serving others in some contagious energetic way, inspiring them to focus on positive possibilities and gratitude.

The enduring message that I received that day was to proudly choose your own path, enjoy life authentically, while being respectful of others' chosen paths.

The lasting effect from this experience helped me to see my father and others for who they were on their life path. I didn't feel obligated to try to "fix" someone else. What a tremendous relief. Support and encouragement can still be offered, without feeling responsible for solving others' challenges, recognizing the boundaries of our role.

I couldn't "fix" Survivor's Guilt for him.

I had to let that go. That wasn't my story.

My life was a uniquely different story, filled with fresh, positive possibilities!

***

The second mystical event enveloped my younger sister, Shelley, on the day our father passed. She was quietly journaling when her pen suddenly began to write without her conscious thought. What started as a reflective moment turned into "automatic writing," as if someone else had taken control of the pen, leaving her bewildered and entranced by the unexpected message:

Daddy passed away today. It is SO huge. I am so grateful I was by his side the last two days. I got to say goodbye and touch his face for the last time. I got to look at him til the end.

He was so strong and stoic and creative, yet such a good businessman. His life was full. He came to America alone but did not go out alone. There were eight or nine women around him when he took his last breath. He was surrounded by love.

I hope you felt the love and that we were all there. I feel so honored that I got to be there. All the responsibility I was holding for you, for your well-being and happiness, left my shoulders that afternoon. It was like a heaviness left me. You are now free. In a way, I am free too. You shed the bodily form and soared, soared, soared into brilliant love and light.

(Automatic writing begins.)

It was extraordinary. I was limited by that body, the heaviness and grief I was attached to vibrationally in the body. The body matches, molds and adheres to the vibration of feelings. The body response out-pictures what is subconscious. It is its job, like a painting of what one creates, first seeing it in the mind. It's a match like a magnet in a way.

Don't worry, I will be with you anytime you want. I am here for you. I can be anywhere and everywhere at the same time. There is no time and space here like it is there. There's no male or female, good or bad, it just is. Colors, beautiful colors like the Northern Lights, like bright stars and energy. It's all just energy, beauty and love. Everywhere and nowhere. So beautiful. LOVE, LIGHT and the most beautiful sounds surrounded by it all.

I did feel the love. I felt so loved.

Mama (Dorothy) *is where she is in this incarnation. She is doing the best she can. It's all love with no time and space there too, but the human experience blocks it, stops it, it's too much for the soul in the body to experience.*

The body is dense, heavy to house the soul for that experience in that particular lifetime. It's all just an experience, just an experience that we grow from or feel pain, even the emotional pain - it's just an experience. It's the attachment we have to labeling it good or bad. It just is and we make up the meaning to it.

Just notice, know that it is all energy. Observe, knowing it just is. It just is. It just is. The experience of knowing it all is love, light and vibration and where are you blocking it?

We all have choice. Yes, I am free of the constraints of the body, but I still have freedom of choice.

I am here anytime, anywhere for you. Just think of me and I will be there. I will be alive in you, to you in non-physical form.

You are so loved. I know you loved me. I felt it and I appreciate it so much. You made my life in that incarnation so much richer and fun.

LIGHT, LOVE, VIBRATION, ENERGY

***

Fast-forwarding to early 2022, a couple months following the passing of our mom, Dorothy, Shelley and I were together in California, curious to receive a channeled message from a medium in Florida whom I had known for years. I had experienced about a dozen "readings" with the medium, in-person and over the phone, during the past decade. We were intrigued to discover if there were any messages concerning our parents from another energetic dimension.

Since 2005, I had trusted meeting with different channelers who possessed a heightened sensitivity to energy vibration as they tapped into a remarkably accurate sixth sense. While it may seem implausible, these individuals demonstrate an ability to communicate with those not living – be it people, animals, or spirit guides. The process hinges on trusting one's intuition, and skills developed through training, meditation, and a willingness to be open to receiving messages.

At my first visit in 2005, I was skeptical. This was a far stretch out of my comfort zone. Looming curiosity won, however, defeating fear of the unknown. The outcome was a firm conviction that this was real communication because what was shared was utterly impossible for the medium to have known about my departed family members.

By early 2022, Shelley was exploring writing her own memoir, examining the effects of being a child of a survivor. I had not yet begun this book, but a tiny spark of readiness was starting to stir within me, influenced by Shelley's enthusiasm for her own project. Eager to gain insights, we reached out to my medium by speaker phone for a channeled reading.

While she knew that our parents had passed, it's significant that she knew nothing about their lives, interests, or personalities. She held no knowledge about Shelley's memoir, or my spark of inclination to begin this book.

Here are relevant excerpts from that experience that I recorded. Part is related to our mom, who had recently passed. Bold face font is added for emphasis, especially from our father:

"She was not typical of her generation.

Charming. Strong-willed. Sharp.

She was a role model of an atypical mom. She had other things in life important to her.

She's good where she is now.

(My notes: Medium says she sees image of a man whose energy is our dad.)

He's well-dressed, polished first impression, but he could have a temper.

He had a lot of responsibility in youth, brought himself a long way, worked hard early, contributed to family. Serious, stoic.

He did have a sense of humor, liked to take care of things, saw things as black-and-white, proud of his accomplishments.

They are together now. (Our parents.)

Both had challenges.

There was a commitment to marriage and this carries over into the spirit world.

Dad had a creative side – he wanted more.

Mom understood business (numbers*). She was in her element with that.*

Dad had questions about his ancestry, his family. It's important to him.

He's watching you both work on this and glad you're doing it.

The search continues, he wants answers also, he needed to know.

He says: "Carry on…"

Dad knows that you're pulling his story all together, bits and pieces. It's still important.

There is a sadness about him.

He lost his dad young and many members of his family at once. He was a young man on his own early. He traveled from country to country and felt alone.

Mom's family – you know them more. Mom didn't really understand Dad's sadness.

Mom wanted more fun from him. She was very social, she liked to be with happy people, it was hard for her when he was sad or serious.

*Someone younger is there with her, a sibling, who passed early. (*My notes: Her brother Stanley was accidentally shot when he was only 21 years old.*)*

She's happy where she is. Freedom in a happy transition. Her body wasn't comfortable at the end.

She knows a lot of people over there in spirit, a social butterfly.

As you heal in whatever you are doing, it is healing to Dad.

(*My notes: The medium asks Shelley a question.*) *Are you writing?*

Your writing will not be only healing to you but to past generations."

***

We all live with a legacy of some sort. We may know the stories handed down, or it may be imprinted into our DNA, our body and emotions, and affect future generations. We also have choices for how we respond to that legacy to create our own life story.

I believe it is important to share stories, especially with children and grandchildren, to understand why someone is the way they are, what makes them special, different, or triggered. It's a gift to share this. Some will receive it right away. Others may take years or never embrace the gift.

History can help us to be and do better. When we know, we must be better. If not, atrocities can repeat or worsen. We have the choice to inform, expand, and grow with new wisdom.

I am forever grateful for the paths paved by ancestors and the blessing of embracing synchronicities that create new stories. I thank you for entering this one life story. You have honored Bernard Joe Rosenfeld and many others. Compassion and understanding are most noble human traits. May we find inspiration to live and demonstrate these every day.

Nancy Rosenfeld

Appendix I:
Map of Europe During WW2

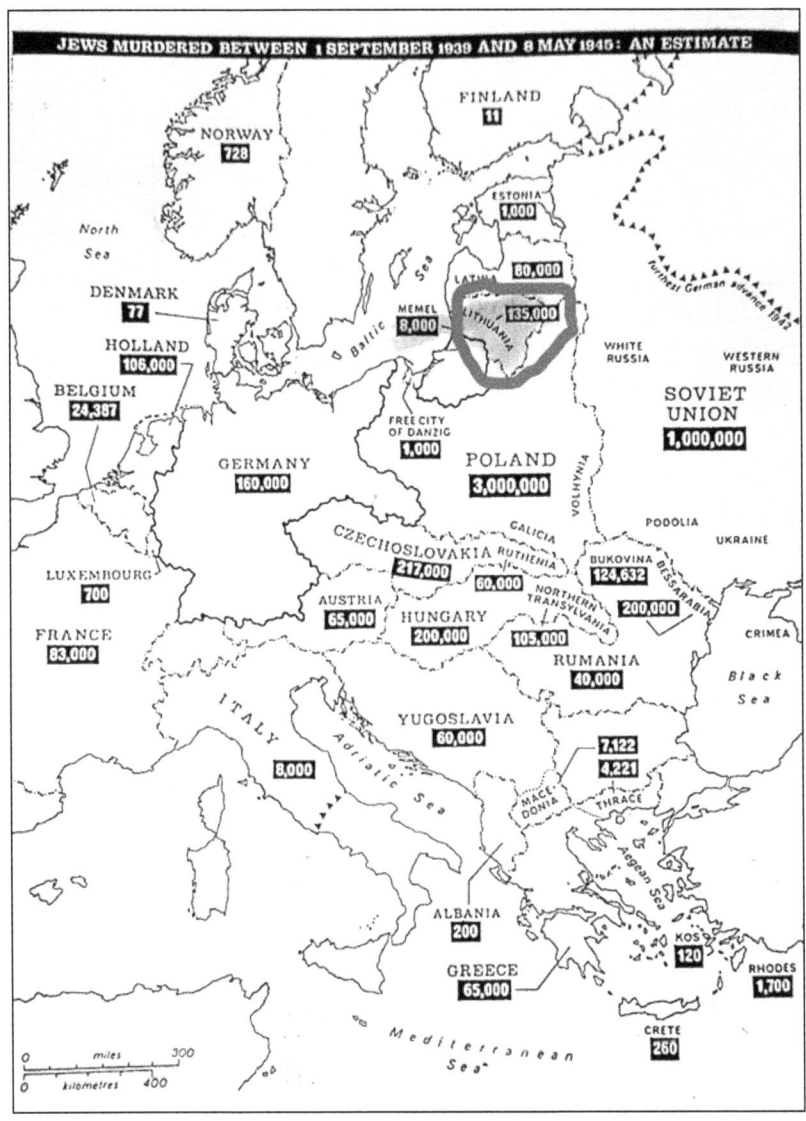

235

Jews Murdered by Country in Europe, Das Dritte Reich und die Juden, Arani Verlag, Berlin, 1955.

Country	Jews 9/1939	Jews Murdered	%
1. Poland	**3,300,000**	**2,800,000**	**85.0**
2. USSR	2,100,000	1,500,000	71.4
3. Romania	850,000	425,000	50.0
4. Hungary	404,000	200,000	49.5
5. Czech	315,000	260,000	82.5
6. France	300,000	90,000	30.0
7. Germany	210,000	171,000	81.0
8. Lithuania	**150,000**	**135,000**	**90.0**
9. Holland	150,000	90,000	60.0
10. Latvia	**95,000**	**85,000**	**89.5**
11. Belgium	90,000	40,000	44.4
12. Greece	75,000	65,000	80.0
13. Yugoslavia	75,000	55,000	73.3
14. Austria	60,000	40,000	66.6
15. Italy	57,000	15,000	26.3
16. Bulgaria	50,000	7,000	14.0
17. Others	20,000	6,000	30.0
Total	8,301,000	5,978,000	72.0

Appendix II:
Bernard's Family List

Father: Nathan Rozenfeldas, Lithuania, born 1878, died 1927

- Three sisters, Seine in Lithuania (lived next door), sister in U.S., sister in South Africa
- Two brothers, one in South Africa, one in Brooklyn, NY, Bernard's Uncle David

Mother: Feige Marcus, died in Holocaust, parents Benche and Riva

- Three brothers: Morris (England), Meyer (Missouri), Isadore Marcus (Arkansas)
- Two sisters: Leah (St. Louis), Elke (Lithuania)

Nathan and Feige had six children (Bernard's siblings), Lithuania

- Taube, born 1912, died in Holocaust with husband and son
- Dvierke, born 1914, died in Holocaust, son taken by Nazi's
- Friedka (Hedva Sada), born 1916, went to Israel 1935, sons Natan, Rani, Yossi Sada in Israel
- Motl, born 1918, barber, Bernard's brother, died in Holocaust
- Beilke, born 1920, died in Holocaust
- Bernard, born 1922, escaped Lithuania, married Dorothy

Bernard and Dorothy's four daughters

- Diane Kramer, born 1951, sons Scott (2 children), Sean (1 child), Jared Kramer (3 children)
- Tina Gross, born 1956, sons Joshua (2 children) and Jonathan (3 children) Gross
- Nancy Rosenfeld, born 1959, son Ryan Daly
- Shelley Rosenfeld, born 1965

Appendix III:
What Does it Mean to be a Survivor?

"Survivor"
By Bernard Rosenfeld, 1987

A survivor is a person who survived when everyone else was killed or died.

I did not begin to think of myself as a survivor until many years later. As I got older, I became more emotional. As the stories of the Holocaust became more and more known, I kept realizing the true meaning of the Holocaust. I started to search for anything that would tell me how and when the ones I loved met their horrible fate.

I became, and still am, obsessed with wanting to feel what they felt. I couldn't take my eyes away from the pictures. The tears would blur my eyes as if to say... don't look.

The price of being alive is very high, too high at times. I almost was glad to feel pain. I wanted to feel the pain that my loved ones endured.

I can visualize some of our Lithuanian neighbors take delight in seeing my mother, sisters, brother, and other friends I grew up with, being dragged to their death or being buried alive. How is it possible for a Christian world to stand by and let this happen, how??? Because it was Jews?

I am thankful for my wife and four lovely daughters and grandsons. God has given me more than I deserve.

The photos I have tell a story of their own, there is nothing I can add that would be more meaningful.

The town I was born in and grew up, I left behind forever. My family and friends lay in some field covered by dirt and grass, fields where I may have walked in my youth. The town too is gone, so I was told.

I will forever think about them, cry for them, but mostly, I wish I could find peace within myself and let them rest in peace for they only found peace in death.

***

Survivor's Guilt Defined

Simply stated, people who experience Survivor's Guilt suffer from emotional trauma after they survive a tragedy when others did not survive. It is considered a serious symptom of PTSD, post-traumatic stress disorder. While not everyone who endures a traumatic event will develop PTSD, some research estimates that as many as 90% of people who lived through events where others died experience feelings of survivor's guilt. People living with this anxiety experience a struggle to turn thoughts to anything else, further increasing anxiety that results in bodily ailments. For Bernard, his physical heart suffered from the intensity of emotional anxiety.

Survivors often question why they escaped death while others lost their lives? They may also wonder whether there was something that they could have done to prevent the deaths of others.

Symptoms may include flashbacks, obsessive thoughts, anger, feelings of helplessness and disconnection, confusion, problems sleeping, stomach and gut issues, headaches, even thoughts of suicide. Survivor's guilt can cause a person to see the world as an unfair and unsafe place.

Bernard did experience anxiety attacks that sometimes could not be stopped from spiraling. Symptoms included racing heart, tightening pain in his chest and gut, severe nausea, with understandable fear and panic. This escalated into worsening conditions with ambulances rushing him to hospital emergency rooms. His cries for help, for relief from pain and nausea, were agonizing to hear. The anguished moaning and crying went beyond the present moment, transmuting aloud the painful sorrow for his family and the torture they endured.

He held an obsession for organization and completing tasks. Driven to complete whatever he focused upon, he felt safer and calmer when in control of his life. His "busyness" could be interpreted as a disguise and distraction to deny thoughts or feelings from deeper inner wounds.

Through the years, Bernard's burying of emotions, trying to run away and hide from the pain of his family's plight, showed up primarily in a physically broken heart. He endured two quadruple bypasses twelve years apart, four stents to open coronary arteries, and a pacemaker. A cardiologist commented after surgery for stents that opening Bernard's chest *"was like finding a jungle of wire,"* amazed at his strength of survival. Bernard also suffered a severe case of pancreatitis in 1988, staying in Intensive Care on morphine for weeks. A spiritual interpretation of this disease is associated with inability to digest the sweetness of life and is also associated emotionally with worry.

Bernard did not have abundant tools or resources to effectively deal with his emotions. Isolated in the conservative deep South, where acceptance and empathy for Jewish immigrants was not widely understood, he chose to remain quiet. Moreover, the decades of 1940 to 1960 were a time when society expected men to be strong. Expressing emotions as a therapeutic release was not yet encouraged.

Other survivors who were more emotionally healed often associated their progress with living among a strong supportive Jewish immigrant presence in their communities. They also appreciated access to knowledgeable individuals to assist in their healing journey. There was no such community in Shreveport, Louisiana for Bernard to share with. He was also busy working to provide for a growing family and demanding business, coping emotionally by avoiding sharing his feelings and past.

Some techniques that can help with survivor's guilt include: allowing feelings to be expressed and accepting that survivor's guilt is not always rational, but is a recognized response to trauma. Seeking professional help. Connecting and sharing feelings with family, friends and support groups. (Bernard waited 48 years before sharing the details of his story and trauma with even his daughters.) Use of mindfulness techniques to slow the mind and body down, be aware, quiet and still, with calm breathing. Getting enough sleep and eating a balanced diet, avoiding drugs and alcohol. Releasing pained energy through hobbies and helping others, which were his primary therapies.

Bernard's self-help gained momentum later in life as he painted more after retiring in the 1980s, stating, *"Art is how I cope."* Writing this manuscript was also a monumental healing catharsis.

He was passionately devoted to serving the local synagogue and donated funds to the Jewish community and others in need. He unquestionably felt it his duty to help others in these ways.

Throughout his entire life, the weight of survivor's guilt burdened his mind, heart, and spirit. Ultimately, embracing peace at the very end as he transitioned to join the family lost as a boy, his journey of hopefulness for magical possibilities was complete.

Appendix IV:
Validating Data

Extensive data exists from first-person accounts of life in European towns during WWII. Records indicate that the Jewish population of Lithuania in 1939, when Bernard escaped that country, was 150,000 Jews. The number of Jews murdered by the end of the war tragically totaled 135,000, 90%. This mass killing was the highest percentage of murdered Jews of all countries.

The majority of deaths occurred in 1941. Poland suffered the highest absolute number of close to 3,000,000 Jewish lives taken, or 85% of its large Jewish population.

The first article below originated in an Israeli publication. Bernard asked his Rabbi in Shreveport, Louisiana to translate it from Hebrew to English. The horrific events took place within 25 miles of Bernard's hometown of Raseiniai, beginning in June 1941, when Germans invaded and brutally initiated their plan to exterminate all Jews. This was also the time when letters to Bernard's family began to be returned.

The second article excerpt was from a Facebook Group: ***Jewish Life Before the Holocaust.*** The family also lived in Raseiniai and tells of the killing pits in August 1941.

***

Article 1: April 13, 1985, Ma'Ariv publication

By Alex Doron (Passed away December 2022)

Twice he faced the Angel of death. And twice he slipped out from between his fingers. This is the story of Joseph ben-Ya'kov, 53 years old (in 1985), of Holon, Israel. Twice he made Aliyah to Israel. The first time on the ship "Exodus", which was returned to Germany by the British in 1947. The second time was on April 29, 1948. Here is his story:

I was born in the town of Krusz, Lithuania, in which about one hundred Jewish families lived. My father earned his living in summer by growing cucumbers, and in winter, he was a butcher. The Germans entered our town on June 25, 1941 and burned down all its houses. I was only 9 years old. Most of the Jews were able to escape a few days beforehand and hid in the houses of various farmers in surrounding villages. A few days after the battle, which occurred near the town, the local military governor distributed proclamations calling the Jews of Krusz to return to their town. They gathered in the one house that had survived the fires, for it had a huge courtyard, a stable, and big storehouses. The Jews remained a week there, until one morning they were commanded to gather in the market place. Their belongings, money, and papers were all confiscated and they were transferred to the Szukazta farm, which was near the town.

We stayed at that farm about two weeks until they took away all the adults, using the explanation that they were needed for work in a nearby city. They were marched to the forest, about ten kilometers away, and were shot. Only 68 children, aged up to 14, and eight adults, including the rabbi of the town, remained at the farm. For some reason, they left no one to guard us, so the youngsters were sent out to herd the local cattle. We obtained some very poor food as charity from local farmers.

Sometime after all the adults were shot, some farmers who visited us told us that our parents had been killed. Most of us refused to believe them.

After about a month, a guard was suddenly set-up at the farm. I then sensed for the first time that something was about to happen, that they were going to eliminate us also. Even at only 9 years old, I sensed this.

Near the granary of the farm, there was a stable and in its loft we kept hay for the cattle. When I recognized that they increased the guards, I slipped away from the view of the guards and burrowed deep into the mounds of hay in that loft. I fell asleep, but was awakened by sounds of shots. I peeked out between the slats of the hay loft and saw how they were taking the children out from the farm, using a list that had been prepared beforehand. I heard them calling my name and the name of my brother. I saw them taking out a group of children. Later, I found out that all had been shot.

The Lithuanians participated with the Nazis who organized this operation. They discovered that eight children and one adult were missing. They began an intense search. Using rifles with bayonets, they checked every corner and also stabbed into the mound of hay where I was hiding. I was lucky that they did not reach me. Unfortunately, they discovered in another pile of hay, another boy. Two sisters and another five boys were able to escape, since they left early with a herd of cows they were tending. Another boy who escaped reached the two sisters and told them what was happening at the farm, but they refused to believe him. One of the boys with them was sent to check whether his horrifying story was true. He did not return. Only then did they recognize the news was correct. They all fled into the forest. There they heard many rifle shots.

Among those who escaped was my brother, Isaac. The next morning, the escapees knocked on the door of a farmer whom they knew and he gave them a little food but refused to hide them. They split up and began to wander among the farmers.

Only two of them escaped, the others were captured during the following three years. One of the two survivors, Ze'ev Leizerin, is now a member of the kibbutz Yagur.

For three days, without food or drink, I hid in the loft. Only when I saw that the guards had left the farm did I emerge. I scrambled to an apple orchard and from there to the forest, through which I walked until I reached the home of a farmer whom I knew from the days when my father bought from him cattle for slaughtering. He fed me, gave me milk to drink, and also gave me apples. However, he was afraid to hide me in his home, since the Germans and the Lithuanians had distributed publications among the farmhouses in which they declared that if they find there any Jew they would wipe from the face of the earth every village in a radius of seven kilometers round that house. I had no choice but to travel on foot 35 kilometers to the nearby town in which my aunt and her family were hopefully still residing.

I had traveled only a short distance when I was attacked by a severe stomach ache, after being without food for three days, hiding in the hayloft, I had eaten all at once an abundance of food. Seventeen times during my walk to Butik, my aunt's hometown, I had diarrhea. Exhausted, with my strength almost given out, I arrived in that town. I knocked at the door of a farmhouse, and asked about my relatives. The farmer told me that all the Jews of the town had been gathered into one camp, three huts which had previously served as army depots. When I arrived there, I found only women and children, 14 years old and younger. They had murdered all the men, and had seized all the goods of the Jews, leaving them only blankets and their clothes. I found my aunt and her two children in the camp. I told them what had happened in Krusz, but the rest of the people in the camp refused to believe me and demanded that I leave them, since I was spreading fear and terror.

After a few days, the guards suddenly ordered us to prepare to move to another camp, which was fit for winter quarters. Everybody was ordered to pack their belongings and put identifying marks on their bundles. A day before we were supposed to move, new patrols appeared with trucks. On top of the truck cabins sat gunners, with another gunner next to each driver. We were boarded onto the trucks, 40 to 50 Jews per truck, standing crushed together, without our belongings, which had been piled together at one spot.

A True Story of Surviving by Synchronicity

I was in the second truck in the convoy, which drove into the forest. There, next to an earthen track was a deep pit. The gunner who sat next to the driver's cabin pushed us out, beating us savagely with the butt of the rifle, so that the women and children would scramble quickly off the truck. On the earthen path, armed Lithuanians waited to pounce on the women and children and beat them with iron rods and sticks. After that, they were placed in line next to the pit. The women were ordered to undress and to walk forward facing the pit. The first ones who did that were immediately killed by a burst of gunfire aimed at them from behind. I noticed then four or five Germans in uniform, whose total task was to photograph the event. They just gave orders, photographed, wrote notes, and laughed. The Lithuanians did the shooting.

I was placed in a line and I began slowly, with shaking hands, to unbutton my shirt as we were ordered. Suddenly, in a split second, I noticed that no man stood near me. There was no Lithuanian guard. I bounded into the trees of the forest and began running. Till today, I still do not know how I succeeded to do this. I escaped from the slaughter into the forest.

Breathless, I reached a peasant's house in the midst of the forest. The peasant told me that he had heard the shooting and the cries of the dying. He feared to allow me into his house, but his Russian wife heard our conversation. She knew a bit of Yiddish, possibly because she had worked previously in Jewish homes. She asked, "Are they killing there, in the forest, also children?" I answered, "They are shooting everyone there, including children." The man gave me a bit of food and ordered me to clear out. I returned to the forest, wandered for many hours until I reached a road upon which more trucks were traveling, full of women and children destined for the same pit of death.

I continued walking, this time along the road. Near the entrance to the forest, at the side of the road lay a couple of armed Lithuanians, who acted as sentinels for this operation, keeping strangers from entering the area until the slaughter was completed. I saw both of them from far off, but continued walking towards them. I looked like a gentile, and I decide to bluff my way through. Suddenly one of the sentinels stood up and asked me where I was going. "Don't you know that today they are shooting here the Jews?" was his reprimand. When I told him that I wanted to visit some acquaintances, he ordered me to return back.

I returned to the peasant's house in the forest, and from there took another direction back to Krusz. I returned to the empty farm with its hayloft, and hid there two days. After that I went to the house of the farmers I knew nearby and after receiving some food, continued to another farmhouse some two hours walking further on.

The farmer took me in for a couple of days, but he also was afraid to help me. He suggested to me that I go to the house of one of his friends in the forest. This I did.

That Sunday, the wife of that farmer walked to the nearby town to pray at the church. When she returned, she told me that she met on her way, two children who crossed the road in a stooped run, then were swallowed up in the trees. She quickly went after them, calling to them that they should not be afraid. One of the two was my brother, Isaac, whom I had not seen for a month.

My brother and I decided that from then on, we should stay together. Each night, for several weeks after that, we stayed at another farm, until winter came. Then the problem arose again how to harbor us together. We again separated. My brother stayed the winter of 1941 and the spring and summer of 1942 in the home of one farmer, where he worked as a cowherd. I did not know anything about him. But, one day the farmer quarreled with his neighbor, who thereupon went to the authorities and informed them that his rival was hiding a Jewish boy. The Lithuanian police hastened to the house of the farmer and demanded that he hand over the youngster who was then herding cows in the fields. The farmer was not able to withstand their torture and he handed the boy over. At that period, I was working for another farmer twenty kilometers away. One day, he returned from market and told me that they had captured a Jewish youngster, and had beaten and tortured him for a long time. The following week, after the farmer returned again from market, he informed me that they had hung the boy. This boy was my brother.

Thanks to my "gentile" visage, the people did not recognize that I was Jewish. Every so often, I changed my refuge and worked among the peasant farmers in the villages. One farmer's wife, for whom I worked for a time, even gave me the birth certificate of her dead son. Thus, I received a new identity. I worked for the peasants for two and one-half years, during the summer herding cows and during the winter, bringing water from the well or feeding cattle and sheep. I did any work that they asked me to do.

On October 7, 1944, the Russians came. Only then did I come out of hiding.

P.S. Krusz may be the town called Krazia on some maps. It is about 40 kilometers (25 miles) northwest of Raseiniai, which in turn is about ninety kilometers (60 miles) northwest of Kovno (now called Kaunas).

***

Article 2: August 31, 2020 excerpt from Facebook Group *"Life Before the Holocaust"* hosted by National Library of Israel

By Natali Beige, Israeli doctoral student researching rural towns in Lithuania during the Holocaust, with permission to share.

On the last days of August 1941, the final liquidation of the Jewish population in the rural town of Raseiniai in Lithuania took place. When the war against the Soviet Union broke out on June 22, 1941, Lithuania was at the forefront of Nazi invasion. From the first days of the war the Jewish communities in the Lithuanian provinces found themselves under rapid progress of persecution and mass destruction. Before the extermination camps and gas chambers, the killing pits of the Eastern front were the preliminary stage in the implementation of the Final Solution, a stage referred sometimes as "Holocaust by bullets".

Raseiniai, located some 70 km from Kaunas, was one of the first Jewish communities in Lithuania and is mentioned in historical documents from 1253. The Hebrew Gymnasium in the town was famously known and attracted renowned teachers from all over Lithuania. Some 2,500 Jews, including the Mordechai Tatz family, lived in Raseiniai with their four children, Sarah, Rivka, Zeev and Gershon. Life was good to the Tatz family. After the First World War, Mordechai became one of the pillars of the community. He had a successful business of transporting timber and grain. The youngest son Gershon, (the author's grandfather) studied at Yeshivas Knesses Yisrael in Kaunas, and was considered a prodigy, and his teachers destined him to greatness.

With the beginning of Operation Barbarossa on June 22, 1941, the Lithuanian countryside was radically transformed from relative peaceful communities of co-existence to the center of unthinkable human atrocities. By the end of December 1941, more then 130,000, men, women and children, among them the Tatz family, were dead, shot and buried in hundreds of mass graves. Although the mass murders took place at industrial pace, the killing process, which included bullets, knives, axes, wooden poles and even stones, was far from modern.

After the first killing wave of the Jewish men on the 29th of July 1941, there were about 50 men and nearly 2,000 women and children left. Until their final days, the Jews experienced the most harsh and severe conditions. They were expelled from their homes and concentrated in improvised ghetto. They were humiliated, beaten, their property stolen, and ultimately, they were murdered with the active help of their Lithuanian neighbors, thus adding another layer of horror to the massacres.

A True Story of Surviving by Synchronicity

On August 28, 1941, local armed units began to load groups of women, children and the elderly onto trucks and drive to the murder site in Kurpiškės Forest. Local residents who were hiding in the trees witnessed the terrible events:

"The women and children had to undress; they were beaten and shoved to the edge of the pit... children's heads were smashed with rocks or against trees. The screams were terrible, the screams of children and women who were wounded and fell to the pits alive. There were women who behaved quietly and proudly, combed their hair and their children's hair before they marched to the edge of the pit."

According to testimonies of the Lithuanians who took part in the killings, the mass shooting lasted two days, from 2 pm to 10 pm, and the next day from 9 am to 4 pm. In an excavation report done by Soviet authorities after the war, more than 2,000 bodies were uncovered.

Thus, in less than three months, the Jews of Raseiniai, with a glorious "Litvak" history of hundreds of years, ceased to exist. The mass graves can be found in two places: near the town of Girkalnis, about 10 km southeast of Raseiniai, where some 1,650 Jews are buried. Another mass grave is located 6 km southwest of the town near the village of Kalnujai, where 1,677 Jews are buried.

About Co-Author Nancy Rosenfeld

Bernard's third daughter, Nancy, shares her father's passion for artistic expression and introspective writing. After a long career in finance, consulting to leadership teams, and speaking nationally on the topic of initiating change, the nomad urge was embraced as she traveled extensively, landing on the tropical island of Maui, Hawaii, where she lives today.

Crafting this book was a spiritual-like endeavor, weaving together her father's original manuscript, filmed interview, and numerous photos, honoring his final words for his story to be shared. His life demonstrated persistence and encouraged a heart-felt collaborative soul promise to be fulfilled.

Nancy is the author of four other books, which include memoir, positive growth, travel adventures, and ancient tribal wisdom. Colorful fluid artwork and candid, inspiring books can be found at www.iamdoingthisnancyrosenfeld.weebly.com. Nancy's books:

- *I Am Doing This! A Travel Adventure Inspires a New Life*
- *A Path to Higher Self: Ancient Tribal Wisdom Shows the Way*
- *A Left-Brain Thinker on a Right-Brain Journey*
- *Finding Joy Amidst the Chaos*

A website has been created to share many of Bernard's photos, offering vivid images that illuminate Lithuanian memories, family gratitude, and superb story-telling. www.50centsforalife.weebly.com.

The co-authors, Bernard in Non-physical, and his daughter, Nancy, thank you for reading and honoring the joy of fulfilling dreams.

Milton Keynes UK
Ingram Content Group UK Ltd.
UKHW021451200524
442976UK00046B/1332